The Gardener's Guide to Growing
HELLEBORES

Graham Rice &
Elizabeth Strangman

David & Charles
Newton Abbot

TIMBER PRESS
Portland, Oregon

Copyright © 1993
Text: Graham Rice & Elizabeth Strangman
Photographs: Roger Phillips (except where otherwise credited)

First published 1993
Reprinted 1993, 1994, 1995, 1996, 1998

Graham Rice and Elizabeth Strangman have asserted their right
to be identified as authors of this work in accordance with the
Copyright, Designs and Patents Act 1988.

First published in the UK in 1993 by David & Charles Publishers,
Brunel House, Newton Abbot, Devon
ISBN 0 7153 9973 X
A catalogue record for this book is available from the British Library.

First published in North America in 1993 by
Timber Press, Inc.
133 S.W. Second Avenue, Suite 450
Portland, Oregon 97204-3527 USA

ISBN 0-88192-266-8

Cataloguing-in-Publication Data is on file with
the Library of Congress

Typeset in England by ABM Typographics Ltd., Hull
and printed in Italy by LEGO SpA

CONTENTS

1

THE LURE AND MAGIC OF HELLEBORES

by Elizabeth Strangman

Christmas rose and Lenten rose are the gardener's romantic names for the best-known and best-loved hellebores. They are nature's gift to gardeners in the dismal months after Christmas, when the weather is cold and discouraging and spring seems a long way ahead. At a time when few other flowers brave the elements, except the lovely but fleeting winter-flowering *Iris unguicularis*, which can be pulled for the house, and the cheerful *Cyclamen coum*, lighting up the garden, only the snowdrops in their prim whiteness and fascinating variety of forms can compete with hellebores.

It is not only their early flowering that makes hellebores so special – it is above all the sheer size and quality of their flowers coupled with their range of colours, from pure whites, primrose yellows, pure greens, through pinks, plums and darkest midnight purples, to slaty blue-blacks in a wonderfully subtle range of hues.

Turn the flowers up and a magical transformation takes place, revealing an almost endless variety of shading, veining and spotting. Of particular delight are the spotted forms, and many of us have been spellbound by the magic of pure white flowers transformed into spotted ones by the gardener's sleight of hand.

Starting to flower so early, hellebores are in full glory for ten to twelve weeks, to be joined in turn by all the other treasures of the spring gar-den. The flowers assume green or subtle pinky, coppery or smoky purple tints as the seed is shed in midsummer. By then the leaves are at their best, from the bold stems of *H. argutifolius* and *H. foetidus* to the finely divided foliage of *H. multifidus* and the bold dark green clumps of the Orientalis Hybrids. Besides all these attributes, hellebores are easy to grow and generous with their seed, offering the promise of many more treasures in years to come.

Picking and floating the flowers adds to the enthusiast's enjoyment. It is hard to imagine anything more beguiling than a lovely bowl filled with different forms to be savoured at leisure in the evening. There are many recipes for the successful picking of hellebore stems – but the recommended burning, pricking or slitting are seldom successful and a shocking waste. Floating the flowers, picked with half an inch of stem, is foolproof and allows you to enjoy the secrets they hide.

Perhaps this is the place to issue a warning – hellebores are addictive, and once intrigued and ensnared by their charms it is hard to break the spell. Most *aficionados* experience withdrawal symptoms if deprived of their annual fix of one or more new treasures.

The seeds of my own addiction were sown in childhood. My father grew a number of Orientalis Hybrids in a semi-wild spinney garden, where the plants he had originally bought from Amos Perry of Enfield seeded around. I remember them in shades of white and pink, and was intrigued and enthralled by their infinite

---

Helleborus × *sternii* 'Boughton Beauty', introduced by Valerie Finnis and seen here in her garden

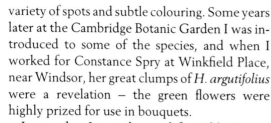

variety of spots and subtle colouring. Some years later at the Cambridge Botanic Garden I was introduced to some of the species, and when I worked for Constance Spry at Winkfield Place, near Windsor, her great clumps of *H. argutifolius* were a revelation – the green flowers were highly prized for use in bouquets.

It was when I started to work for Hilda Davenport-Jones at Washfield Nursery that I first saw a large range of colours and markings. We used to save seed from the best plants, grown isolated in separate areas of the garden. In the mid 1960s I persuaded her to allow me to hand-pollinate with the aim of improving the colours by selec-

tion, always keeping the best and using these as parents to line breed. A trip to Yugoslavia in the spring of 1971 was naïvely greeted as a chance to sort out the species in my own mind. It did not work out like that, and I came home convinced of the enormity of the task and the need for a great deal of meticulous fieldwork – something which is still important today.

Even after twenty-five years of working with hellebores, their lure and magic remain a potent force. It is hard to imagine life without the annual surge of 'hellebore fever' as spring approaches and the new seedlings join old favourites in flower.

FOUR WARNINGS

At this point we should perhaps warn readers of a few small surprises in store and give some explanations.

Except in the botanical section, Chapter 2 (page 8), we have used the word *petal* throughout the book, in spite of the fact that a hellebore flower is in fact made up of sepals. But this is, after all, a book for gardeners, and *petal* is the term gardeners use; being botanically correct and using the word *sepal* might cause confusion.

Secondly, to emphasise that most of the hellebores we grow are not simply forms of *H. orientalis* but hybrids, we draw attention to the fact that the botanical name *H. × hybridus* is a valid one for these plants. However, having pointed out its existence we now all but abandon it, preferring to use the more colloquial phrase of Orientalis Hybrids rather than this unfamiliar and clumsy botanical name.

Two completely new botanical names will also be found here. The plant previously known as "H. × *nigriliv*" is now called *H. × ballardiae*, while the plant formerly known as "H. × *nigristern*" is now known as *H. × ericsmithii*. The reasons for this change can be found in Chapter 7 (page 69). The double quote marks, by the way, are used to distinguish old and invalid species and cultivar names.

Although it will be met with later, perhaps this is the place to introduce the word *pedate*. This term is used to describe the way in which the hellebore leaf is divided. At the point at which the leaf joins its stem, the leaf is split into a number of divisions, some or all of which are themselves divided. Sometimes this structure is easy to see, sometimes it is less clear, and occasionally the structure may be almost *palmate*, that is, having all the divisions arising at the point where the leaf joins its stem.

Finally, we are conscious that in many areas where hellebores grow, place names can be confusing. This is not just because spellings seem frequently to vary from map to map – with the dramatic political upheavals in what was Yugoslavia and in the former Soviet republics in the Caucasus, the names of provinces and even the countries themselves are causing confusion as the English-speaking world learns to use names in local languages.

In Yugoslavia we have generally used the 1989/90 edition of the excellent map published by Roger Lascelles; otherwise we have tended to use the most modern names with which we expect our readers to be familiar – although, needless to say, we have occasionally broken our own rules.

2

ECOLOGY AND BOTANY

Hellebores are primarily European plants. Their range in Europe stretches from western Britain (though not Ireland), eastwards through central and southern Europe and the Iberian peninsula, into the Ukraine and eastern Romania. It also extends eastwards along the Black Sea coast of Turkey and into Russia, and there are two outposts, a small one straddling the Turkish/Syrian border and a larger one in China. In most of north-western Europe only two species, *H. viridis* and *H. foetidus*, are found, while the Balkan region sees the greatest concentration of species. Two island enclaves in the Mediterranean boast their own pair of distinctive plants.

Holidaymakers in these parts are unlikely to stumble across hellebores in the way that they might encounter, for example, cistus or ground orchids. This is partly because of the relatively undemonstrative demeanour of many species, partly because of their localised, often mountain distribution, and also because of the restricted habitats of many species.

Many Mediterranean and all the Balkan species grow away from the coast, where the less adventurous visitor is unlikely to venture, and they flower early in the year before many tourists arrive. They grow in relatively inaccessible mountain regions and in woodland or shaded habitats among scrub, where they are less obtrusive. Many of those growing in apparently open situations are likely to be hidden by bracken in summer. In many areas the accompanying flora of those growing without tree or scrub cover indicates that the site was once wooded. However,

there is always the chance of spotting the foliage by the roadside. Majorca, the area most likely to be visited by British tourists, is in fact one of the least likely places to see hellebores, for they grow only in a few exceptionally inaccessible spots.

In some areas of Britain the bold and distinctive stinking hellebore, *H. foetidus*, will be a familiar sight on country walks while the positively demure *H. viridis* tends to be more secretive. The distribution of both remains patchy and they are absent from large areas of Britain.

Gardeners tend to think of hellebores as shade-loving plants and for many species this is fair, though it is clear that in the wild this shade is not necessarily provided by trees: low scrubby areas are often favoured. Seeing some species flowering early in the year on open, sunny slopes fosters an idea of their love of sunshine, but see them later in the season and they are almost always overgrown by bracken or by meadow grasses and herbs, which create at least as much shade as trees. Many also grow among rocks, which provide a little shade and a cool root run. A few species, like *H. foetidus*, grow in both extremes of habitat, woodland fringes in Britain and hot slopes in Spain, while *H. vesicarius* grows in conditions which are parched in summer.

Most species seem to grow in soils with a certain amount of humus and which are not unusually soggy in winter. Apart from *H. vesicarius* none have a preference for hot dry conditions; even *H. lividus* prefers the damper spots in the Majorcan mountains. A few do tend to appreciate damper spots, and both *H. viridis* and *H. thibetanus* cam be found in quite moist conditions.

Hellebores are most often found on alkaline soils, and there is a definite correlation between limestone rock formations and good hellebore areas. However, they are also found on deep alluvial soils, which can be acidic, and although they are sometimes seen tucked in among limestone rocks, they make better plants where the soil is deeper and richer.

BOTANY AND CLASSIFICATION

Hellebores belong to the buttercup family, *Ranunculaceae*, one of the most diverse in the plant kingdom. This family includes, in addition to *Ranunculus* (the buttercups), such unlikely cousins as *Aconitum* (the true aconites), *Actaea* (baneberry), *Aquilegia* (columbines), *Clematis*, *Delphinium* and *Thalictrum*, so it is a relief to find that the hellebore's closest relatives do have certain similarities. Even a superficial glance at the flowers and foliage of *Eranthis* (winter aconite), *Trollius* (globe flower) and *Caltha* (marsh marigold) reveals their close relationship with hellebores.

Hellebores differ from winter aconites in having basal or stem leaves and more than one flower on a stem; winter aconites have only a simple ruff of leaves immediately behind the flower. Hellebores differ from globe flowers in their funnel-shaped nectaries; globe flowers have flat nectaries with a pouch at the base, marsh marigolds have no nectaries. Both globe flowers and marsh marigolds may also have more than five sepals.

Some botanists have proposed the creation of a separate family, *Helleboraceae*, for hellebores, together with their close, and not so close, relatives. Fortunately, this has not found much favour.

FLOWERS

The flowers of most plants are composed of four parts – sepals, petals, stamens and carpels. The sepals are the protective scales which form the outside of the bud; the petals are usually showy and brightly coloured and serve to attract pollinators; the stamens produce pollen and the carpels receive pollen and eventually form the seedpods containing the seeds.

In hellebores, instead of being large and brightly coloured, the petals have become modified into nectaries which are very short and shaped rather like flattened horns; they are usually green or amber in colour.

With the petals modified into nectaries, these generally bee-pollinated flowers would be at a loss to attract insects so the sepals have become enlarged to look like petals; the outer two continue to function partially as sepals and enclose the remainder of the flower before it opens. These sepals are green in most species, although they may also be white, pink, purple or even yellow and in some forms may be spotted or marked. Even when the sepals are not green, the outer two may be noticeably green-tinted. As the flowers age the sepals fade to green, when they photosynthesise in the same way as leaves, helping the seed-pods to swell.

There are usually five sepals, which may be oval, elliptical or even spade-like in shape, and together they form a flower which is more or less cup-shaped or bell-shaped, sometimes very rounded or sometimes very starry.

The nectaries form a ring at the base of the sepals. Very occasionally they elongate and take on the colours of the sepals, giving a slightly anemone-centred form, or they may revert to a larger, petaloid form, this being the origin of some of the doubles. Inside this ring of nectaries are the stamens. These are usually present in large numbers, sometimes over 100, and when the flower first opens they are tightly clustered around the base of the carpels. As they mature they elongate, starting with those on the outside, and arch out over the nectaries releasing their yellow pollen.

In the centre of the flower are the carpels or seed-pods. Depending on the species and its general vigour there may be anything from two to eight carpels in a ring, but they are not usually attached to each other, except at the base in a

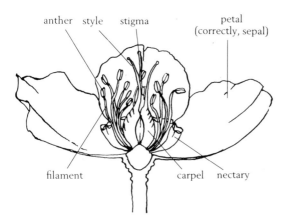

anther   style   stigma   petal
(correctly, sepal)

filament   carpel   nectary

Section through hellebore flower

few species. Each carpel consists of three parts. At the tip of each is the stigma which receives the pollen, and this tops the curved style which in some forms contrasts strongly in colour with the sepals and anthers. The stigma is receptive before the pollen in the same flower is released, so encouraging cross-pollination.

At the base of the style is the slightly inflated ovary. After fertilisation this swells up, and when the seed is ripe it splits along the inner edge to release the seeds. In *H. vesicarius* the pods become impressively inflated.

Except in species such as *H. foetidus* and *H. argutifolius*, no more than six or seven flowers are usually carried on any one stem, and plants flowering for the first time or growing poorly may produce fewer; one flower on a stem is quite common with *H. niger*. In most species the flowers hang down gracefully and bell-like, although in some forms they may look outwards more horizontally.

All hellebores flower in the winter or spring from buds formed the previous summer. Occasionally, young and newly divided plants may produce flowers in the summer at the expense of the display a few months later, and these precocious flowers are usually atypical. Hellebores are pollinated by honey-bees, bumble-bees and other solitary bees, which are attracted to the flower primarily by its colour and then find the bonus of sweet nectar, especially valuable early in the season when many species flower.

Hellebore seeds are black or tawny brown and may be almost round or slightly kidney-shaped; perhaps they are best described as mouse-dropping-shaped with a noticeable white appendage called an elaiosome along one edge. This contains sugars and fats and is attractive to ants, which can transport the seeds for some distance.

STEMS AND LEAVES

The flowers are carried on stems which may be as tall as 4ft (1.2m) in *H. foetidus* and *H. argutifolius* or as short as a few inches in a number of other species.

Four species, *H. argutifolius*, *H. foetidus*, *H. lividus* and *H. vesicarius*, have leaves on their flowering stems, giving the first two in particular a rather shrubby appearance. The first three have relatively woody stems which persist over the winter; these are replaced the following season by new shoots from ground level which start to grow during the spring. The leaves are carried alternately up the stem but are often withered at the base by flowering time. The plants of this type are often known as the caulescent group (literally 'with stems'). *H. vesicarius* carries leaves on its stems but these die back each year; it also has leaves which arise at the base.

Most species have no main stems carrying leaves, only flowering stems, and these are sometimes referred to as the acaulescent group ('without stems') although they do have bracts at the points where the flowering stems branch. These can be quite similar to the leaves, though smaller, or much simplified and undivided.

Most hellebores, except the three caulescent species with their overwintering leafy stems, have leaves which arise at ground level. In many species the leaves are more or less fan-shaped in general appearance. In most the leaves are pedate, that is, divided at the point where the leaf blade joins its stem and with most of the divisions again divided. Although all hellebores have this basic structure and most are instantly recognisable, they vary enormously. In many species, such as *H. niger*, *H. orientalis* and *H. atrorubens*, the central leaf division remains entire while the others are divided. In some forms of

H. multifidus the leaves are constantly redivided, creating a noticeably feathery appearance.

In the past, botanists developed systems for classifying hellebores based on the shapes and divisions of the leaves. These ideas have been discredited, as fieldwork has shown that leaves with varying degrees of division and dissection and with leaflets of varying shapes can sometimes be found not only on adjacent plants in a colony of what would otherwise be regarded as one species, but even on the same plant.

Leaves are usually toothed to a greater or lesser extent. This toothing is striking in *H. argutifolius*, and usually only in *H. lividus* are the leaves without teeth altogether. They are usually leathery in texture and the pattern of veins is often clearly visible on the undersides.

The species with overwintering stems obviously retain their leaves in winter, as do both *H. orientalis* and *H. cyclophyllus* together with some forms of *H. odorus*, while *H. vesicarius* is again the odd one out as it retains its leaves all winter but dies down completely in summer.

ROOTS

Most hellebores produce a dense rhizome with the leaves and stems arising at its tips. The scars from previous years' shoots are visible along the top. Roots are produced all the way along the rhizome, but the most active arise from the newest growth and are pale brown in colour. Roots arising from older parts of the rhizome are darker, often black, and although remaining alive are less active.

The roots themselves are fleshy, with more fibrous growth at the tips, and the root hairs are clearly visible on the palest, youngest roots. The root system of most species is very large and tends to delve deep into the soil, allowing the plants to tolerate drought well. This means that hellebores are difficult to move without leaving much of the root system behind. The roots of *H. vesicarius* are especially fleshy, and act as a food and water store during the dry summers in its natural habitat.

CLASSIFICATION

Botanists use a number of characteristics to divide hellebores into groups of similar species.

1 Striking features of the structure of the plants, such as the presence of stems.
2 Whether or not the individual carpels are joined to each other at the base.
3 The shape and surface appearance of the pollen grains.
4 The shape and size of the seeds.
5 The ability of the plants to hybridise.
6 Distinctive features of the leaves, such as the degree of dissection and their hairiness.
7 Flower colour.

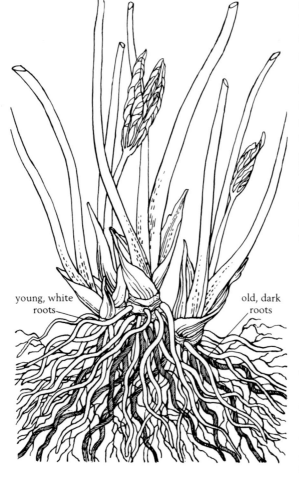

young, white roots

old, dark roots

Hellebore plant showing the emerging leaves, the crown and the root system.

Brian Mathew, in his invaluable monograph, has divided the genus into six sections:

Syncarpus The name refers to the fact that, uniquely among hellebores, the three carpels are joined together for half their length. This section contains just one species, *H. vesicarius*, which is quite different from all other species. No hybrids involving this species are known.

Griphopus The name is derived from *gryphos* (a gryphon) and *pous* (a foot) and relates to the resemblance between the narrow leaflets and the feet of a gryphon. This section also includes just one species, *H. foetidus*. Occasional hybrids with the species in the following section have been recorded but are not fertile.

Chenopus The name derives from the Greek *chen* (a goose) and *pous* (a foot) and describes the leaves, which are divided into three broad leaflets. The two other stemmed species, *H. argutifolius* and *H. lividus*, belong here. When crossed, the two species in this section produce fertile offspring. They have sometimes been treated as one species.

Helleborus The ancient Greek name for the plant, and probably originally applied by them to *H. cyclophyllus*. Much later, botanists made the very distinct *H. niger* the type species of the genus, and so the section containing it must carry the genus name. *H. niger* produces infertile offspring when crossed with the two species in the previous section.

Helleborastrum The name indicates a similarity to, but not an exact likeness with, plants in the section Helleborus. This is by far the largest section and contains the following nine species, all of which cross with each other to give fertile offspring: *H. atrorubens*, *H. cyclophyllus*, *H. dumetorum*, *H. multifidus*, *H. odorus*, *H. orientalis*, *H. purpurascens*, *H. torquatus* and *H. viridis*.

Dicarpon The name of this section was derived from the fact that its only species was thought to be consistent in having just two maturing carpels. There is just one species in this section, *H. thibetanus*. Its ability to hybridise is not yet known.

NOMENCLATURE

There is a great deal of confusion, especially among gardeners, about the names of some hellebores, and quite a few names which are clearly invalid are still in common use. It is understandably annoying when a plant has to have its name changed, but it does not happen merely on the whim of some mischievous botanist. Far from it.

Many name changes come about through increased understanding of the relationship between one plant and another following extensive research. As well as traditional herbarium techniques of studying the structure and distribution of plants preserved as dried specimens, this research increasingly involves detailed work in the field studying wild populations. Laboratory work is also becoming more important, and this may involve studying genetic structure, using scanning electron microscopes to examine pollen grains and other details, and even the analysis of the constituents of natural oils.

Botanists must follow the rules laid down in two authoritative documents: the International Code for Botanical Nomenclature, which concerns wild plants, and the International Code for the Nomenclature of Cultivated Plants, which concerns named garden forms. These codes are intended to impose order on what would otherwise be the impossibly chaotic world in which anyone could call any plant exactly what they liked – we would have several names for one plant and several plants with the same name.

The following erroneous or confusing names have appeared in catalogues and seed lists in recent years or are still used by gardeners. For a comprehensive list which includes many older names, see Brian Mathew's book.

Helleborus abchasicus: Now classified as a subSpecies of *H. orientalis* originating from the western Caucasus mountains and correctly known as *H. orientalis* subsp. *abchasicus* (without the first 's' which is often used).

Helleborus antiquorum: An invalid name for typical pale-flowered *H. orientalis*.

Helleborus atrorubens: The plant most gardeners know as "H. atrorubens" is an unusually early-flowering, purple-flowered plant with green tints. It has usually lost most of its leaves by flowering time, which can be as early as mid December. Unfortunately this name correctly belongs to a less familiar species from Yugoslavia so cannot be used for this plant, which is now known as *H. orientalis* subsp. *abchasicus* 'Early Purple', although there are a number of similar plants grown in gardens which are all known by the incorrect name of "H. atrorubens" (see page 43).

Helleborus caucasicus: An invalid name for typical pale-flowered *H. orientalis*.

Helleborus colchicus: An invalid name for *H. orientalis* subsp. *abchasicus*.

Helleborus corsicus: A long-used but ultimately incorrect name for *H. argutifolius*. The name *H. corsicus* was first used in 1813 but occurs only in a list and is not accompanied by a description. So although the name *H. argutifolius* was not used until 1824, under the code which governs these things *H. argutifolius* is the name we must use, since it was published with both a description and an illustration. Sorry, but it can't be helped.

Helleborus guttatus: Wild plants with white flowers and varying degrees of reddish spotting are now correctly known as *H. orientalis* subsp. *guttatus*.

Helleborus × hybridus: This is a general name coined in 1894 to cover hybrids between *H. orientalis* and any other species. This is a convenient name when we need one to cover this great variety of plants. In practice, however, the full name is usually shortened and, for example, *Helleborus* 'Susanna' is written instead of *Helleborus × hybridus* 'Susanna'. It remains useful in botanical contexts.

Helleborus intermedius: An old, invalid name for the northern form of *H. torquatus* from Bosnia.

Helleborus kochii (or H. kotchyi): An invalid name for typical, pale-flowered, but early-blooming *H. orientalis*.

Helleborus lividus* subsp. *corsicus: Another old name for *H. argutifolius*. Some botanists felt that *H. argutifolius* and *H. lividus* are sufficiently alike to be distinguished only as subspecies of the same species, *H. lividus*. Under that scheme *H. argutifolius* borrows the name it cannot have when treated as a species in its own right! Sounds crazy, but there it is.

Helleborus olympicus: Usually thought of as an invalid name for typical white-flowered *H. orientalis*, but William Robinson said it had 'large rose-coloured flowers, and good habit, [and] is very similar if not identical, with one grown as *H. abchasicus*. . .'

Helleborus serbicus: An old, invalid name for *H. torquatus* which sometimes reappears in the form *H. multifidus* subsp. *serbicus* (see page 62).

Helleborus × torquatus: *H. torquatus* is not a hybrid but a wild species in its own right. At one time, the only plants in cultivation were self-sterile and this led to the supposition that the plant was an interspecific hybrid; it was also sometimes listed as *H.* 'Torquatus'.

3

CULTIVATION

Hellebores are tolerant plants, and given a good start in life are easy and very rewarding. They will grow happily on any soil from chalk to clay and even in the thin lifeless material found in many London gardens. But hellebores are no different from other plants in that they appreciate tender loving care and improved soil, rather than being relied upon to give their best wherever an insensitive gardener may carelessly plant them. Given the careful cultivation we describe they will surely thrive; and being as tough as they are, a less than thorough attention to detail will not prevent them giving a reasonable display.

SOIL AND SITUATION

Although all hellebores are happiest on limy soils, acid soils can still grow good plants. In some ways this is surprising, as in the wild *H. orientalis* often grows in acid conditions, but in gardens a pH of about 7.0 seems ideal. A simple soil test kit from the garden centre will give you a good enough idea of the pH level of your soil and also suggest how much lime to apply to bring it up to the level you require. Elizabeth gardens on acid soil, with the help of lashings of spent mushroom compost.

Chalky, gravelly and heavy clay soils can all grow good hellebores, but the addition of plenty of organic matter during preparation is essential to give them the open structure and good water-holding capacity they enjoy. In very dry, sharply drained soils hellebores will usually manage to cling to life, but as well as plenty of muck or compost before planting, they need extra nurturing in the form of regular mulching. In some gardens, gravelly or sandy conditions are exacerbated by shallow tree roots, from pines perhaps, or sycamores. Raising the soil level using logs or stone is one answer, and hellebores can then be grown in a special, humus-rich mix.

A raised bed can also be an attractive and practical solution to the hellebore's one true bane, bad drainage; this they will not tolerate. But 9–12in (23–30cm) of leafy soil mix over well-forked soil will enable them to grow without the threat of wet feet leading to terminal decline.

Another simple and practical solution to bad drainage is either to make use of existing trees or to plant deciduous trees specifically to take water out of the soil, a method used very successfully by E. B. Anderson and discussed in his book *Seven Gardens*. Do not plant the hellebores too near the base of the trees, as they will then suffer in the poor light – reserve these spaces for cyclamen, which revel in such inhospitable spots. To make the best use of the shade cast by deciduous trees and their helpful root systems, it pays to make beds around them extensive and flowing in outline rather than a simple tight circle around the trunk. Greedy, shallow-rooted trees like sycamores should not be utilised, and of course on light soils the effect of too many tree roots will be detrimental.

On a larger scale, double digging or even the blissfully forgotten bastard trenching will certainly improve drainage but could ruin the gardener. In some gardens this will mean digging with water lapping over the top of your boots; laying tile drains is the best solution but can be difficult and expensive. To be realistic, few gardeners have the energy or the industry to go in for bastard trenching or tile drains and less arduous preparation is usually sufficient.

Although hellebores can be encouraged to

grow well in most soils, in the poorest conditions it pays to stick to *H. foetidus* and the Orientalis Hybrids. Even then, thoughtful preparation and regular care will reward you with contented and floriferous plants.

Most hellebores are tolerant of both sun and shade, and although they are often happy to be on the dry side in summer, all except *H. vesicarius* hate to be baked. They appreciate shade from the midday sun and a place under deciduous trees with a tall canopy of foliage is ideal; if planted in full shade under low branches their growth will be slow and flowering poor. A good alternative to a high canopy is a bed on the west or north side of a house or wall. Many of Graham's hellebores are planted towards the edge of a canopy of mature apple trees and seem to thrive except when bombed by windfalls. Unfortunately, sooty mould growing on honeydew secreted by the aphids on the unsprayed apples can disfigure the hellebore foliage in summer.

Although most hellebores, with the exception, perhaps, of *H. dumetorum*, sometimes appear to be growing in full sun in the wild, in the majority of cases they are shaded by tall meadow flowers or bracken during the hottest months of the summer; so do not be fooled into thinking they require full sun in the garden.

H. cyclophyllus, *H. odorus* and *H. multifidus* subsp. *hercegovinus* are three which do prefer a more open spot, and the more retentive the soil in which they are growing, the more sun they will take. *H. viridis* and *H. dumetorum* are definitely best in the shade of deciduous trees, and *H. atrorubens* prefers partial shade, as do *H. purpurascens* and *H. torquatus*.

Although *H. foetidus* is usually found in partially shaded spots in the wild in Britain, in warmer regions like Majorca it grows on hot dry slopes and this is a clue to its very tolerant and adaptable nature in gardens. It will thrive in poor soil, although never matching the impressive specimens that can be found in richer conditions. Partial shade is also suitable for *H. lividus*, *H. argutifolius* and *H.* × *sternii*, although all are best in full sun where there is no tendency for them to become drawn.

HARDINESS

Almost all hellebores are hardy in most of Britain. In the United States the situation varies according to the climatic zone, but what we say about Britain applies also to the Pacific northwest of the United States (see also page 146). Only *H. lividis* and *H. vesicarius* are best treated as tender in Britain, while *H. multifidus* subsp. *hercegovinus* is perhaps the least hardy of the others and needs thoughtful planting in colder regions.

In some cold gardens, especially if exposed to biting winds, the flowers and even the stems of *H. cyclophyllus* and some forms of *H. multifidus* may be damaged. If sheltering the whole garden is impracticable, planting in the lee of an evergreen shrub can be very helpful; like all plants with large leaves, hellebores appreciate some shelter from the fiercest winds. Another way of alleviating the worst effects of biting winds and long cold spells is to cover the plants with dried bracken fronds. This is a much kinder material, both on the eyes and to the plants, than straw, which not only looks ugly but blows around the garden and harbours slugs.

PREPARATION AND PLANTING

The majority of hellebores are long-lived plants. If you lift a hellebore plant for division or knock a young plant out of its pot, you will notice the roots growing strongly downwards rather than spreading sideways. The implication of this is that while regular mulching of the surface is a useful part of their seasonal care, deep cultivation and improvement of the soil before planting is vital. This will give the roots plenty of rich material where they need it to provide both moisture and sustenance.

Double digging represents the perfect standard which few of us will ever attain. But if you are an energetic gardener with time on your hands, or have someone to do the digging for you, then your hellebores will certainly appreciate such thorough preparation.

For most of us single digging of the bed is a less

unattractive prospect, and this is perfectly adequate provided that when the holes are dug for the individual plants they are dug deep and the bottom of the hole is well broken up.

Organic matter is a crucial part of good preparation, and leaf-mould is the best choice. Again the ideal is not available to us all, so good, well-rotted garden compost will do very well. But our recommendations should not put you off using whatever organic matter is available if you find leaf-mould or garden compost hard to come by.

Spent mushroom compost is good but is very limy, and if your soil is already alkaline its use may cause problems for other plants. It is imperative that mushroom compost be sterilised by your supplier, otherwise you may be plagued with mushroom fly larvae which have a taste for the fine roots of garden plants as well as for mushrooms. Farmyard or stable manure is good, although it *must* be well rotted (at least a year old), and the contents of old growing bags can also be used although it helps to put the compost, roots and all, through a shredder or sieve before use.

Your organic matter should go in the bottom of the trench when (single or double) digging the bed during the first stage of preparation. Later, when digging holes for planting individual hellebores, a planting mixture should be used. This should consist of equal parts of leaf-mould or garden compost and old loam-based potting compost with the addition of a fertiliser such as bonemeal or Osmocote; add a soil insecticide such as bromophos to forestall attack from soil pests. The individual holes should be large, 18in (45cm) across and one spit deep, with half a bucket of the planting mixture worked into the base of the hole before setting the plant in place.

The level of planting is important. The final soil level should be 1in (2.5cm) above the point at which roots break out from the crown. With pot-grown plants you simply plant them so that the surface of the root-ball is level with the surrounding soil. After planting and watering in with a whole canful of water, give the plants a 1–2in (2.5–5cm) mulch of weed-free organic matter such as mushroom compost or bark. This will not only prevent the new plants being engulfed by weeds, but will retain moisture and, eventually, be absorbed into the soil to replace existing organic matter as it is burned up. A generous feed with a balanced liquid fertiliser in the spring after planting will encourage strong growth.

Many gardeners plant their hellebores too close to each other. The Orientalis Hybrids soon make a broad foliage cover, and if planted with 3ft (90cm) between crowns the foliage will still meet in a year. Wider spacing is perhaps advisable, as this will leave plenty of room for the plants to develop and for smaller shade-loving plants like primroses and wood anemones to be planted in between.

Hellebores vary in their speed of growth and development. The stemless species from the Balkans can be very slow, needing three or four years from germination to flowering; they also appreciate slightly better drainage, better growing conditions generally and a little cossetting. The Orientalis Hybrids are much quicker, as is *H. niger*, while the *niger* hybrids, *H. foetidus*, *H. argutifolius* and *H.* × *sternii* are also very quick but not so long-lived.

GENERAL CARE

It may seem strange coming from the authors of a whole book on the subject, but hellebores do not require a great deal of specific attention during the year. So having noted that our enthusiasm for the tolerance and adaptability of the hellebore at the start of this chapter was swiftly followed by such detailed instructions on planting as to bely the assertion, you may raise your eyebrows when we say that they do not require a great deal of attention through the seasons. Well, like making love or playing the clarinet, anyone can do it badly, but here we set out to explain how to grow hellebores well.

Apart from dealing with pests and diseases (page 17), hellebores need little regular routine work and there are only a few times during the year when they need special attention.

Over the years there has been much debate

about exactly what to do with hellebore leaves in winter. Of course you can do nothing, simply leave them in place, but then you risk them carrying black spot disease through the winter ready to infect the flowers as they emerge in spring. From the aesthetic point of view, although the Orientalis Hybrids are evergreen, by flowering time the foliage can be disfigured by black patches and dead and battered leaflets; such tattiness is hardly an ideal setting for the flowers.

The best approach is to cut off some leaves during the autumn and early winter when the garden is put to bed, concentrating on removing dead leaves and any showing signs of blackening, plus those lying across each other or crossing the centre of the plant where the flowers will break. By Christmas time they should be thinned out sufficiently to leave a good circle.

However, as our winters become windier it may be wise to remove them entirely at this stage to prevent newly planted specimens becoming rocked at the root and also to prevent the leaves of more mature plants rubbing on the ground; this constant movement can damage nearby plants as well as create an unsightly smear on the soil.

Thin the leaves further as the flower stems emerge, then just before they are in full flower remove all the old leaves. The new leaves will start to emerge to continue photosynthesis soon after, so it is easier to remove or cut back all the old ones before the new ones emerge. This avoids bruising new growth or even cutting out the wrong stems. All old foliage is best burnt as a precaution against the carry-over of disease.

To compensate for the removal of the last of the leaves the plants deserve a good mulch. Although the main root system will be some way down, bacteria, worms and the percolation of rainwater will eventually turn your surface mulch into something the roots will appreciate.

On acid soils, sterilised spent mushroom compost is the perfect material to use as its extra lime will help reduce the acidity. On neutral or limy soils use leaf-mould if you have it, but remember that beech leaf-mould from a chalky soil will be a great deal more limy than oak leaf-mould from an acid soil. Well-rotted, weed-free garden compost or manure, or one of the non-peat mulches available at the garden centre, are good alternatives.

Before you mulch, take the opportunity to thin out any seedlings. Remove all those actually growing in the clump and thin any of those remaining which you would like to retain to 2–4in (5–10cm) apart.

Autumn is a good time to check labels, as frost and the winter rains are usually responsible for the final disappearance of your lettering. Reliable labelling is especially important if you intend to breed from your plants, but also to satisfy the eager inquiries of visitors as to the origins of plants that take their fancy. Your memory will never compensate for the lack of good labels.

Although the foregoing advice refers particularly to the Orientalis Hybrids, it applies also to stemless species. Given conditions so much better than they are used to in the wild, these species tend to grow more strongly in cultivation. In the wild they are often forced to grow in poorer places, owing to pressure from people, building and cultivation in particular, and become overcrowded and surrounded by their own seedlings. The result is that they do not flower well or make vigorous leaf growth and seldom develop into large mature clumps.

One advantage that many wild plants have over plants in gardens is that they are covered with snow and so stay completely dormant in winter. In Britain at least, our stop-go winters render them more susceptible to frost and biting winds and cold damp conditions lead to black spot attack.

Much of the advice in this chapter can also be applied to *Helleborus argutifolius*, *H. × sternii* and *H. foetidus*. These species may also need to have dead or damaged foliage removed any time. The tall stems of these species die after flowering and seeding, and by then they look extremely messy. If you do not require seed these stems should be cut out at ground level; alternatively this can be left until the seed has been collected, though by then they usually look very tatty.

Specific advice relating to individual species will be found under their own entries in Chapter 6, starting on page 42.

PESTS AND DISEASES

In some books the section of pests and diseases is a long and dauntingly detailed one; not here. For although hellebores do suffer from one or two especially difficult problems, generally they are trouble-free if grown well and suffer from relatively few ailments.

Aphids: Hellebores have their own special aphid, *Macrosiphon hellebori*, but they are also attacked by other species with less specific tastes. The aphids congregate almost exclusively on the undersides of the leaves and on the inside of the flowers as they age. The first obvious sign of attack may be the discarded white skins on the lower leaves and on the ground, or a rather sticky coating on the flowers and leaves.

Growth of seedlings in the frame can be severely affected by relatively small numbers of aphids, while the foliage of established plants can become coated with congested colonies of the little beasts, leading to distortion of leaves and possibly the spread of virus infection.

Small infestations can be squashed with the fingers, but otherwise the best remedy is to spray with a soap-based product or use a chemical spray containing pirimicarb, which harms the fewest beneficial insects. Either way, it is important to direct the spray to the underside of the foliage, and if this is not practical a systemic product such as one containing dimethoate should be used instead.

Black death: In recent years a completely new disease of hellebores has appeared in the gardens of a number of enthusiasts. This takes the form of black marks between the leaf veins and also between the veins of the bracts. Sometimes it appears as a mass of separate spots, rather like sooty mould, but which does not wipe off. It also appears as larger marks in a small area of leaf bounded by veins, often in a rectangular strip

running out to the leaf edge. Sharp-edged black streaks may also appear in the flowers.

The origin of this problem is something of a mystery. A number of laboratories have confirmed that there is no fungus or bacterium present, and eelworm has not been found either. Virus remains the most likely culprit.

Suspecting that this problem may be caused by a virus, most growers have dug up and burned their plants as the disease has taken hold, worried that all their plants might rapidly become infected. But there is some evidence that the disease does not recur in the year following the original infection.

Black spot: This is the most damaging and the most widespread problem with which hellebores must cope, the number one enemy – the fungus *Coniothyrium hellebori* is the main culprit. It attacks the foliage, stems and flowers of all species; particular individuals are often especially susceptible and any plants growing poorly are the most likely to suffer.

Black or dark brown blotches appear on both sides of the leaves, gradually coalescing to form large dead areas and eventually affecting the whole leaf, much of which may turn yellow and die. As the initial small spot enlarges, it may develop striking concentric rings. The infection can then spread to the rest of the plant, killing the tissue at the base of both the leaf petioles and the flower stems and causing the whole plant to collapse. Mild infections may cause only blackening on the flowers and bracts.

Moisture is essential for the germination of the fungus spores which start the infection, so this problem is usually at its worst on plants grown outside in the winter months and on seedlings in frames which are poorly ventilated.

Those parts of the leaf initially infected can be removed, while in gardens where this disease is often a problem it pays to remove all the old foliage in the autumn. As a precaution against infection, give two sprays at fortnightly intervals during the autumn and another two after Christmas. Spray immediately after the autumn clear-up, when infected foliage should be removed, then top-dress to set the plants up for the winter. If infection still takes place, apply a curative spray at once.

The RHS recommends mancozeb as the fungicide with which to spray, and we have also used benomyl, which deals with botrytis too. It generally pays to vary the chemical used as this helps to guard against a build-up of immunity to any particular one. Always use a systemic fungicide in winter. Systemics are longer-lasting and more effective in seasons when unexpected rain can nullify all the work of spraying. A really good drenching is preferable to a token spray; 'spray to run off' is the usual recommendation. It is important to spray both sides of the foliage and direct the spray into the crown of the plant to give protection to the flower buds as they emerge.

There is no doubt that removal or thinning of mature leaves increases the air flow around the plant, helping prevent dank conditions and creating less congenial conditions for fungal attack. It is also important to remove all old flower stems and dead leaves, which can act as hosts.

While often thought to be confined to the stemless species and hybrids, the disease can also affect the foliage of *H. foetidus*, *H. lividus*, *H. argutifolius* and *H. × sternii* and may attack their stems at soil level; these then collapse, and the plant is ruined. With this group of species, removing the old shoots as soon as possible after flowering helps prevent infection moving from the old to the new growth.

Botrytis: This is not a serious problem with hellebores, although it can be troublesome when growth has been already damaged. Precocious early leaves which have been damaged by frost are susceptible, as are flowers burnt by icy winds. Cut off damaged growth as soon as it is noticed.

Chafers: Chafers of various sorts, some of which turn into may-bugs, pose most problems when new beds are made in lawns and when there are overgrown areas near the beds where hellebores are grown. Adults lay their eggs around the crown of the plant in summer, and the larvae spend up to five years feeding on roots and rhizomes, the soft, white, brown-headed, C-shaped grubs eventually reaching 1½in (4cm) in length. These are the usual culprits when flower or leaf stems suddenly come away in your hand, but the adults may also attack buds and foliage.

Regular forking of the new beds to let the birds have a feast is a useful preventative. Mixing bromophos into the soil when planting is a valuable precaution, but normal cultivation plus the removal of weeds will usually deal with the problem in the end.

Mice: These are the other deadly menace to hellebores besides black spot; with no warning whatsoever they can do an enormous amount of damage in just a single night. They have a connoisseur's taste for young seedlings at the seed leaf stage, so take precautions and have traps set ready in the frame. To avoid killing birds or trapping children's fingers, have a 5in (12.5cm) pot to hand to place over each trap when the frames are open during the day.

Mice are also partial to seeds at the three-quarters ripe stage and will strip flowers off a plant, leaving piles of tell-tale post-banquet debris, after climbing the plants and nipping through the stems just behind the flowers. It pays not only to set traps but to scatter a handful or two of unwanted flowers around so that they have plenty to eat and are less likely to climb for the hand-pollinated seed you really want to keep. Traps will need regular checking in case a whole family is sharing a binge.

Slugs and Snails: Although hellebores are rabbit and stock proof, there are stages at which they are susceptible to slugs and snails. Seedlings are especially liable to be eaten, from the stage at which the seed leaves emerge up to pricking-out stage and even after potting. Frames should be baited with pellets, or traps set. The young emerging foliage is also susceptible, and the flower buds can be ruined by slugs and snails eating them even before they emerge from the soil.

Pellets containing methiocarb should be scattered around the plants from the autumn onwards and replenished when they are washed away; alternatively traps may be set and kept baited. In wet springs slugs may even climb the flower stems and nibble the buds; they may also eat the nectaries and even make a home in the flower – this is especially troublesome in early flowers.

As. a general precaution, keeping the area around frames free of weeds and debris and clearing borders thoroughly in the autumn allows the beasts fewer hiding places.

Smut: A few growers have recently had a problem with smut, probably caused by *Urocyistus floccosa* – an allied fungus attacks winter aconites. This disease is especially prevalent in hot summers and causes the leaf petioles to buckle slightly and to split vertically, the 1–2in (2.5–5cm) cracks revealing a mass of black smutty spores.

So far this disease is still uncommon and while plants are not usually killed by it, it is important to cut away and burn the infected leaf to prevent infection of other parts of the plant and of neighbouring plants. It is thought that this particular smut fungus does not permeate the whole plant, so removal of the affected leaf should be sufficient to prevent further spread. However, the spores remain viable in the soil for some years and may infect tender shoots as they push through.

Vine weevil: As our winters become less severe and insecticides sold to the nursery trade for its treatment have been withdrawn, vine weevil has become an increasing problem in beds out of doors. Often the grubs are introduced on primroses or auriculas bought from small, poorly run nurseries, and they can then spread in woodsy

beds where they have long been known to attack rhododendrons.

The roots of the plants are eaten and the plants then suffer from drought and lack of nutrients; in severe cases they may become loose in the soil. Foliage may also be eaten by adults, which nibble rounded holes in the edges of the leaves. Once the beds are infested there is nothing that can be done, although spraying foliage regularly with HCH can reduce the population of adults. Biological control involving the use of parasitic nematodes, while well established for use on cyclamen grown as pot plants in uniform conditions, is unpredictable in its efficacy out of doors and is much less successful. In the greenhouse, adults can be caught manually when feeding at night.

Prevention is the best cure, and gardeners are well advised to wash the soil off the roots of primulas, auriculas, hardy cyclamen and saxifrages if there is any doubt about the hygiene standards of the nursery from which they are bought.

Virus: So far virus has not been a major problem with hellebores, although it may be a reason for the loss of vigour and the difficulty in propagation of some old clones. Occasionally a plant is discovered with pale, glossy, unusually stiff foliage and noticeably jagged toothing, and this is probably the result of virus infection. Pronounced yellow veining is also probably a sign of virus, and some plants treasured for their variegated foliage, such as the variety 'Graigueconna', are probably infected with virus.

There is no cure except the bonfire but the control of aphids will help prevent infection, as many viruses are carried by aphids from plant to plant. Keeping weeds under control is also an advisable precaution, as they can act as reserves of infection.

4

PLANT ASSOCIATIONS

Any plants that break into flower so early in the year ensure that we look to the spring with relief while winter still envelops us. The subtle colours of hellebores and their demure demeanour perfectly match the light and mood of winter-into-spring. Even on their own they create a comforting and inspiring picture. But one of the other reasons that hellebores hold such a special place in the affections of so many gardeners is that they are such a joy to plant with.

Although they belong to the spring garden whose flowers bring so much excitement, hellebores dare to give their best in midwinter while the electric blanket is still in nightly use. The range of good companions at flowering time is a large one: bulbs such as snowdrops, leucojums, anemones, chionodoxas and scillas, dainty woodlanders such as hepaticas, cyclamen, dentarias, primroses and pulmonarias, shrubs such as willows, forsythia, hamamelis and ribes.

One of the striking things about seeing hellebores in the wild is that so many of the plants with which they grow naturally are good garden plants themselves. This is clear from the sections under each species heading where wild partners are listed, in Chapter 6. Vincas, pulmonarias, epimediums, primroses, hepaticas, ferns, and many more garden plants for partial shade and leafy soil, grow with hellebores in the wild and make ideal garden companions for them.

SHRUBS AS BACKGROUND

The perfect situation for hellebores in the garden is under tall tree cover with a background of shrubs, either bold evergreens like camellias or mahonias, or deciduous shrubs with interesting twiggy branches, coloured bark or early flowers. Remembering that they are easy plants to grow given shade from midday sun, they are equally happy planted among shrubs or in the shade of a wall or fence.

Placing the right hellebore in front of the right shrub is perhaps a good starting point: a rich purple like the 'Queen of the Night' strain in front of *Ribes sanguineum* 'King Edward VII' could so easily clash, but striking up through the low branches of a mature *Hamamelis* × *intermedia* 'Pallida' – that would be different. In general choose pale-flowered shrubs to show up dark-flowered hellebores, and if possible place pale hellebores, especially yellows, against a rich evergreen background or in front of early-flowering shrubs in similar or complementary shades.

Other good shrubs to associate with hellebores include:

Acer species with good bark, such as *A. davidii* and *A. palmatum* 'Senkaki'

Camellia hybrids, especially those with smaller flowers

Hamamelis, especially those with a spreading rather than an upright habit

Hydrangea species, especially the lacecaps

Magnolia kobus

Mahonias

Philadelphus coronarius 'Aureus'

Physocarpus opulifolius 'Luteus', or 'Dart's Gold' whose colour lasts longer

Prunus serrula and the paler *P. maackii*, for their ornamental bark

Prunus × *subhirtella* 'Autumnalis'

Rhododendrons

Salix daphnoides and *S. magnifica*

Viburnum species, deciduous and evergreen

Second thoughts must go towards pruning the shrub in such a way as to ensure that there is a background of flower low down against which the hellebore flowers can be seen; this is especially tricky when you remember that the whole planting will be looked at from 5–6ft (1.5–1.8m) above ground.

A HELLEBORE BORDER

One simple and very effective approach to grouping hellebores is simply to plant all the best together, as Helen Ballard has done in the classic border planted on the north side of her Herefordshire farmhouse. Here the colours grade into each other and the hellebores are interplanted with snowdrops, hardy cyclamen and peonies. In such mixed plantings the pure green-flowered plants associate well with any of the other colours but are particularly lovely with the apricot and primrose-coloured forms. Primrose yellow and dark imperial purple are particularly pleasing, showing each other off to great effect.

Mature clumps of hellebores thrive under magnolia, aucuba and *Danae racemosa* at Great Dixter in Sussex

Pale colours are lovely to gather for a softer effect – white and apple-blossom pink through to plum show up especially well on dull winter days. Pinks and slaty blue/blacks would compliment each other well. The polypodiums are at their best from late summer right through the hellebore flowering season, and their lovely fresh green would be ideal meandering through all these hellebores.

In less shady places, later-growing perennials can be interplanted so that early in the year you see simply a bed of hellebores while other plants come to the fore later. Plants such as *Geranium phaeum* and *G. sylvaticum*, *Iris chrysographes*, *Tricyrtis formosana* var. *stolonifera* and *T. latifolia* and *Strobilanthes purpurea* start into growth in late spring and can give useful shade and 'coolth' in midsummer, shading the hellebores from the midday sun.

SPRING ASSOCIATIONS

Plants which grow naturally in woodland and at the woodland edge enjoy the same conditions and humus-rich soil as do hellebores. Many of these are late winter- and spring-flowering plants and, to start with some general thoughts, the following plants should provide ample possibilities:

Anemone blanda, A. nemorosa, A. ranunculoides and *A. trifolia* in their various forms, especially the earlier-flowering ones

Cardamine species, from the small *C. trifolia* to *C. kitaibelii*

Crocus, especially those with a tendency to self-sow

Cyclamen coum, C. hederifolium and *C. repandum*

Epimediums

Erythroniums

Fritillaria camschatcensis and *F. pontica*

Galanthus, particularly in their many special forms

Hepatica nobilis and *H. transsilvanica*

Leucojum vernum

Narcissus, especially in their smaller, earlier forms

Polygonatums

Polypodium australe and *P. vulgare* forms

Primula, especially primroses and the more elegant of the polyanthus

Pulmonaria, especially those with good leaves later in the year

Sanguinaria canadensis

Scillas

Tiarella cordifolia and *T. wherryi*

Trilliums

Uvularias

SUMMER ASSOCIATIONS

In the summer these flowering mixtures become pictures of cool foliage, the shady summer scene taking over from the light and sparkle of spring. The large distinguished leaves of the Orientalis Hybrids or the more intricately cut species mix well with spotted pulmonarias, cool elegant hostas, and lacy ferns, together with the more linear shapes of lilies, polygonatums and irises. Small silver-leaved plants like the more compact forms of lamium galeobdolon make attractive contrasts, as do the bluer-leafed dicentras.

In America, especially in the north-west, May- and June-flowering Pacific Coast irises are often grown with hellebores. In the UK we tend to think of this group of irises as lime-hating and not entirely hardy, but they are proving more tolerant of lime than at first we thought and with a good autumn mulch are hardy in many areas. They appreciate the same leafy, partially shaded conditions in which hellebores are usually grown, so we should try them more often. Other ideas for summer groupings include:

Anemone sylvestris

Astilbes

Clintonias

Dicentras

Euphorbia palustris

Gentiana asclepiadea

Geranium, especially *G. sylvaticum* forms such as 'Album', 'Amy Doncaster' and 'Baker's Pink', together with the various forms of *G. phaeum*

Iris chrysographes

Ophiopogon planiscapus 'Nigrescens'

Thalictrums

Veratrums

AUTUMN ASSOCIATIONS

Towards the end of the season, as the first of the old hellebore leaves are cut away, there are still plants to grow among and around them. These include:

Arum italicum for its fruits

Aster macrophyllus 'Twilight'

Colchicums

Cyclamen hederifolium

Disporum smithii for its fruits

Iris foetidissima for its foliage and fruits, especially the white-fruited form

Tricyrtis

LOW-MAINTENANCE ASSOCIATIONS

Hellebores are not the most demanding of plants, and gardeners with busy lives need equally self-sufficient plants to grow with them. Among the plants which like the same conditions, associate well with hellebores and look after themselves are:

Asarum europaeum
Asplenium scolopendrium
Blechnum spicant and other species
Brunnera macrophylla
Camellias
Cardamine heptaphylla
Dryopteris forms
Epimedium, evergreen types and forms of *E.* × *versicolor*
Fragaria daltoniana
Hostas
Myosotis scorpioides 'Mermaid'
Omphalodes verna
Onychium japonicum
Polystichums
Rhododendrons
Symphytums
Viburnum farreri
Vincas
Viola labradorica 'Purpurea'

COLOUR PLANNING

The most thoughtful approach is to plant individuals or colour groups with complementary companions. What follows is a range of suggestions, mainly for the Orientalis Hybrids in their various shades, reflecting the tastes of each of us – but not necessarily the tastes of both! One thing to be kept in mind is that hellebore foliage spreads out widely after flowering. The great advantage of this is that it provides cover for primroses and other more insistent shade-lovers nestling underneath, but plants which themselves make substantial foliage growth can make uneasy neighbours.

APRICOTS

These are relatively new colours in hellebores, so they give you a chance to try some completely new associations. Hamamelis, especially the darker cultivars like 'Jelena' or 'Diane', make good background shrubs, as do shrubs with yellowish-green stems such as *Cornus stolonifera* 'Flaviramea', or 'Kelseyi' with its red-tipped winter shoots.

Creamy-veined *Arum italicum* 'Pictum' makes a good neighbour, as do fresh ferns such as *Polypodium australe* or *P. vulgare* 'Pulcherrimum'. If you prefer an altogether lacier effect the various forms of *Polysticum setiferum* 'Divisilobum' are ideal.

Flowers in sympathetic shades include erythroniums such as *E. californicum* or the more vigorous and yellower 'Pagoda', and epimediums such as *E.* × *warleyense* 'Ellen Willmott' or *E.* × *versicolor* 'Sulphureum'. If you like to replicate the particular shades of these hellebore flowers, then primroses can match them well. You could choose the dainty 'Lady Greer' or the slightly more substantial 'Beamish Foam' in pink flushed with lemon, while 'Lambrook Cream Peach' should be good if you can get it.

Other plants to grow with apricot hellebores include:
Anemone × *lipsiensis*
Primroses such as 'Old Double Sulphur' or the pink-tinged 'Sue Jervis'
Milium effusum 'Aureum'
Narcissus 'Jenny'
Viola odorata 'Sulphurea'

BLUES

Choosing a background for hellebores in blue shades can be difficult, as their colours tend to be rather retiring. Sympathetic shrubs, for example blue-leaved rhododendrons such as *R. fastigiatum* and *R. lepidostylum*, will create a harmonius atmosphere, and the dark-stemmed *Salix daphnoides* would be suitable.

Slaty blue hellebores can easily suffer from overpowering neighbours, so companions must be carefully chosen. Blues with blues is a reliable formula, and pale blue pulmonarias like 'Mrs Kittle' or 'Roy Davidson', both of which have wonderful spotted leaves, will match well. Blue wood anemones like 'Blue Bonnet' or 'Blue Beauty' will wander through prettily, and the stunning but easy *Corydalis flexuosa* will certainly ensure that visitors stop and look.

Harmony in the foliage of neighbouring plants is a good way of augmenting blue hellebores, and the unusually glaucous foliage of *Dicentra* 'Langtrees' would be a sympathetic companion, likewise the silvery-painted *Athyrium niponicum* 'Pictum'. Pewter-leaved forms of *Cyclamen coum* would also fit in well, and among snow-drops the broad, glaucous leaves of *Galanthus elwesii* would make a delightful undercarpet. In fact any of the more glaucous-leaved snowdrops would be suitable, and as blue hellebores de-mand close inspection perhaps a variety like 'Comet' would be good; it needs careful scrutiny before the narrow green lines on its outer petals are revealed.

Snowdrop flowers provide contrast, and if that is your taste a little white primrose like 'Schneekissen' might be suitable or perhaps 'Garryarde Guinevere' would be sufficiently dainty. The rosy-pink *Cardamine pentaphyllos* would fit in well, as would a deep carmine pink *Cyclamen coum*.

Other plants to grow with blue hellebores include:
Adiantum pedatum and *A. pedatum* Asiatic form
Narcissus 'Dove Wings'
Primroses such as 'Blue Horizon' or 'Blue Riband'
Puschkinina scilloides
Sanicula caerulescens
Scilla bifolia and the paler *S. mischtschenkoana*
Tiarella wherryi

GREENS

Green hellebores make a surprisingly impressive impact in the garden, whether you grow *H. odorus* or one of the larger-flowered green hybrids. Yellow-flowered *Cornus mas* makes a fine background shrub, as does the evergreen *Daphne laureola* with its yellowish-green scented flowers. The red stems of *Cornus alba* 'Sibirica' are stunning with green Orientalis Hybrids, as they are with *H. foetidus*.

Winter aconites make a good carpet, while clumps of a small, early narcissus like 'Cedric Morris' look wonderful (although you may think these yellows a little strong, in which case the daintier *Hacquetia epipactis* is perhaps more fitting). *Galanthus* 'Merlin', with its green inner petals, is perfect, or the cool elegance of the strong and beautifully proportioned 'S. Arnott'. White and green always gives a clean, sharp look, and in addition to snowdrops you could try *Pulmonaria officinalis* 'Sissinghurst White'.

Other plants to grow with green-flowered hellebores include:

Anemone trifolia
× *Chionoscilla allenii*
Crocus tommasinianus, especially pale-flowered forms
Epimedium pinnatum and its subsp. *colchicum*
Mahonias
Osmaronia cerasiformis
Pulmonaria longifolia 'Dordogne'
Ranunculus ficaria 'Brazen Hussy'

PINKS

Hellebores come in such a range of pinks that we could refrain from suggesting planting partners for fear of a mismatch with your par-ticular plants. There are rose, apple-blossom, coral and now peachy pink shades, so carry a mature flower around your garden and match it to prospective neighbours.

But, ever eager for a challenge, we plunge in by suggesting a few shrubs as good neighbours, the sweetly scented *Viburnum* × *bodnantense* 'Dawn', for example. *Sarcococca hookeriana* var. *digyna* is also sweetly scented, and its variety 'Purple Stem' not only has its younger stems coloured purple but the backs of its leaves and its petioles are purple too and make a very suitable background. The rich red stems and foliage of a good form of *Euphorbia amygdaloides* 'Rubra' makes a superb background. The pale pink

A good pink hellebore seedling with naturalised snowdrops at East Lambrook Manor in Somerset

forms of *Prunus mume* are also suitable, although they appreciate shelter. Some of the early-flowering rhododendrons are also worth considering if your soil is acid, but you may feel that the pinks of varieties like 'Praecox', *R. dauricum* 'Midwinter' and *R. mucronulatum* are a little too strong.

You can harmonise by choosing pinks for under and around your hellebores too. Pink primroses like 'Lambrook Pink' or 'Lingwood Beauty' would be ideal, but darker colours like 'Tawny Port' or even the very rich 'Dukyl's Red Cowichan' are also suitable. Pink *Anemone nemorosa* would wander among the plants pleasingly; *Jeffersonia dubia* is more clump-forming; *Epimedium grandiflorum* in its lilac shades would be pretty.

Pink and blue is always a reliable combination, and pulmonarias like 'Blaues Meer' or *P. angustifolia* subsp. *azurea* with their bright blue flowers and modestly sized unmarked leaves should fit the bill. Appropriate foliage like the narrow black straps of *Ophiopogon planiscapus*

var. *nigrescens* should also be considered, or the prettily marked *Erythronium dens-canis* with its pink flowers to follow.

Other plants to grow with pink hellebores include:

Cornus alba 'Sibirica'
Epimedium × *rubrum*
Scilla siberica 'Spring Beauty' and *S. mischtschenkoana*
Pulmonaria officinalis 'Sissinghurst White'
Trillium chloropetalum rubrum

PRIMROSES AND YELLOWS

As a background, shrubs such as *Salix fargesii*, with its 6in (15cm) upright catkins, or the more rounded twiggy habit and yellow clusters of *Cornus mas* are good. The deliciously fragrant *Daphne pontica*, with greeny yellow flowers, or the lemony *Hamamelis* × *intermedia* 'Pallida',

26

with an equally intoxicating scent, make a very harmonious backdrop. Alternatively, a variegated holly such as 'Silver Queen' will set off yellow hellebores well.

Primrose hellebores generally need quiet companions. Powerful colours will often distract, and native wild primroses and their double forms make harmonious neighbours. 'Barrowby Gem', if you can get it, would be ideal for its long flowering period and wonderful scent. With pulmonarias, choose your variety according to the shade of hellebore. The palest primrose hellebores are best with a pale pulmonaria like 'Blue Mist', but the stronger yellows can take the darker 'Frühlingshimmel'. Few are rich enough for the strongest blues and those with purplish overtones. Pale wood anemones like *A. nemorosa* 'Robinsoniana' would be lovely, while the unusual form with green, leafy flowers known as 'Green Fingers' would be a welcome underling for a spotted yellow, as both deserve a close look.

As well as the polypodiums mentioned earlier, one particular fern comes to mind – *Adiantum pedatum*, with its dark, almost black stems and its arching, neatly divided, fresh green fronds.

Other plants to grow with primrose and yellow hellebores include:
Epimedium × *warleyense*
Hacquetia epipactis
Iris foetidissima
Narcissus 'Rip van Winkle'
Scilla mischtschenkoana
Viola labradorica 'Purpurea'

REDS

Choosing a background for red-flowered hellebore varieties is not easy. They often show up poorly against dark evergreens, and the flowers of many pale-flowered shrubs clash. Some of the early rhododendrons should be suitable, as would the rich pink *Prunus mume* 'Benichidori', which is happy in a little shade, and *Salix gracilistyla* 'Melanostachys'. *Euphorbia* × *martinii*, with dark green, red-tinted foliage, makes a stupendous background.

Choosing companions in matching shades can be difficult, as red hellebores often have purple or bronze tints which create unease. That said, *Euphorbia dulcis* 'Chameleon' and *Epimedium* × *rubrum* will provide foliage in the right tones. The early flowering *Pulmonaria rubra* has the bonus of fresh foliage to follow.

Choose pink partners carefully, depending on the exact shade of both. *Pulmonaria* 'Dora Bielefeld' is a good choice, some of the Barnhaven 'New Pink' polyanthus should be suitable, or perhaps, in a richer, darker mode, *Vinca minor* 'Burgundy'.

For more of a contrast, pale blue *Pulmonaria* 'Frühlingshimmel' or wild primroses would be suitable, while a carpet of snowdrops would certainly make an impact.

Other plants to grow with red hellebores include:
Anemone blanda 'White Splendour'
Cyclamen coum
Primula vulgaris 'Ladybird', 'Captain Blood' or other dark doubles, or Barnhaven polyanthus 'Rustic Reds'
Pulmonaria officinalis 'Sissinghurst White'
Scilla siberica 'Alba' or 'Spring Beauty'

PURPLES

Choosing good shrubs to make an appropriate background for the dark purple hellebore varieties is especially important, as their rich colouring could easily disappear in front of the wrong colour. *Corylopsis sinensis* 'Spring Purple', with its yellow tassels and purple-tinted young growth, would be ideal. The stems of that unusual willow *Salix daphnoides*, in purple overlaid with a white bloom, would also be a good choice, though pruning every couple of years would be necessary to keep the whole plant to a modest size and ensure that the best stem colouring is down at hellebore level.

Rich purple and pale blue is an attractive spring combination, and the soft lilac-blue of *Primula vulgaris* subsp. *sibthorpii* is ideal, as are pale blue pulmonarias like Amy Doncaster's palest sky-blue 'Blue Mist'. Wood anemones like *A. nemorosa* 'Royal Blue' will meander in and out perfectly, and from among the bulbs try the undeservedly neglected pale blue *Scilla mischtschenkoana*, whose spelling you will have to learn to write down for visitors.

Purple and white provides a contrast not all gardeners appreciate, but if it fits your taste try *Pulmonaria officinalis* 'Sissinghurst White'; the foliage also goes well later in the season. Snowdrops are good too, preferably a fairly stout and upright one – 'Lime Tree', which is a late version of *G.* × *atkinsii*, perhaps, or 'Magnet'. The vigorous *Anemone blanda* 'White Splendour' can nestle prettily right under a dark hellebore.

This brings us on to purple and yellow, and there are plenty of primroses to suit, ranging from the wild species to one of its various double forms such as 'Old Double Sulphur', or you could try *Anemone ranunculoides* and its pretty double form. There are many daffodils to choose from, 'W. P. Milner' or 'Queen Anne's Double', for example, and Bowles' golden grass, *Milium effusum* 'Aureum', can be allowed to self-sow among the clumps.

The various hellebore plants going round as 'Atrorubens' at least have earliness in common, and flowering as they do before most other hellebores, their companions must be chosen with care. The choice is small, limited to snowdrops and little else; *G.* × *atkinsii* is early and easy to find, and has the merit of spreading well. The hellebore spreads too, so if they are planted closely and then both are left alone, eventually they should mix.

Other good plants to grow with rich purple hellebores include:

Anemone apennina and *A. nemorosa*
   'Robinsoniana'
Cardamine kitaibelii and *C. trifolia*
Chionodoxa luciliae
Erythronium revolutum
Geranium maculatum
Primula, especially primroses such as 'Alba
   Plena', 'Blue Riband', 'Chartreuse', 'Garryarde
   Guinevere', 'Ingram's Blue' and 'Miss Indigo'
Scilla siberica 'Spring Beauty'
Viola labradorica 'Purpurea'
Lamium galeobdolon 'Silberteppich'

WHITES

Camellias are excellent shrubs to back white-flowered hellebores, and 'Cornish Snow' is especially suitable. With masses of small white flowers set off by its good evergreen foliage, it is far more elegant than the large-flowered hybrids. *Rhododendron* 'Bo-peep' would be a good alternative for rhododendron fans. Among other shrubs, consider corylopsis, *Hamamelis mollis* and the equally well-scented *Sarcococca confusa*. *Daphne pontica* would be a fine choice, or perhaps the relatively unknown *D. albowiana*, which seems to differ mainly in its red rather than black fruits.

If you like contrast you can be bold with white hellebores and try darker pulmonarias like the rich and sparkling 'Bertram Anderson' form of *P. longifolia*; alternatively you could be more subtle with 'Blue Mist'. A good white could take *Scilla siberica* 'Spring Beauty'; *Cyclamen coum* and almost any anemones that fit in with other nearby plantings would also be suitable. Some whites are very early and could be underplanted with choice aconites such as *Eranthis hyemalis* 'Guinea Gold'.

The purity of the best whites will also take the pinkish purple of *Corydalis solida*, though there will be little opportunity for foliage contrast as the corydalis dies away by midsummer.

Matching white with white, in the form of variegation, works well, and the white-veined, arrowhead leaves of *Arum italicum* 'Pictum' make a good choice, as does the more delicate *Disporum sessile* 'Variegatum'. Snowdrops and *Cyclamen coum* 'Album' can intermingle among them all.

Spotted whites invite us to pick up the colours of the spots in nearby plantings, but this might tend to encourage too many heavy colours. A good form of *Euphorbia amygdaloides* 'Rubra' is ideal. Better, perhaps, to plant a group of hellebores in white, purple or red, and spotted white, then underplant them all with sky blue or primrose yellow.

Turning up the flowers to examine them is one of the joys of spotted hellebores, so snow-

(*Above*): A good yellow hellebore seedling with *Pulmonaria* 'Fruhlingshimmel' at Washfield Nursery. The red wool on the hellebore marks a hand-pollinated flower
(*Right*): *Helleborus argutifolius* growing in the garden at Dower House, Boughton House, with *Lamium maculatum* 'Beacon Silver' and *Corydalis cheilanthifolia*

drops demanding the same close attention make good neighbours. The Greatorex doubles like 'Ophelia', with their unusually neat centres, or another double such as 'Hill Poë', with its curious white flared centre, come to mind.

Other plants to grow with white hellebores include:
Cardamine quinquefolia
Epimedium × *versicolor* 'Sulphureum'
Narcissus 'Charity May' or 'Thalia'
Narcissus moschatus
Primula 'Barnhaven New Pinks'
Pulmonaria 'Blue Ensign' and *P. officinalis* 'Sissinghurst White'
Tiarella cordifolia

OTHER HELLEBORES

Christmas roses, *H. niger*, are more difficult to place with other plants effectively, although trimming off all the foliage before the turn of the year helps reveal the flowers and allow companions a little space.

Primroses are less successful companions for *H. niger* than they are for the Orientalis Hybrids, as the foliage is so low that little space is left for anything to squeeze under. If they really did flower at Christmas we would indeed be stuck, for the choice then is severely limited. *Cyclamen coum* can be slid in close, a speckling of magenta or pink among the white, and the little yellow *Hacquetia epipactis* together with hepaticas in their pinks and blues would also make good companions. But perhaps bulbs like scillas or *Crocus tommasinianus* 'Whitewell Purple' are the best minglers.

In winter, the stinking hellebore, *H. foetidus*, is sometimes seen alone in a desolate border full

of dormant summer plants; it looks silly in winter and it gets in the way in summer, although it can serve as a host for one of the classier *Clematis integrifolia* selections like 'Tapestry'. But in a similar border with a carpet of bulbs or the background of a wall, an evergreen shrub or even the dense twigginess of a deciduous shrub, then the effect is quite different. Here the familiar wild species will make a specimen plant of the highest quality – all on its own. Red- and yellow-stemmed cornus are fine companions.

The red-tinted 'Wester Flisk' cries out for neighbours, even from before the flowering shoots have started to extend. 'February Gold' or 'February Silver' daffodils can be stunning partners.

In terms of plant association, the Corsican hellebore, *H. argutifolius*, is similar to the stinking hellebore in its flowering season and growing habit. But the Corsican hellebore is better out in the full sun than in shade, for in shady situations it grows too tall and this accentuates its natural tendency to flop.

In full sun in a dry garden with other Mediterranean plants this, or *H.* × *sternii*, really comes into its own. A well-drained soil will help keep its stems to a relatively modest 2½–3ft (75–90cm) in height, but unfortunately increases its

tendency to lose its lower leaves.

For spring, as it comes into flower, the dwarfer forms of *Euphorbia characias* are good, while the red-tinted *E.* × *martinii* is perhaps even better, its rounded habit contrasting well with the jagged foliage of the hellebore. A shrub such as *Cistus incanus* subsp. *creticus* will neatly hide bare stems as long as the hellebore is supported to prevent the stems collapsing on to the cistus after snow. Silver foliage like that of glauciums or artemisias is good too, while sages, lavenders or rue would all be appropriate neighbours, although these too may need protection from hellebore branches.

Later in the year, when the old flowering stems have been cut out, the Corsican hellebore makes a good support for a climber such as an annual Mediterranean pea – *Lathyrus chloranthus* or *L. clymenum*, for example, but not the perennial peas, which make so much growth that they will surely bring the hellebore crashing down. That intriguing biennial *Adlumia fungosa* is another choice, or perhaps the yellow-flowered climber *Dicentra macrocapnos*. In colder parts of the United States, this species is grown outdoors exclusively as a foliage plant, the ferocious winters killing the flower shoots to ground level.

5

PROPAGATION

Having bought or raised an exciting plant there is, unfortunately, no easy or fast way of propagating it and this explains why the best-quality hellebore plants are expensive to buy. New forms of shrubs can be propagated quickly by taking cuttings; not so with hellebores. And unlike the usual run of herbaceous plants, they cannot be divided up regularly or increased by other methods such as stem or root cuttings. Perhaps this is one of their fascinations. In practice this leaves us just two viable choices, seed and division, with the faint possibility of a third method, micropropagation, for the professional laboratory in the future.

Ultimately, it comes down to a simple choice. Hellebores can be propagated from seed in relatively large numbers, but seed will always produce a certain amount of variation. Division will at least ensure that all the offspring are identical, and although it is a very slow process it remains the only way of increasing named forms or special individuals.

DIVISION

The prime reason for propagating hellebores by division is to ensure that all the new plants are identical to the parent. You may have an old plant which is not thriving, and division can revive it. Or you may have an especially lovely or interesting plant you wish to propagate to make a larger planting or to pass around to friends.

As hellebores are slow to recover after division, many gardeners are understandably reluctant to disturb their plants, preferring instead to take pieces off the side when fellow enthusiasts plead persuasively or their natural generosity takes over. This is a big mistake and can lead to

disaster. It results in the healthiest and most vigorous shoots being given away, leaving the warm-hearted gardener with the weakest growth from the middle of the clump as reward for his generosity. This is one of the main reasons why supposedly long-established clumps in gardens sometimes look so feeble, and it is ironic that the most generous gardeners may end up with the poorest plants themselves. No, it is best to divide the clump properly and ensure that both you and your friends have strong, vigorous pieces to grow on.

TIMING

The clue to the correct time for dividing plants lies in their pattern of growth. The Orientalis Hybrids make a great deal of root growth in autumn and winter while the species, most of which naturally lie dormant under the snow in winter, make their main root growth in spring.

The ideal approach is to divide the plants just as root growth is beginning, as this ensures that they settle down as quickly as possible after recovering from the inevitable shock. So the Orientalis Hybrids can be divided as early as the end of August but are most often done in early September. In general, the earlier the better is a good rule as this enables the new divisions to catch as much of the potential time for root growth as possible, growing into bigger and better plants for the following spring.

The flower buds will already be formed when the plants are divided, so that the young plants will flower the spring after division. But do not be alarmed if they then take a year or two off flowering – this is particularly likely with divisions from old clumps. Regard it as a promising sign that they are building up strength.

We should say here that the species in the caulescent group, *H. argutifolius*, *H. foetidus* and *H. lividus*, do not divide easily. For one thing, division presents a practical problem owing to their lack of a clearly divined system of rhizomes, and anyway it hardly seems worth the bother when they set seed so generously and the variation between seedlings is relatively slight. Although it is probably perfectly possible to divide *H. vesicarius*, why take the risk with such a treasure when you can rely on the, admittedly few, seeds produced. Brave souls may try division in early autumn, this being a plant from a Mediterranean climate starting into growth with the autumn rains.

Like many species in the wild, *H. niger* lies dormant under the snow in winter and divides best in early spring. The *niger* hybrids like *H.* × *nigercors* and *H.* × *ericsmithii*, with their rather different habit of growth brought about by the influence of the other parent, divide best in the early autumn, though it is a difficult process.

The Balkan species (*H. atrorubens*, *H. cyclophyllus*, *H. dumetorum*, *H. multifidus*, *H. odorus*, *H. purpurascens* and *H. torquatus*) always divide best in early spring, in that period between starting into first growth and before the leaves are developed – ideally, before the flowering stems elongate. This can be as early as the end of January or early February in a mild winter. Catching them just as they start into growth minimises the damage and gives them longer to settle down before having to support leaf growth.

TECHNIQUE

Before doing anything, there are three crucial factors to consider. First, it is important to choose the right plants to divide; second, division must be done at the right time of year; and third, the weather conditions on the day must be suitable, as described below.

At flowering time, make a decision as to which plants need division and mark them specifically for division with clear labels; by September they all look alarmingly alike and you may well end up dividing the wrong plant. Do not waste time dividing poor forms, choose only the very best.

Division is not a job to be rushed, and ideally you need plenty of time with no interruptions to do the job well. Choose a dull, still, cool day and preferably a dank and drizzly one; if the season is dry, water the plants thoroughly a couple of days before digging them up. Avoid days which are hot and dry or particularly windy, but if this proves to be a counsel of perfection never be put off, simply move operations to a cool, shady shed and have a hand sprayer ready to help prevent roots drying out. Plants for division should be in good health and sprayed against aphids.

First of all dig up the marked clump, which is sometimes easier said than done. It is helpful to tie all the leaves together loosely first then fork all round the plant before starting to lever it out. It is surprising how heavy a mature plant ready for division can be, so have forks, string, knife and barrow to hand from the first. Lever out the plant using a large digging fork and shake the clump well. If your soil is heavy, use the fork to comb off as much soil as possible, taking care not to damage the roots more than necessary.

Even if you intend to split the plant into only a few large pieces it is a great help to wash all the soil off the plant. Washing makes it so much easier to examine the growth of the plant and to see exactly where to make cuts. The root system of an old plant with its mass of congested rhizomes is impossible to fathom when covered in soil. Although at Washfield Elizabeth finds an old baby bath or a small galvanised bath indispensable for washing off soil, a large bucket should be adequate.

If you intend to divide a large strong clump into just a few plants, a small spade will be ideal; sharpen it with a file before you start. On the other hand, if you wish to divide an old clump or break up a young plant into as many pieces as possible, Elizabeth finds the ideal tool to be a wide-bladed, sharp knife – having broken the tip off many a narrow blade!

Once the plant is dug and washed, never rush. Take time to look at the plant very carefully and to decide which are the easiest and most obvious places to cut. In some plants you may find the new growths climbing over each other so that their noses are under other growths; these will need teasing apart carefully.

If you need only a few plants, cut in the obvious places. If you want to obtain the maximum number of splits, start by making as many cuts as possible in the old rhizomes in the middle of the plant, as this will give you good long lengths of rhizome on each division. Be as careful as you can not to damage roots, and most especially not to damage young roots. Cut off any old dead rhizome and damaged roots.

It helps the young plants establish themselves well if each has at least one mature leaf, so try to keep this in mind when deciding where to cut. If there is a choice, leave two small leaves rather than one large one, as a large leaf is inclined to catch the wind and act like a sail – if the young plant is loosened in the ground the new roots may be damaged.

Have a bucket or bath of crumbled and wetted peat to hand in which to place divisions immediately – this will cut down on the chance of the roots drying out, which is to be avoided at all costs. It is a good idea to place the divisions in size order in the bucket, as this makes it easier when it comes to planting out or potting up and minimises root damage.

It is very important that you write any additional labels now, at the time of dividing, rather than leave it until later. Each nursery row will need a label, but if the divisions are to be potted up it is best to use one label per pot rather than one per batch; this will avoid a confusing muddle, infuriating after lavishing all this care on the plants.

DEALING WITH DIVISIONS

Once the divisions are made, they can be potted up or planted out immediately. Better still, however, Elizabeth has found that bedding them down carefully in a bucket of peat for about ten days encourages the prompt growth of strong young roots; in this time the divisions can make as much as 2in (5cm) of new root. This

A fine white-flowered hybrid at Washfield Nursery which has been the parent of hundreds of good plants

technique is not necessary with larger divisions which are destined to be planted straight back in the garden, but is especially valuable when you're trying to make as many divisions as possible from a single plant. If you have divided several plants on the same occasion, it is best to keep them in separate containers as this avoids the possibility of mix-ups. Keep them in a shady place out of the wind, spray them over thoroughly with water every evening, and make sure the peat never dries out.

You now have a break while the new roots form. This time can be used to prepare the ground for planting, whether the divisions are to go back in their permanent places in the garden or in prepared nursery rows. There is also time to check on the numbers and type of pots you will need if potting up. Small divisions can go into 6½in (2 litre) standard pots, though they are happiest in long pots which are an inch narrower but a useful 2in (5cm) deeper. These are sometimes sold as rose pots. You need a good open compost for potting; a good mix is made up of equal parts of sterilised loam, fine grade bark, medium grade peat and grit (5mm crushed beach) with thirty or forty granules of Osmocote in each pot.

Any good open compost will do, but it needs to be rich in humus though well drained and sufficiently open for young roots to grow in easily. If your usual compost is a peat-based one from the garden centre, continue to use it. Hellebores are not unusually choosy, and any humus-rich mixture which is reasonably well drained will do.

If replanting in beds or borders, this is your only chance to prepare the ground well. Dig the area deeply and plant in the same way as you would specimens in the border (page 13). Plant firmly with the nose just under the soil and water in well, twice – or ideally three times. Don't forget to replace the label, with the date of division added.

When planting in nursery rows, add lime if necessary, make a large deep hole, and add plenty of humus-rich planting mix. Be careful not to cramp the old roots and take care not to damage the young roots which have developed while the divisions were in their peat. Plant the best divisions at the front of the row immediately behind the label, grading down to the smallest at the end of the row. In this way there will be no danger of parting with the best pieces without realising.

After planting or potting up, ensure that the divisions are well watered and watch for aphids, which are particularly debilitating for young plants; likewise black spot.

There is no point in dividing inferior plants, but if you feel you need practice, or to gain confidence, it is quite a good idea to dig and divide a not too precious plant first and then tackle a cherished plant after that experience.

RAISING HELLEBORES FROM SEED

Hellebores can be raised from seed in three ways. You can simply collect seed from a mixed planting of good plants; this will produce better seedlings than seed collected from poor plants, but the results will be unpredictable and if you have speckled plants in your collection many of the seedlings will also be speckled.

If the seed is saved from different colours grown in isolation from one another, the resultant plants will be broadly similar. Alternatively you can hand-pollinate; this is the most exciting and the most creative option, as it can produce improvement in colour and form. It is the only reliable option with the species.

Fortunately, hellebores germinate very easily, and you only have to look at the forest of seedlings which often appears under mature plants to realise that hellebores are not difficult to raise from seed. Some are more generous than others, but given the right conditions none, except *H. vesicarius*, is difficult. For in spite of their early flowering season, their generous supply of nectar attracts honey-bees and bumble-bees to pollinate on any days when the weather encourages them to fly.

The reproductive cycle of the Orientalis Hybrids and many of the species is such that they flower early in the year, the seed ripens by midsummer and falls to the ground around the plants, and all will germinate by Christmas. Plants will occasionally flower just over a year later if grown well; the majority will bloom after two years, and all should flower in their third year.

If allowed to reproduce in this way, self-sown seedlings can show an interesting variety of colours, but unless different colours are kept separate and unless you are very selective, they tend to produce muddy colours, a preponderance of spots and ultimate disappointment. Over the years your new plants are unlikely to improve and may well be less attractive. When it comes to species, only seedlings from plants grown in complete isolation from possible hybridisers by hooding and self-pollinating by hand can be relied on to come true.

To get the best from your plants and to improve them, they should be either self-pollinated or crossed with selected partners. The seed from each cross should then be kept separate and sown separately. Fortunately the procedure for crossing or self-pollination is not difficult, so anyone seriously interested in growing hellebores should not propagate them from open-pollinated seed. A couple of hand crosses which take only a few moments will yield enough seed for most people (see page 75).

SEED COLLECTION AND STORAGE

As soon as the seed-pods are seen to start to split, the flowers should be cut off and upended in a brown paper bag to allow the pods to open fully and drop their seeds. Beware of using manila envelopes, as the gluing at the bottom sometimes leaves gaps through which seed can escape. The brown paper bags commonly used in shops, roughly 7in x 10in (17.5 x 25cm) or a little larger, are very cheap to buy and being deeper than they are wide, help prevent spills. The bags should be kept indoors in the dry for a couple of weeks and then emptied on to a large white sheet of paper so that the seed can be separated easily from the stems, pods and other debris.

The seed can then be stored in small brown envelopes, for example those sold as school dinner money envelopes, again in a cool dry place. But seed will need to be stored only for a relatively short time, as sowing should take place in the second half of June or in early July; germination will then be excellent. If seed is stored for longer than a few weeks, germination is reduced when the seed is eventually sown. It seems clear that the seed does not die but goes into a state of dormancy from which it is reluctant to be roused. From this you will deduce the reason for the poor germination of seed bought from seed companies, which usually arrives in autumn or winter, many months after the ideal sowing time.

The usual way of treating such seed is simply to sow it as usual when it arrives, leave the pots outside and wait, sometimes for ever, for germination to take place. More often occasional seedlings appear at unlikely seasons while the rest of the seeds remain stubbornly inactive. Storing seed in the fridge between its harvest in the summer and its dispatch by the seed company in the autumn seems to have little positive effect, perhaps because hellebores require a warm spell after sowing and taking up water followed by a reduction in temperature – not the other way round.

The one exception to these rules seems as usual to be *H. vesicarius*, seed of which remains viable for up to two years, although it is still preferable to sow it soon after harvest.

SEED SOWING

The routine for sowing seed of the herbaceous hellebore species is not a complicated or a difficult one but is worth explaining in detail. *H. vesicarius* is, again, the exception and is dealt with separately.

Seed is sown in the second half of June or early July, shortly after it is collected. Seed received in autumn and winter is best sown as soon as you receive it. Hellebore seed does not need a winter's freezing to spark germination, this is a myth; most will germinate naturally before Christmas, with the exception of *H. niger*. Some gardeners sow seed straight in the open ground, but careful sowing in pots will give the best results.

At Washfield Elizabeth sows in 6½in (16cm) clay pots. John Innes seed compost is perfectly suitable for hellebores, but if you buy it in a bag rather than mix it yourself, you may need to improve it with extra bark or extra grit if what you find when you open the bag does not meet with your approval. If you are used to a different mixture for seed-sowing then stick with it; fresh seed is far more important than which particular seed compost you use.

Each pot is crocked, the crock covered with 1in (2.5cm) of grit, then filled with compost to just under the level of the top; it is then tapped down firmly and levelled off lightly. Do not use another pot or a firming tool; you need plenty of air in the compost and watering will compact it quite sufficiently.

A 6½in (16cm) pot will take about thirty seeds. It is important always to space the seeds about an inch (2.5cm) apart in case potting up is delayed, and this also minimises root damage

This lovely hybrid growing in the garden at Washfield Nursery was the result of crossing a 'Pluto' hybrid with 'Early Purple'

when the seedlings are pricked out. You can move the seeds about with the point of a pencil to ensure they are well spaced. If you have too many seeds do not sow them more thickly; it is far better to split them into two batches and sow them in separate pots.

After sowing, cover the seed carefully with ½in (12mm) of grit. Elizabeth is lucky enough to have a local supply of 5mm crushed beach from which she sieves out the finest and coarsest and uses the rest for seed covering, but any sharp grit is suitable. Make sure the surface of the grit is level, then label each pot with the date of sowing and all other relevant information.

The pots then need watering, and this is best done by soaking from below. Ensure that the water is no higher than 2in (5cm) below the top of the pot or the seed could float up through the grit. Remove the pots gently once the grit shows wet. Then plunge the pots right up to their rims in grit; any similar material would do, but avoid sand as it tends to compact and grow lichen. Plunging encourages an even, cool and moist atmosphere. Do not plunge the seed pots in the garden or in soil, as worms will get in and disturb the seedlings.

Graham uses 5in (12.5cm) plastic pots. Most gardeners have some around, but they should be full-depth pots rather than half pots or pans, which are unsuitable as they do not allow the seedlings enough root room. About twenty-two seeds will go in a 5in pot. Do not use pots smaller than 4in (10cm), taking about a dozen seeds, and try to use only one size of pot; small pots and pots in mixed sizes will be more difficult to manage. Plastic pots need not be plunged but can simply be stood on the grit in a frame. Whether you use clay or plastic pots, be sure that the grit is wet when the pots are stood out, and take care to stand them level to prevent water washing the seeds about so that they congregate in patches.

A humid microclimate around the seeds appears to facilitate germination, and some sort of cover such as a slate or similar material is ideal. At Washfield Elizabeth uses asbestos rounds cut to the size of the seed pots, and these are ideal, but few of us would be happy to cut up asbestos considering the health problems associated with it.

The joy of these lids is that they act as protection from cats, inquisitive birds and the destructive fury of heavy rain, which can scatter grit and seed far and wide. The beauty of using clay pots is that in hot dry weather the pots can be watered overhead with no danger of disturbing the seed – the lids are left on and the compost absorbs the moisture from the plunge through the sides of the clay pots.

Seed sown in plastic pots without the benefit of pot lids should have two coverings. The first cover should be a frame of wire netting to keep out rabbits, birds, mice and cats. Make sure none of the pots are under the struts or they will suffer from drips. In nature seedlings are covered in snow after germination, and this insulation blanket creates a relatively constant temperature rather than the stop-go conditions of the average British winter. So to help equalise conditions the frames also need a glass or polythene cover for use during the worst winter weather.

Start checking for germination in October and inspect the pots three or four times a week. If your seed was fresh and it was sown promptly, all species and hybrids should have germinated by Christmas with the exception of *H. niger*, seedlings of which will appear in the New Year.

AFTER GERMINATION

As soon as germination starts, bring the pots from the plunge into a frame or cold greenhouse

to give protection from the elements, and give them plenty of light. A cold greenhouse with plenty of ventilation is suitable, but be sure to cover the ventilators with wire netting to guard against birds, mice and cats and to fill any ground level gaps in the blockwork. Elizabeth simply removes the pot lid and moves the pots to a frame. There is no need to plunge the pots, and they can go in as tight as possible unless they were sown too thickly, in which case a little extra spacing would be useful.

It will be as well to have an emergency covering to hand in case of hard or prolonged frost; the shade frame used later in the season against the sun is ideal. Otherwise old carpet, coconut matting or other insulation is suitable. Try and make sure the frames are open as much as possible, as stale and stagnant air is the seedlings' worst enemy. The lights can be removed completely on blue sky days unless the winds are too bracing. In recent years we have experienced some very strong, cold, drying winds on sunny days, when the frames can become quite hot if left closed. The answer is to prop them open, securing them well by tying them down or weighting them with concrete building blocks or something equally heavy and stable.

As the seedlings continue to grow you will need to pay more attention to watering, and the seed pots may need watering more than once a week. The seedlings are now very vulnerable to slugs and mice. One mouse can make a feast of hundreds of precious seedlings in one night's gorging, so set a trap in each frame. Better still, set two in case they have a party and friends are invited along for a feast. Make sure slug bait is set regularly, preferably using one based on methiocarb which also kills millipedes and leatherjackets.

The seedlings must be protected against the worst of the weather and against pests until March. They will then be ready for potting up just as the first true leaf, or leaves, are showing.

Seedlings can be planted direct into the open ground from their seed pots, but potting them up will give them a better start in life; it is far, far better to take a little extra trouble and grow them on in individual pots, protected from the hazards of life in the open, to produce sturdy, healthy plants which will grow away strongly after planting out.

Tip the ball of roots out of the pot, remove the crock and grit, then gently squeeze it a little to loosen the roots. Then, taking care *never* to handle them on the stem, pick up each seedling by a leaf and pot to just below the seed leaves. Pot gently, simply tap the pot sharply to settle the compost, and press down firmly. Finally top-dress with grit to serve as a mulch and prevent the compost compacting. Ensure that the label from the seed pot is transferred to the newly potted seedlings.

It is vital that seedlings are never handled by the stem below the growing point, however gently. The stem is easily bruised, and within a few days it blackens at the point where it has been touched and bends into a gentle arch with the seed leaves hanging down facing the pot. Apart from the blackened area where the stem bends over, the rest of the seedling may remain green for some time. But you might just as well throw it away at once.

Pot up the seedlings in spring, ideally when the seedlings have one true leaf; if left too late there is an increased danger of root damage which can set back seedlings of slower-growing species especially badly. Start with the most advanced pots, tipping out and potting up one potful at a time to avoid the danger of confusion. Always pot up a few more seedlings than you think you need, half a dozen perhaps, in case of accidents.

Pot the seedlings individually into 3½in (9cm) pots. If you are short of space you can use boxes, but the disadvantage of this is that the roots are far more likely to become tangled and this can lead to damage when you come to separate them for planting. Choose deep boxes, either deep plastic seed trays or tomato boxes treated with a plant-friendly wood preservative. If the tomato boxes you are able to beg from your local greengrocer have the base made of a single piece of hardboard rather than slats, drill some drainage holes. Prick out a maximum of

fifteen seedlings to a standard-sized seed tray, twenty-four to a tomato box. Any standard potting compost is suitable.

By the end of April all the seedlings should be potted up except those of the rather slower species like *H. dumetorum* and *H. purpurascens*, which may not be ready until early May. After potting they can all be lined out in the frame with the same protection given to newly germinated seedlings – a glass or polythene light, mouse-traps and slug pellets. Although there is unlikely to be any need for extra frost protection it might be necessary to shade the frame on hot sunny days.

After a few days kept closed, the frame can be opened up on all sunny days and the seedlings allowed gentle rain whenever possible, taking care not to expose them to heavy rain or hail, which will lead to bruising of the foliage. The frame can also be opened day and night in mild weather and should always be left slightly open except on nights when a severe frost is expected. The seedlings will be ready to plant out as soon as the roots start to show through the bottom of the pots. Those in clay pots will probably need water at least once a week if the weather is mild, those in plastic will need watering less frequently.

There are exceptions to this approach. Seedlings of *H. argutifolius*, *H. atrorubens*, *H. foetidus*, *H. lividus* and of *H. niger* crosses often make so much root so quickly that they are best pricked out into a slightly larger pot, 4in (10cm) rather than 3½in (9cm), to prevent them becoming pot-bound.

The treatment for *H. vesicarius* differs rather more from the normal procedure. The seed is best space sown 2in (5cm) apart and then left in the seed pot until the following September or October after germination. As the seedlings start to grow in the autumn they can be potted individually into deep pots for planting out the following spring.

SELF-SOWN SEEDLINGS

The simplest method of raising hellebores from seed, although the most unreliable, is simply to allow bees to pollinate the flowers and then let the resulting seed germinate beneath the plants. This has the advantage of involving the gardener in no effort whatsoever, but in most cases the results will do little more than reflect this lack of diligence. For bees can carry pollen a long way, and not only will they bring pollen from other plants in your own garden, but they may well bring it from inferior plants growing in gardens nearby.

Most hellebores self-sow to some extent, but some are more prolific than others. The most generous with their seedlings are *H. argutifolius*, *H. foetidus* and *H. orientalis*. If you grow just one form of *H. foetidus* then you can rely on self-sown seedlings coming reasonably true and you should get plenty of them. But if you grow more than one form, 'Bowles' Form' as well as 'Wester Flisk' perhaps, they will probably cross and you will find yourself with a variable batch of seedlings. At least *H. foetidus* does not cross with other species.

By contrast, the Orientalis Hybrids will cross not only with each other but also with quite a number of other species, so the offspring of plants growing near other forms and species will be highly unpredictable. About the only help we can give is that you usually find that seedlings showing dark staining on stems will be the darkest-flowered. As a rule the plant we know as "Atrorubens" often flowers so early that few bees are around to pollinate and so self-sown seedlings are relatively uncommon.

On its own *H. argutifolius* is a prolific self-sower, and although it can be crossed with *H. niger* by hand, natural hybrids are rare. However, it will cross with the closely related *H. lividus*, and where the two are in the same garden, even if *H. lividus* is grown in the greenhouse and *H. argutifolius* some way away, hybrids (*H. × sternii*) will undoubtedly turn up in spite of *H. lividus* starting to flower rather earlier.

It is striking how few self-sown seedlings of *H. niger* appear compared with *H. orientalis* and its hybrids. They seem to appear regularly in Graham's garden but only in small numbers. The various forms cross with each other of course, but will not usually cross with anything else, although one plant in Graham's garden has produced two self-sown seedlings which are clearly hybrids with the plant of *H. lividus* which was flowering in the greenhouse a few yards away. As to the stemless species like *H. cyclophyllus* and *H. odorus*, these will cross with other species and with the Orientalis Hybrids so there is no guarantee that they will self-sow true.

To put it bluntly, it may be easy simply to let the plants self-sow but it will be impossible to predict the quality of plants resulting from such uncontrolled cross-pollination – except to say that chance seedlings will rarely be as good as their parents. Despite talk of serendipity!

Once the seeds have germinated around the plants it is vital they are not left there permanently. Only in the wildest parts of the garden can they be left to mature around their parents, as the colours will mix and poor forms will only increase. It is especially important to remove seedlings growing in the crown of the parent plant, for if these are allowed to mature it will soon become very difficult to distinguish them from their parent. At flowering time the interloper may be all too obvious, but to remove the seedling at that stage will involve digging up the whole plant and pulling it to pieces – something to be avoided if possible.

So the seedlings should be removed while still young. Given that open-pollinated self-sown seedlings are unlikely to produce plants of the highest quality, they do not deserve the most favoured treatment. The best approach is to thin them out soon after germination to 3–4in (7.5–10cm) apart. When they have two true leaves they can be lifted carefully with a handfork; at this stage they will move easily with a small root ball and can be planted either into nursery rows or into deep boxes. You can pot them up individually if you prefer, but we suggest you reserve this treatment for seedlings of known parentage.

Choose deep boxes as recommended earlier. Any reasonable compost will do; a mix of equal parts of a loam-based potting compost such as John Innes Number 3 and a peat-based potting or multipurpose compost is the best com-

An exceptional dark blue-black seedling raised by Helen Ballard and seen here in her garden in Worcestershire.

promise between suitability and availability. Prick out fifteen seedlings to a standard-sized seed tray, twenty-four to a tomato box. Take care not to overfirm the seedlings and always handle them by their leaves. Water them in well, having added a liquid feed to the water as this gives the roots instant access to available plant food and helps them grow away quickly.

If you have a frame for the boxes so much the better; they can receive the same treatment as described earlier. Otherwise an open but sheltered place outside will do, alongside the greenhouse perhaps; but try to choose a spot not exposed to icy winds and one sheltered from the worst of the rain and hail. These may not be your most cherished seedlings, but they deserve a little care and consideration. Stand the boxes on grit or raise them up off the ground on wood blocks to allow good drainage and prevent worms getting in.

PLANTING OUT AND GROWING ON

When the roots start to appear through the bottom of the pots or boxes the young plants are ready to go outside. In general, plants known to come true can be safely planted out straight into their permanent positions, but it is advisable to grow on those of more doubtful origins in a holding bed and await developments. Once they flower you can select the right plant for the right spot. Plants of *H. foetidus* and *H. argutifolius* can safely be planted out in their final positions without an intermediate stage for assessment if you are sure there has been no chance of crossing, especially as these species are not easy to move once established.

You can treat *H. niger* in the same way, and also species which you are confident have not crossed or which you have grown from wild collected seed. However, the Orientalis Hybrids and any others whose purity may be in question should be lined out for a few years in a nursery bed until they can be assessed. This ensures that only your very best plants go into your beds and borders.

Prepare the nursery beds in the same way as beds for permanent planting. Seedlings can be planted out as close as 10in (25cm) apart, although 12in (30cm) is better, as once they have grown to flowering size and been assessed they will be lifted and moved to their final homes. Planting in staggered rows with the plants 10in (25cm) apart in each direction makes the most of the space available.

Many *nigers* and a small percentage of Orientalis Hybrids will flower one year after germination, as will hybrids between *H. niger* and *H. × sternii*, *H. argutifolius* and *H. lividus*. Almost all the seedlings of Orientalis Hybrids will flower after two years, although those with a high proportion of species blood may take longer. The seedlings of the stemless species will rarely flower before three years and not always then.

Once planted out, seedlings still need care and occasional attention. Slugs can be troublesome

and aphids can multiply very rapidly unless dealt with promptly. Wind can burn soft young foliage, so a sheltered spot is especially useful to ensure that the development of seedlings is unimpeded by such unnecessary damage. Black spot too can disrupt the growth of developing seedlings, and regular protective spraying is a great help in preventing and controlling infection. The loss of a leaf to black spot is of greater significance to a seedling than to a mature plant with far more foliage.

You may prefer to pot on young plants, in which case the Orientalis Hybrids can be moved from their 3½in (9cm) pots into 6½in (2 litre) pots. The slower-growing species are better moved into 5in (12.5cm) pots and kept in the frame.

MICROPROPAGATION

A number of companies have experimented with propagating hellebores in the laboratory using micropropagation techniques. This work followed two main paths, and while a small number of plants have been produced of some of Helen Ballard's Orientalis Hybrids, problems were encountered in producing them efficiently and at a sufficiently reasonable price. The batch of plants produced in this way that we have seen also suffered from the basic flaw of not being identical, either to each other or to their parent. These problems seem to have led to the work fizzling out.

There has also been some work on *H. × nigercors* with the commercial cut flower trade in mind, but there has been little progress along this route and it may now be many years before micropropagated plants of either group are available.

6

THE HELLEBORE SPECIES

The hellebore species can be a minefield both for the gardener anxious to ensure that his plants are correctly named and for anyone studying them in the wild. For in any wild population the range of forms is often so great that there are always plants which are outside the range of variation attributed to that species.

Here we will follow Brian Mathew's classification and nomenclature as described in detail in his indispensable monograph. However, it is becoming increasingly clear that more time and observation is needed before the species can be fully understood, for although Brian sets out a clear and practical approach, when plants are examined in the wild there always seem to be contradictions. Some species are not only inherently variable but may also hybridise with each other, and with so few forms grown in cultivation it is not difficult to gain a lopsided view of the species from those plants found in gardens.

Few wild species are as showy as the many hybrids and selected forms grown in gardens, and few gardeners except hellebore specialists grow more than one or two. So with the continuing problems in their identification and classification and the fact that they are so much less widely grown, we make no apologies for treating them relatively briefly while research continues with the aim of clarifying the situation.

HELLEBORUS ARGUTIFOLIUS
Helleborus argutifolius Viviani

This is one of the most widely grown species and is valuable as both a foliage and a flowering plant, while it is sufficiently tough and adaptable to be happy in a wide range of gardens. It is sometimes still known as *H. corsicus*, but this name is incorrect.

This is an imposing plant with stems reaching 3–4ft (90cm–1.2m) in height, and a mature plant can be 4ft (1.2m) across. The stiff, leathery leaves are divided into three sharply spined leaflets, the central one oval and the outer two slightly curved in outline. From January until March or April the stems are topped with heads of between twenty and thirty green cup-shaped flowers 1–2in (2.5–5cm) across. Recent collections have confirmed that some wild plants have a slight pinkish tint.

Growing wild in Corsica and Sardinia, *H. argutifolius* is found in a wide range of habitats including the shoreline, roadsides, woods and in

Helleborus argutifolius
Actual diameter 8in (20cm)

the *maquis*. Among the plants with which it grows in the wild, *Crocus corsicus, Cyclamen repandum, Euphorbia characias* subsp. *wulfenii* and *Lavandula stoechas* would make good companions in the garden.

This is an adaptable plant, thriving in sun or shade and in a variety of soils, but is at its best in full sun in rich but well-drained conditions. It is least happy in heavy clay, and in shade the stems tend to grow too tall and collapse. Even in the open, staking mature plants is a wise precaution as the stems can be broken by autumn gales or frozen snow. Black spot can be a problem on overwintering stems, and precautionary spraying is advisable.

Self-sown seedlings are usually produced freely and germinate well, even in cracks in paving or other inhospitable places. But if seeds are not required, it pays to cut out the old stems when the flowers are over as this shows off the foliage and helps prevent black spot. Many plants die after five or six years, so replacement seedlings should be raised; they are quick to mature so you should not be left with an unsightly gap for long.

In the garden *H. argutifolius* looks good in front of *Eleagnus × ebbingei* 'Gilt Edge' and alongside the red-stemmed *Cornus alba* 'Sibirica'. Mediterranean plants such as *Euphorbia characias*, cistus and rue make good neighbours, and it also makes a specimen plant. This is one of the few species which are good for cutting.

There are no named varieties, although the large-flowered form from Bodnant garden in North Wales was awarded a First Class Certificate by the RHS in 1960. Montrose Nursery in North Carolina have been developing forms which are especially hardy.

HELLEBORUS ATRORUBENS
Helleborus atrorubens Waldst. & Kit.

There has been some confusion between this relatively demure species and the much larger, purple-flowered form of *H. orientalis* subsp. *abchasicus* often grown under this name. This

Helleborus atrorubens
Actual diameter 10½in (27cm)

latter plant is now correctly known as 'Early Purple' (see page 111) and is quite different from this altogether more delicate plant.

Helleborus atrorubens will be unfamiliar to most gardeners. It reaches about 12–18in (30–45cm) in height, with bold, circular leaves pedately divided into five main leaflets; they die away in winter. The outer one on each side is divided again to make anything between nine and fifteen elliptical divisions, typically eleven to thirteen, which are toothed, especially towards the tips. Some plants have purple-tinted young leaves. The flowers, which tend to face outwards rather than hang, appear in February and March on characteristically widely branched stems and are usually rather starry and about 1½–2in (4–5cm) across. They vary in colour and may be green or more often reddish-purple-backed or occasionally deep purple.

In the wild this species grows only in northwest Yugoslavia, where it is found on the edges of woods and in meadows bordering woods, especially where the soil is deep and rich. Among its many interesting wild companions are *Asarum europaeum, Cyclamen purpurascens, Epimedium alpinum, Gentiana asclepiadea, Hepatica nobilis, Lamium orvala, Lunaria rediviva* and *Pulmonaria officinalis*.

A mature planting of *Helleborus argutifolius* growing at the Chelsea Physic Gardens in London

(*Right*): Wild species. All the flowers in this selection are from species plants of known wild origin collected and grown by Will McLewin. The four different forms of *H. torquatus* are all from its northern area in Bosnia

H. torquatus

H. torquatus

H. torquatus

H. torquatus

H. atrorubens

H. torquatus

H. multifidus
subsp. *hercégovinus*

H. dumetorum

Plants appear at 1/2 life size

46

The former country of Yugoslavia, where so many hellebore species are found, showing its constituent provinces

This species thrives in leafy soil in partial shade and is not difficult to grow, although it seems especially prone to slug and bird damage so appreciates the protection of slug pellets and a little fine brushwood.

Helleborus atrorubens is an interesting rather than flamboyant plant, but in its best forms its purple-flushed flowers with their green-tinted interiors are well worth close inspection. Understandably it appreciates neighbours which are not overwhelming, and in addition to its wild companions, which include the form of *Geranium phaeum* known as 'Samobor', with bold dark marks on its foliage, try an early primula such as 'White Wanda', or snowdrops.

HELLEBORUS CYCLOPHYLLUS
Helleborus cyclophyllus (A. Braun) Boissier

This impressive plant is one of the two most widely grown green-flowered species, but even so is still found mainly in the gardens of specialists. It is often confused with *H. odorus*

and it is so difficult to separate the two that it is tempting to think of them as northern and southern forms of the same species.

Helleborus cyclophyllus
Actual diameter 12in (30cm)

.The emerging leaves of *H. cyclophyllus* have fine silvery hairs underneath while the mature foliage is round in outline, arching over from the centre to the edge. Each leaf is usually divided into seven main segments, with the outer two divided again giving up to eleven leaflets, although from eight to twenty-five segments have been found on wild plants. The leaves usually die away in the autumn.

Flowering is in February and March, sometimes earlier, on stems up to 16–22in (40–55cm) high, and each flower is about 2–2¼in (5–6cm) across. The flowers are usually green, though they may occasionally be cream or almost yellow in colour, and the carpels should not be joined at the base. Some plants may have a scent reminiscent of *Ribes*.

The unfused carpels, the absence of overwintering foliage and the more southerly distribution should distinguish *H. cyclophyllus* from *H. odorus*. *H. cyclophyllus* is found in an area from northern Greece extending into the northern Peloponnese, much of Albania, southern Yugoslavia and southern Bulgaria. It is also found in Corfu, and the plant distributed by Blackthorn Nursery as *H. odorus* may belong here.

It grows mainly around the edges of woods or in scrub and sometimes on grassy slopes, but is typically a plant of the mountains. At its classic location on the slopes of Mt Parnassus in Greece it can be seen with such delights as *Colchicum triphyllum*, *Corydalis bulbosa* and *C. solida*, *Crocus biflorus*, *C. sieberi* and *C. veluchensis* in a variety of shades, *Fritillaria graeca*, *Muscari botryoides* and *M. neglectum*, and *Scilla bifolia*. Here it occurs so widely and is so well established that it seems certain that it is indeed the black hellebore referred to in classical Greek literature.

This is not a difficult plant to grow but it appreciates shelter from spring frosts and drying winds. Repeated frosting is debilitating and apt to leave this species susceptible to attack from black spot. In the garden it would look wonderful with *Muscari latifolium* and *Crocus chrysanthus* 'Cream Beauty', and also with *Euphorbia polychroma* and *Digitalis grandiflora*.

HELLEBORUS DUMETORUM
Helleborus dumetorum Waldst. & Kit.

This is one of the wild species least often seen in gardens, mainly because its flowers are small and green – not a popular combination. But for hellebore enthusiasts it is a delightful plant with its own quiet charm.

A slender plant reaching 8–12in (20–30cm) in height, the deciduous foliage has three central leaflets which are undivided while the outer two are divided into four, or occasionally just three, segments, making eleven to thirteen altogether. The overall shape of the leaves and their individual segments is rather variable, but the leaflets are usually rather slender and the narrower they are, the smaller the teeth along the margins.

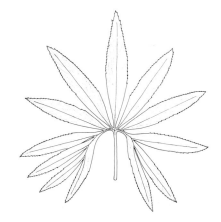

Helleborus dumetorum
Actual diameter 8in (20cm)

H. dumetorum flowers in February and March and the flowers are the smallest of all the species, about 1–1½in (2.5–4cm) across and usually rather starry in shape. They are green in colour, nodding and unscented.

The distribution of this species stretches from Croatia and Slovenia, into southern Hungary and south-east Austria then into Romania towards the Black Sea. Generally this is a plant of scrub, light woodland or other shady places, especially clearings in beech woods, with plants such as *Anemone nemorosa*, *A. ranunculoides*,

Helleborus cyclophyllus growing wild on its classic site of Mt Parnassus in Greece

Crocus vernus, Epimedium alpinum, Euphorbia polychroma, Galanthus nivalis, Omphalodes verna and *Vinca minor*.

In the garden this is a shade lover and likes a rich, leafy but not waterlogged soil, though even when perfectly suited it tends to be slower growing than other species. It is not often listed by nurseries, and like *H. atrorubens* is best grown away from plants whose bright colours would overwhelm it. *Anemone nemorosa* 'Vestal' or 'Virescens', primroses and snowdrops are ideal.

HELLEBORUS FOETIDUS
Helleborus foetidus Linnaeus

Known as the stinking hellebore, this is one of Britain's two native hellebores although it also occurs as a garden escape. A number of forms are grown in gardens, many originating in southern Europe, and all are impressive and easy plants for winter and spring, with good foliage and plenty of flowers.

The stinking hellebore can make a plant up to 4ft (1.2m) across, with stems up to 2½ft (75cm) tall carrying dark green leaves which are divided into slender leaflets, most of which are slightly curved and toothed along most of each side. Towards the top of the plant the leaves become more bract-like. The foliage has an unpleasant smell when broken and this gives the plant its common name.

The pale bracts are a feature in themselves before the flowers open, and the flowers are almost cylindrical, although the petals become more flared as they age. Each pale green flower is about ¾in (2cm) long and the same wide, with a brown or reddish-purple band at the tip or just short of it. The flowers are occasionally sweetly scented, but are more often rather catty.

(*Above*): *Helleborus dumetorum* (WM 9025) collected by Will McLewin and flowering here in his garden in Stockport. (*Right*): *Helleborus foetidus* growing wild in a beechwood in Gloucestershire

The stinking hellebore grows in much of Europe, from Hungary in the east, to Switzerland, through south Germany, west to Britain and Portugal, and south to the Balearic islands. It is one of the most widespread of all hellebores.

In Andalucía in southern Spain, companions for *H. foetidus* include *Cerastium tomentosum, Echium albicans, Erinus alpinus, Narcissus assoanus, Ornithogalum reverchonii, Paeonia broteroi, Papaver rupifragum* and *Saxifraga gemmulosa*. In Northamptonshire it grows in mixed blackthorn and hawthorn hedges with wild roses and brambles, *Anthriscus sylvestris, Arum maculatum, Galium mollugo, Geranium dissectum, Hyacinthoides non-scripta, Mercurialis perennis, Rumex acetosa, Veronica chamaedrys* and *Viola riviniana*.

This is a very adaptable plant, and although it

is at its happiest in humus-rich soil in partial shade, good specimens can also be found in dry shade and in full sun. In very wet conditions it may rot off and die. As with *H. argutifolius*, the plants are not long-lived, but seedlings are easy to raise. Black spot can be a problem, not only at the base of the stems but on the leaves, flowers and bracts, so precautionary spraying is wise. Mature plants may need support, especially if growing in shade.

This plant is impressive from autumn to late spring with its foliage, bracts and flowers, and in good conditions will retain its leaves down to ground level, when it looks well with white crocuses, snowdrops, the variegated *Symphytum* 'Goldsmith', pulmonarias, ajugas or evergreen epimediums.

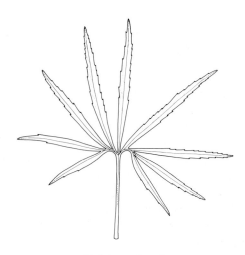

Helleborus foetidus
Actual diameter 9in (23cm)

NAMED FORMS

'Bowles' Form' In *My Garden in Autumn and Winter* the great plantsman E. A. Bowles wrote: 'I have great hopes of a panful of seedlings raised from some pods I gathered among the rocks where *Primula allionii* and *Lilium pomponium* grow wild and happily in the Valley of the Roja. It struck me as a far more beautiful form than I was accustomed to, the leaves more finely divided, the whole plant more vigorous and stately, and the flower heads wonderful indeed for size and number of blossoms.' Fortunately this plant is still available occasionally, although seedlings must be selected carefully and poor forms discarded.

'Green Giant' A tall variety with pale green, finely divided leaves and green bracts which are brighter than usual. This variety originated with Will McLewin.

'Italian Form' Not easy to distinguish from 'Bowles' Form', which itself originates in Italy, and probably the same. Plants under this name usually have an exceptional number of flowers on unusually large plants.

'Miss Jekyll' Sometimes called 'Miss Jekyll's Scented Form', the leaflets are unusually narrow and the flowers sweetly fragrant – or they should be, though even hand-pollinated seedlings may not in fact be sweet and the scent may also vary with the time of day.

'Sienna' Originating from near Sienna in Italy, the leaves are dark, the bracts pale and the whole flower head is especially bold and upright. A very impressive variety introduced by Will McLewin.

'Sierra Nevada Form' A form originating in the Sierra Nevada, with relatively few flowers which are larger than usual and carried on unusually dwarf plants reaching little more than about 12in (30cm) in height.

'Sopron' Distinct in its dark metallic foliage and large, open flowers without the usual dark markings at the tip. The bracts are narrow, and both bracts and flowers are noticeably pale. Originating from seedlings collected by Will McLewin near Sopron in the north-west of Hungary.

'Tros-os-Montes' The large, dark foliage has leaflets which are especially serrated and the flower head is pale and rather wispy. The flowers themselves are green but with no dark tips. Selected by Will McLewin from seedlings collected by Jim Archibald on the border between Spain and Portugal.

'Wester Flisk' A form with strikingly red-tinted stems and leaf petioles, the colour stretching right up into the flower heads in the best plants. The leaves are greyish-green. This variety originated at Wester Flisk on the Firth of Tay; the picture on page 108 shows a plant growing at Wester Flisk and typical of those to be seen there. This plant is rather less red than some seen recently which are the result of rigorous selection for the best colour (see page 106).

HELLEBORUS LIVIDUS
Helleborus lividus Aiton

This is probably the rarest of all hellebores. There seem to be very few plants remaining in its natural habitat, and although it is grown in gardens, many of the plants listed by nurseries and grown in gardens are probably hybrids with *H. argutifolius*. It is, however, a very beautiful plant with a lovely combination of flowers and foliage.

Its growth habit is similar to that of the more familiar *H. argutifolius* but the plant is much shorter, about 15in (38cm) in flower. The leaves are deep green, sometimes with a steely hue, veined in silver on the upper surface and flushed pink below. Each leaf is divided into three elliptical leaflets, sometimes with a few small, widely spaced teeth along the edge.

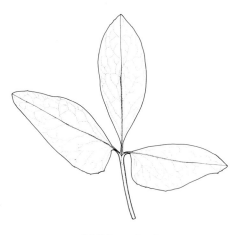

Helleborus lividus
Actual diameter 9in (23cm)

Flowers start to open in December and continue until March, and the 1–1½in (2.5–4cm) cup-shaped flowers are basically apple green inside and pink or purple-flushed outside, though they can vary; eventually they open out flat. The pink tint to so much of the plant is a very distinctive feature.

In the wild *H. lividus* grows only in Majorca, and possibly on the nearby island of Cabrera, but it is now very rarely seen in spite of Majorca being such a Mecca for botanists. It is restricted to the mountains of the north-east coast, often along river beds, on damp cliffs or among boulders, mostly in very remote areas. Grazing and development have restricted its distribution in recent years. It is sometimes found with that other well-known Majorcan endemic, *Paeonia cambessedesii*.

This species is best grown in pots in the alpine house, in a mixture of four parts of John Innes Potting Compost Number 2, one part grit and one part fine bark or leaf-mould. Seedlings should be potted on steadily; a 15in (38cm) pot is probably the largest you'll need. They look best in clay pots, and a top dressing of grit helps keep moisture away from the crown and shows the plants off well. Pots can be stood outside from June to September. Watch for black spot in winter and give a liquid feed three or four times while the plant is outside.

After five or six years grow on a seedling as a replacement (division is almost impossible) but ensure that *H. argutifolius* is not around to cross-pollinate and give you *H.* × *sternii* instead.

H. lividus is a fine plant to grow alongside cushion plants, other early flowering alpines and spring bulbs, or it can be grown in a Mediterranean bed.

HELLEBORUS MULTIFIDUS
Helleborus multifidus Visiani

This can be a confusing species for the gardener (not to mention the botanist!). There are four subspecies:

Helleborus multifidus subsp. *multifidus*
H. multifidus subsp. *bocconei* (Tenore)
  B. Mathew
Helleborus multifidus subsp. *hercegovinus* (Martinis) B. Mathew
Helleborus multifidus subsp. *istriacus* (Schiffner) Merxmuller & Podlech

They all have more or less green flowers, and although the finely cut foliage of some plants is very distinctive, so few plants of all four subspecies are available to gardeners that there is little chance to get to know them. All lose their leaves in winter.

52

Helleborus lividus growing in a raised bed in the cold greenhouse at Washfield Nursery

Between them these four subspecies cover much of Italy and western Yugoslavia. In a clockwise direction their distribution runs from subsp. *bocconei*, which stretches from Sicily up into central Italy, then there is a gap before subsp. *istriacus* takes over in north-east Italy and continues across the border into Yugoslavia; then in the northern Adriatic mountains subsp. *multifidus* takes over, with subsp. *hercegovinus* growing furthest south in Bosnia Hercegovina. The distribution pattern is important in distinguishing between subspecies.

It is the finely cut foliage of subsp. *hercegovinus* which many gardeners tend to associate with this species, although the foliage of some of the other subspecies is less distinctive.

Starting in Italy, subsp. *bocconei* has about twenty leaf segments, although mature well-established plants may have rather more. The shape varies from almost linear to elliptical, and the edges are coarsely toothed. The flowers are usually little more than 1½in (4cm) across in the wild, though good forms can be 2–2½in (5–7cm) across. They vary in shape from rounded to starry, and generally open from January to March. They are usually green at first, before paling to greenish-white but never becoming yellow. Martyn Rix reports seeing a double form growing in the wild near Florence. They have an elderflower scent.

This plant is found in scrub and woodland in central and southern Italy and Sicily, but prefers relatively light shade. Interesting plants seen growing with it include *Allium flavum, Anemone apennina, Cardamine bulbifera, Hepatica nobilis, Lathyrus vernus, Primula vulgaris, Ranunculus millefoliatus* and *Scilla bifolia*.

Straddling the border between Italy and Slovenia, the leaves of susbp. *istriacus* are the least divided of all: twelve divisions are usual, twice that occasional. The divisions are broad, up to 1½in (4cm) wide, the undersides of the leaves are hairy and sometimes the young leaves have coppery tints. The flowers are relatively large, sometimes reaching 2in (5cm) in the wild, and they may be purple-tinted on the outside. Some plants are difficult to distinguish from *H. odorus*.

This plant is also found in scrub and lightly shaded places alongside such plants as *Crocus vernus* subsp. *albiflorus, Cyclamen hederifolium, Hepatica nobilis, Muscari comosum, Primula veris* and *Pulmonaria angustifolia*.

Further south in the coastal mountains, though not near the sea, subsp. *multifidus* is found. This subspecies is distinguished by its more finely cut foliage – between thirty and forty segments are common. The flowers are usually 1–1½in (2.5–4cm) across and a dark, almost metallic green. This plant grows in the same general area as *H. torquatus*, and intermediates occur with the flowers edged or veined in purple, sometimes quite strongly. We tend to agree with those botanists who have not found it possible to separate this plant from *H. torquatus*,

H. purpurascens

H. viridis
subsp. *viridis*

H. atrorubens

H. multifidus
subsp. *bocconei*

H. multifidus —
subsp. *multifidus*

H. multifidus subsp.
multifidus

H. multifidus
subsp. *istriacus*

H. odorus

H. cyclophyllus

H. orientalis
subsp.
abchasicus

H. orientalis
subsp. orientalis

54

which they have classified as *H. multifidus* subsp. *serbicus*.

As well as in the usual lightly shaded spots, this subspecies is also found in more open situations on grassy or bracken-covered slopes, often in thin rocky soil. Among its companions in the wild are *Asarum europaeum, Cardamine pentaphyllos, Cytisus purpureus, Daphne mezereum, Erythronium dens-canis, Gentiana asclepiadea* and *G. verna, Iris graminea* and *I. pallida, Paeonia peregrina, Paris quadrifolia* and *Primula elatior*.

Furthest south, subsp. *hercegovinus* is found in the mountains of south-east Bosnia Hercegovina. One feature of this plant stands out – the lacy leaves. Jim Archibald, a dedicated counter of leaflets on wild plants, found a leaf with an astonishing total of 185 divisions. We have to say that 100 is more common, and it takes plants a few years to build up to that number. But even 100 makes a very attractive foliage plant, and an unjustly neglected one. The young leaves are usually slightly hairy on the undersides.

The flowers, which appear in February and March, are usually less than 2in (5cm) across, yellowish or pale green and cup-shaped or starry in shape.

This plant is found in open, rocky places as well as lightly shaded scrub or woodland.

Helleborus multifidus subsp. *multifidus*
Actual diameter 9in (23cm)

Among its companions are *Allium senescens, Arum nigrum, Crocus tommasinianus, Cyclamen hederifolium, Euphorbia myrsinites, Muscari comosum* and *M. neglectum, Satureja montana* and *Scilla pratensis*.

All four subspecies can be grown in light shade in rich but well-drained soil, although subsp. *bocconei* and subsp. *hercegovinus* in particular require a little more shelter from icy winds. You should expect subsp. *hercegovinus* to be especially slow-growing and also more susceptible to black spot than the others.

The most sought-after of these plants are those with especially lacy leaves, which make wonderful foliage plants. The leaves arch over to soil level so are best placed at the front of the border where they can be admired.

HELLEBORUS NIGER
CHRISTMAS ROSE

Helleborus niger Linnaeus

The Christmas rose is the showiest and certainly the best known of the wild hellebores, but it can be difficult to grow well and it can hardly be said to be a regular in flower on Christmas Day. Snow rose is perhaps more appropriate.

There are two subspecies:
Helleborus niger subsp. *niger*
Helleborus niger subsp. *macranthus* (Freyn) Schiffner

H. niger is a very widespread species, and over much of its range subsp. *niger* is the one that is found. Generally it is a mountain plant and grows in an area stretching from the Alps of Switzerland, southernmost Germany and Austria, through Slovenia, and into Croatia together with northern Italy. By contrast, subsp. *macranthus* grows only in northern Italy, although it may cross the border into Slovenia.

The Christmas rose is evergreen and reaches 9–12in (23–30cm) in height, with dark leathery leaves pedately divided into seven, eight or nine segments which are usually untoothed except sometimes towards the tips. The leaves are usually taller than the flowers, except when flattened by snow. The large flat flowers are usually carried singly on strong stems from January to April and can be anything from 1½ to 3in (4 to 7.5cm) across, mostly rounded in shape. Although usually white with a green eye, the flowers may be pink on the back or turn pink as they age.

This plant grows in a variety of habitats, mostly in woodland but also out on open slopes. In its more usual wooded situations it grows with plants such as *Anemone nemorosa, Asarum europaeum, Cardamine kitaibelii, Cyclamen purpurascens, Daphne mezereum, Epimedium alpinum, Gentiana asclepiadea, Hacquetia epipactis, Helleborus atrorubens, Omphalodes verna, Primula vulgaris* and *Veratrum nigrum.*

The other subspecies, subsp. *macranthus,* is similar but is distinguished by its slightly blue-tinted leaves edged with tiny teeth and its larger flowers, sometimes as much as 3¾in (9cm) across.

In the wild it grows with an unusual variety of other plants including *Campanula sibirica, Clematis recta, Coronilla emerus, Cyclamen purpurascens, Cytisus purpureus, Erica carnea, Euphorbia nicaeensis, Gentiana clusii, Gladiolus imbricatus, Iberis sempervirens, Inula ensifolia* and *Lilium bulbiferum* var. *croceum.*

Many gardeners find the Christmas rose difficult to grow well, although it is often the garden which is more of a problem than the gardener. It does not like acid soil, neither does it care for poor, impoverished or dry conditions and it does not usually thrive in full sun. So, by contrast, we can safely say that it likes limy, humus-rich soil in dappled shade or under a north wall with a good moisture supply. Lime can be applied where necessary, and both heavy clay and sandy soils can be improved with plenty of organic matter, preferably leaf-mould, forked in before planting and as a regular mulch. On acid soils mushroom compost is a better mulch.

Some plants, once known as var. *altissimus,* hold their leaves above the flowers, and while this protects the flowers from muddy splashes, it hides them from view. If you want to cut the flowers, the leaves are best left in place, otherwise all the leaves in the centre of the clump are best cut away shortly before the first flowers open. Christmas roses resent disturbance, but if you must move them, do so in early spring. Slugs can be very destructive and voles can eat the buds before they come through.

Bulbs such as winter aconites, scillas, snowdrops, crocus which naturalise well such as *Crocus tommasinianus,* and some of the small primulas like 'Wanda' make good neighbours.

Over the years many varieties have been named, but few true forms of the older ones are still to be found, partly because plants which should be propagated by division have been raised from seed.

Helleborus niger
Actual diameter 12in (30cm)

56

'Blackthorn Strain' A vigorous seed strain developed by Robin White by crossing 'White Magic' with 'Louis Cobbett'. The flowers are carried on tall, dark stems and are pink in bud, opening almost white and turning pink as the flowers age. The pink colouring varies slightly from plant to plant.

'Eva' A spectacular plant with flowers 4½in (11cm) across and slightly pointed petals. This was selected by Norman Hadden and given to Margery Fish.

'Foliis Variegatis' A plant with an irregular pattern of cream variegation was found in Slovenia and given this name by Leon Doyen. It was found to be infected with virus but it is not certain that the virus causes the variegation. Barr and Sons listed a plant of this name in 1889 which was said to have variegated young foliage, so perhaps the Slovenian plant should have a new name to avoid the admittedly slight risk of confusion.

'Harvington Hybrids' A strain raised by Greenfingers Nursery, said to start flowering early, in December, and continue to April.

'Higham's Variety' A reliably Christmas-flowering form introduced in 1985 by Carol Klein, who obtained it from her grandfather Henry Higham who worked in private service early this century.

'Ladhams' Variety' Described by Sir Frederick Stern in his book *A Chalk Garden* (1960) as 'the most robust [form] with substantial flowers which are not so liable to be damaged by bad weather as some of the other forms: it comes true from seed'.

'Louis Cobbett' Often said to be a

pink-flowered form, but although the buds are pink the flowers are only pink-flushed on the backs. This is nevertheless a captivating plant with very dark red stems.

'Madame Fourcade' A dwarf, large-flowered variety with pale foliage raised in the nineteenth century but not seen for many years. Plants originating in Holland have appeared again recently, and although the flowers are not large, they appear regularly before Christmas, and sometimes in November.

'Marion' A double-flowered variety with about twenty-five pure white petals. This was found as a chance seedling in the garden of Mick Sandell of Wateringbury in Kent, and named for his wife. It breeds fairly true, although some seedlings are more double than others.

'Pixie' A semi-double, anemone-centred variety with short, quilled petals clustered in the centre of each flower. This form was found by a gardener in Essex and given to Don Mann.

'Potter's Wheel' A seed strain developed by Hilda Davenport-Jones from a plant given to her by Major G.H. Tristram. An exhibit of seven plants was given an Award of Merit by the RHS in February 1958 and the flowers were described as follows: 'The immense flowers measure from 4 to 5 inches across, with broad glistening white, overlapping sepals, the bases of which, together with the nectaries, are a deep, clear green. The pleasant colour effect is admirably set off by the cluster of golden stamens in the centre of the flower.' (See page 109.)

'Praecox' A form said to flower

regularly before Christmas and still grown in Germany.

'St Brigid' A variety with tall dark green leaves which protect the flowers from damage. Discovered in a garden in Kildare, Ireland, in the middle of the nineteenth century, it was thought to be extinct but Anne Watson, who runs a nursery in Yorkshire, is now building up stocks following its rediscovery in Ireland. (See page 110.)

'Sunset' Plants under this name derive from a group of pink- and red-flowered plants discovered by Will McLewin in Slovenia. Those distributed are divisions of wild collected plants and plants grown from wild collected seed, and while all should show some pink colouring it will vary from plant to plant.

'Trotter's Form' A large-flowered, pure white form which flowered for ten months of the year in Inverness-shire, where it was raised by Dick Trotter. It was introduced by Jack Drake, founder of the well-known Inshriach Nursery.

'White Magic' Originally said to be a cross between *H. niger* and *H. orientalis*, this is in fact a very prolific seed strain of *H. niger* with the flowers held on dark strong stems and with small, distinct, bright green leaves. It was raised in New Zealand. (See page 110.)

In addition to those mentioned above, the following varieties have been referred to in recent literature but are unlikely to be still in cultivation: 'Apple Blossom', 'De Graff's Variety', 'Flore Roseo', 'Minor', 'Miss Kearney', 'Mrs Stanhope', 'Oxford Variety', 'Riverston', 'Rubra', 'Snowflake', 'The Bath Variety', 'Vernalis' and 'Wardie Lodge'.

HELLEBORUS ODORUS
Helleborus odorus Waldst. & Kit.

The showiest and the easiest to grow of the green-flowered species, *H. odorus* is quickly becoming more popular as it becomes more widely available. As its name implies, it is scented, but our assessment on different occasions has varied from '*Ribes*', 'quite sweet', and 'a little bit elderflowerish' through 'cheap soap' and 'a fraction catty' to 'almost nothing'!

Sometimes making quite a substantial plant over 20in (50cm) high, the young leaves of *H. odorus* are covered in silvery hairs and they are also often slightly copper-tinted. It generally loses its leaves in the winter. Mature foliage has five broad divisions and the outer ones are again divided to give between nine and eleven segments. Flowering is early, December to March, and the flowers are 1½–2½in (4–6.5cm) across and even in shape. They are basically green in colour, though this may vary from a rich dark shade to the colour of unripe 'Golden Delicious' apples and a luminous yellow-green; occasionally there may be coppery tints.

This species is easily confused with *H. cyclophyllus*, and the main distinguishing features are these.

Distribution – *H. odorus* is the more northerly, occurring in northern Bulgaria and across the border in Romania as well as in much of Yugoslavia, except in the south and in the coastal mountains. *H. cyclophyllus* takes over in southern Yugoslavia and extends down into Greece.

Carpels – In *H. odorus* the carpels are joined at the base for a few millimetres while in *H. cyclophyllus* they are not.

Foliage – *H. odorus* has leaves which overwinter, while in *H. cyclophyllus* they die away in the autumn.

However, we have to say that none of these features is entirely consistent – in particular, *H. odorus* may not be evergreen where there is winter snow cover.

One of the best forms of *H. odorus* seen in recent years has been distributed by Robin

The form of *Helleborus odorus* from Corfu distributed by Blackthorn Nursery is here seen flowering on the nursery

White. It has bright yellow-green flowers and originates in Corfu. However, this plant seems to exhibit some of the characteristics of *H. cyclophyllus* so its exact status is in doubt.

In the wild *H. odorus* is found in woodland, on the edges of woods, in scrub and out on grassy slopes. Among its many interesting companions are *Anemone ranunculoides*, *Colchicum autumnale*, *Cyclamen purpurascens*, *Euphorbia cyparissias*, *Fragaria moschata*, *Helleborus niger*, *Iris pallida*, *Isopyrum thalictroides*, *Lathyrus vernus*, *Orchis morio*, *Pulsatilla pratensis* var. *nigricans*, *Scilla bifolia* and *Vinca minor* in a variety of shades.

This easy species grows well in partial shade, although it will thrive in full sun if the soil is rich. It quickly builds up into bold clumps, especially in good soil conditions, and is valuable for its early flowers. It looks good in front of *Cornus mas* 'Aurea', and can be planted alongside *Epimedium* × *perralchicum* 'Fröhnleiten', cream

Helleborus odorus
Actual diameter 16in (40cm)

Helleborus orientalis subsp. *orientalis*
Actual diameter 16in (40cm)

Helleborus purpurascens
Actual diameter 11in (27cm)

primroses or the old white 'Harbinger', *Hacquetia epipactis*, *Ajuga reptans* 'Variegata' or the metallic bronze 'Braunherz'. Dwarf bulbs like *Crocus tommasinianus* and *Scilla bifolia* are also worth trying.

HELLEBORUS ORIENTALIS
Helleborus orientalis Lamarck

Although most of the hybrids grown in gardens are derived at least in part from *H. orientalis*, the wild species itself is rarely encountered. This is not unexpected, as the hybrids are so much better as garden plants, but it is helpful to understand the wild species because the characteristics of the three main types are echoed in some of the more popular garden forms. The species is divided into three subspecies:

Helleborus orientalis subsp. *orientalis*

Helleborus orientalis subsp. *abchasicus* (A. Braun) B. Mathew

Helleborus orientalis subsp. *guttatus* (A. Braun & Sauer) B. Mathew

All are evergreen perennials making about 18in (45cm) in height, with pedately divided foliage in which the central leaflet remains undivided while some or all of the others are divided to varying degrees, giving a total of seven to eleven coarsely toothed, leathery segments. The flowers are 2–3in (5–7.5cm) across, slightly nodding and eventually opening flat; the carpels are not joined at the base.

In subsp. *orientalis* the flowers are usually white with some green or cream tints and the nectaries are usually green. In subsp. *abchasicus* the flowers are tinted with red and the nectaries are purple or green with purple marks. In subsp. *guttatus* the flowers are similar to those of subsp. *orientalis* except that they are spotted to varying degrees in red or purple; usually three petals have more spots than the other two. 'Guttatus' is sometimes used as a cultivar name but this is misleading, as it is used to cover such a wide variety of plants.

All three subspecies grow in a similar variety of habitats. At high altitudes they grow in open grassy situations while lower down they are found in scrub, rhododendron thickets, hazel coppice, deciduous and coniferous woods and even on roadsides. They all prefer limy soil but also tend to grow on deeper, richer soils than other species.

The distribution of the three subspecies needs further study, but subsp. *orientalis* grows in a long stretch from north-west Turkey along the Black Sea coast into the central and western Caucasus mountains. Among its companions are *Cornus mas*, *Cyclamen coum*, *Daphne pontica*, *Fritillaria pontica*, *Galanthus plicatus*, *Paeonia mascula* subsp. *aretiana*, *Primula vulgaris* subsp. *sibthorpii*, *Rhododendron luteum*, *R. ponticum* and *Trachystemon orientale*.

The other two subspecies occur only in the Caucasus, with subsp. *abchasicus* tending to be concentrated at the western end of the Caucasus mountains. In the central and eastern Caucasus it tends to be replaced by subsp. *guttatus*, which grows with *Campanula alliarifolia*, *Cyclamen coum* subsp. *caucasicum*, *Epimedium colchicum*, *Omphalodes cappadocica*, *Ruscus ponticus* and *R. colchicus*, and *Trachystemon orientalis*.

These plants are not difficult to grow. Their cultivation is covered in detail in Chapter 3 (page 13), with plenty of ideas for plants to grow with them in Chapter 4 (page 20). A very large number of varieties have been named, many of them hybrids with other species, and these are described in Chapter 9 (page 84).

HELLEBORUS PURPURASCENS
Helleborus purpurascens Waldst. & Kit.

At its best this can be a lovely plant, especially as it often starts to flower very early in the season with the opening buds pushing the soil aside.

This undeservedly neglected species reaches about 12in (30cm) in height and dies down completely in winter. The young leaves are hairy underneath and then develop a distinctive shape with all the leaflets joined at one point, palmate rather than pedate as in other species. Each leaf has five main divisions, divided to give about twenty-five or sometimes more elliptical or linear toothed segments.

(*Above*): *Helleborus thibetanus* growing in a forest clearing in the mountains of Baoxing in Sichuan, China

(*Left*): Both its pale pink flowers with their dark veins and its unusually large bracts make *Helleborus thibetanus* a very distinctive plant

The 1½–2in (4–5cm) flowers can start to appear in mid December at just above ground level, and are generally cup-shaped and rather variable in colour. There are two main forms grown: one has flowers which are purple outside and green inside, while the other has flowers which are dark bluey purple outside and a similar but paler shade inside. You may also come across forms with flowers in brownish or various pinky purple shades or even grey-blue outside, and sometimes green within; the flowers often have a slightly metallic sheen.

This is a widely distributed species, growing over much of eastern Europe including Hungary, Romania, much of the Carpathian mountains, western Ukraine, south-eastern Poland and eastern Czechoslovakia. It seems to prefer more open situations than most species, and grows in grassy alpine meadows with plants such as *Aconitum lasianthum*, *Ajuga pyramidalis*, *Campanula persicifolia*, *Centaurea atropurpurea*, *Clematis alpina*, *Dianthus barbatus*, *Digitalis grandiflora*, *Lilium martagon*, *Lychnis viscaria*, *Pulmonaria rubra*, *Pulsatilla halleri* and *Trollius europaeus*.

In the garden it can be grown more successfully in full sun than many species, but it will also do well in leafy soil in dappled shade. The emerging flowers and foliage can be badly attacked by leaf spot, so it makes sense to spray as a precaution. A good form of this species is invaluable for its early flowers, and as it becomes more widely available will also be more appreciated. Good garden companions include the plants with which it grows in the wild plus, perhaps, *Cardamine trifolia*, *Hepatica transsilvanica*, *Omphalodes verna* and *Viola odorata*.

HELLEBORUS THIBETANUS
Helleborus thibetanus Franchet

We are delighted to report that this almost unknown species is at last being grown in Britain. Several botanists have looked for it, but thanks to the persistence and generosity of Japanese botanist Mikinori Ogisu we have news of the plant in its wild habitat. Using the clues in Père

David's diaries as a guide, he found several colonies around Moupin in Sichuan province, China, where Père David himself first discovered this plant over 120 years ago.

Helleborus thibetanus
Actual diameter 9in (23cm)

Although superficially most like *H. orientalis*, this is a most distinctive species. The leaves are pedately divided with seven divisions, each edged with saw-like teeth. They start to grow rapidly once the flower stems are well developed, but then die down by the end of July. The bell-shaped flowers are around 2–2½in (5–6.5cm) across and have just two, or sometimes three, carpels. They open in March in the wild, the rather pointed petals opening white and rapidly fading to pink with dark veins and finally to green. The bracts are much larger than those of other species. The seed ripens in early May, and produces no visible cotyledons when it germinates.

This species is known only from the Chinese provinces of Gansu, Hubei, Shaanxi and Sichuan. Around Moupin in Sichuan province, it grows in scrub in damp, rocky clearings and many of the plants are shaded by *Matteuccia struthiopteris*. Other plants with which it grows include astilbes, hemerocallis, *Fritillaria davidii* and a *Petasites* sp.

When plants are eventually available we feel sure this species will thrive in partial shade in a humus-rich soil that does not dry out. Seed arrived in Britain in 1991 but it could be many years before plants are available from nurseries.

HELLEBORUS TORQUATUS
Helleborus torquatus Archer-Hind

Helleborus torquatus is a delightful but problematic plant. The rich purple colouring of some of the wild forms is not only attractive in itself but by hybridisation has been brought to the Orientalis Hybrids, including 'Pluto' and the purple- and blue-flowered types. But this is a confusing plant both in gardens, where hybrid impostors are common, and in the wild where its status is unclear.

Brian Mathew has explained the history of this confusing plant and its nomenclature in his book, and it seems to have been bewildering gardeners and botanists since the middle of the nineteenth century. Until recently most of the plants in circulation were derived from three collected by Walter Ingwersen and Dr Richard Seligman on Mt Kopaonik in Serbia in 1929, and it is these plants which make up so-called 'classic' *H. torquatus*, if only to gardeners. They still grow at Washfield Nursery. All are deep violet-purple outside and green within.

It is now clear that this is a very variable species, but to some extent the variations tie in with its two distinct areas of distribution. The constant factors are that the leaves die away in the winter, the foliage is roughly circular in shape, pedately divided (although the number of segments may vary between twelve and eighty), the young leaves are hairy and may be purple-tinted, and the flowers are 1¼–1½in (3–4cm) across.

However, plants from northern populations in Bosnia Hercegovina and Croatia tend to have

Helleborus torquatus
Actual diameter 18in (45cm)

narrow, almost linear, leaflets while those from southern populations in Crna Gora (Montenegro) and western Serbia tend to have broader leaflets.

The flowers of those in the north tend to be small and rather conical in shape. In colour, Elizabeth has found plants which were green inside and out or with a few brown tints; brown outside and green striped with brown inside; purple outside and blue-green inside (sometimes striped with purple) or, very rarely, purple both inside and out. The form which is purple outside, sea green inside and veined in purple is especially attractive, though the flowers are small.

Further south in Crna Gora (Montenegro) and western Serbia the flowers are more open and the colour range is a little different. Elizabeth found more smoky intermediate shades between the greens, browns and deep violet-purples, and the green interiors were richer and rarely had dark stripes.

It is important to remember that most plants in the wild are relatively unremarkable in colour and only a very few would be regarded as gardenworthy. The fact that these have tended to be introduced to gardens has perhaps given us an unbalanced view of the species.

This is one of only three species so far which has yielded double-flowered plants in the wild. In 1971 Elizabeth found two plants, subsequently named 'Dido' and 'Aeneas', in Crna Gora (Montenegro). Just to emphasise the confusion surrounding this plant, botanists at first thought they were forms of *H. purpurascens*, and

these double forms are still sometimes found in gardens under this name.

The problem with this species is that the purple flowers are supposed to be its most significant distinguishing feature. But this is not a constant factor, and plants with green flowers, indistinguishable from the *H. multifidus* subsp. *multifidus* growing in the next valley, are common. Hence the inclination of some botanists to treat *H. torquatus* as a form of *H. multifidus* which they call subsp. *serbicus*. When peace has returned to the area, more detailed field work may clarify the situation.

In Bosnia *H. torquatus* is usually found in scrub and thin turf with, among other things, *Anemone nemorosa*, *Buglossoides purpurocaerulea*, *Cytisus demissus*, *Globularia cordifolia* and *Primula vulgaris*. In Crna Gora it is usually found in deeper soils, on woodland margins or in scrub, and among its companions are *Acanthus hungaricus*, *Corydalis solida*, *Crocus vernus*, *Erythronium dens-canis*, *Hepatica nobilis*, *Isopyrum thalictroides*, *Primula vulgaris*, *Pulmonaria officinalis*, *Scilla bifolia* and *Viola odorata*.

This species is not difficult to grow, although it can be slow. It appreciates a humus-rich soil in partial shade, although it will tolerate more sun than most species. Good companions include *Anemone nemorosa* 'Blue Queen', *Cardamine pentaphyllos*, *Galanthus nivalis* 'Scharlockii' or double forms, *Narcissus* 'W.P. Milner', *Primula vulgaris* subsp. *sibthorpii*, *Scilla bifolia* and *Trillium luteum*.

There are a number of named clones which are propagated by division.

NAMED CLONES

'Aeneas' One of the two double-flowered plants found by Elizabeth in Montenegro. Each flower is 1½in (4cm) across with between fifteen and seventeen petals, and there are no nectaries. The buds are rich emerald green and coppery brown, and the open petals are green with brown veins on the outsides and are apple green on the insides. The young leaves are green.

'Dido' The other of Elizabeth's Montenegran doubles, this is a little shorter than 'Aeneas' at 10–12in (25–30cm). The flowers are almost 2in (5cm) across, with nineteen petals which are brown or purple-brown speckled with a green edge on the outside and a sharp green inside. The young foliage is reddish-brown.

'Little Stripey' Found by Elizabeth in Bosnia, the flowers are deep violet-purple on the outside and

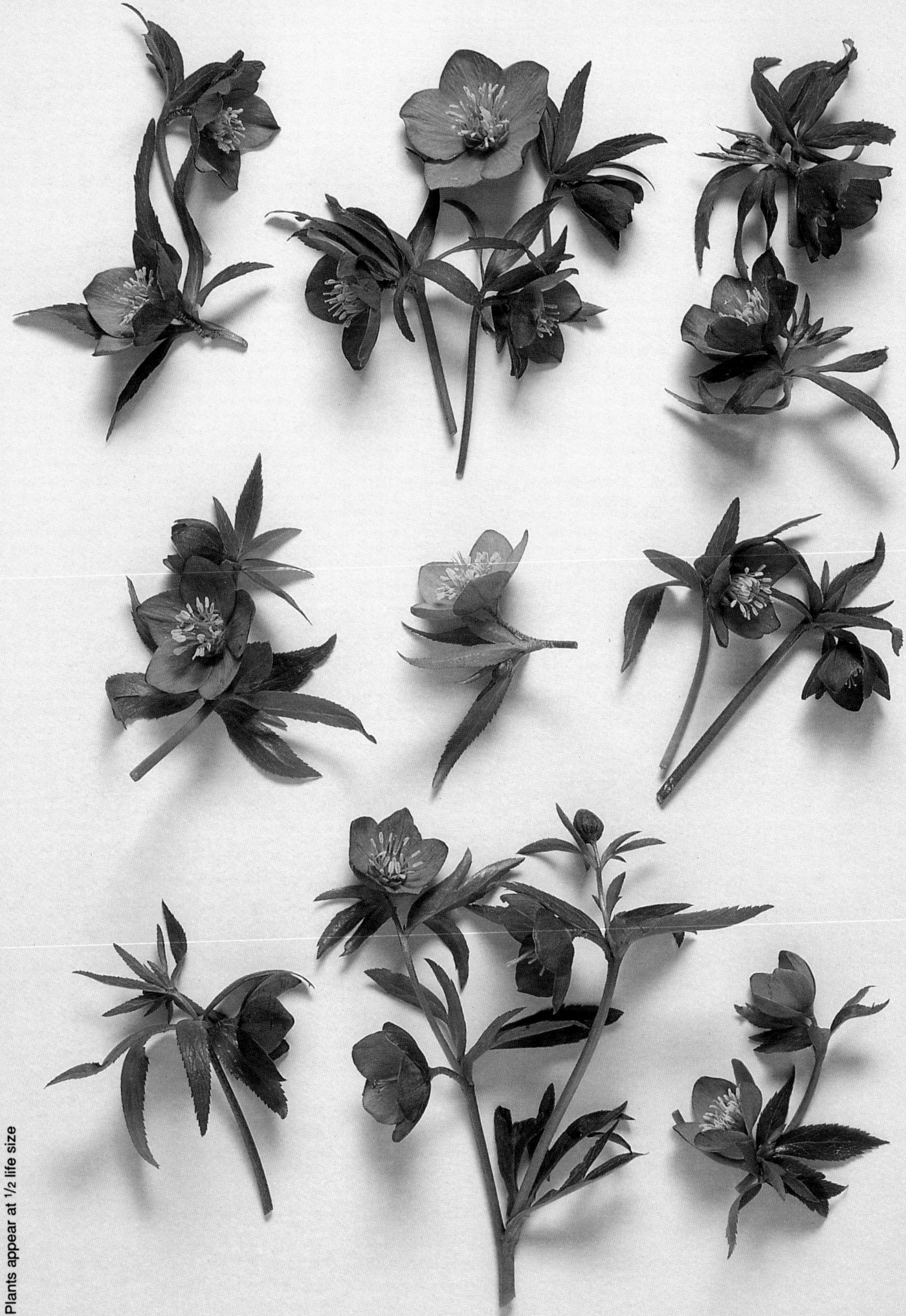

Plants appear at ½ life size

(*Above*): *Helleborus vesicarius* flowering in Will McLewin's garden, where it is planted in a sheltered spot outside and covered with a temporary frame in winter

(*Right*): The extraordinary inflated fruits of *Helleborus vesicarius* at Washfield Nursery

(*Left*): *Helleborus torquatus* from Crna Gora (Montenegro), Serbia. Grown at Washfield Nursery and at Kew, the flowers in the top row come from plants collected on Mt Kapaonik in 1929

pale blue-green inside with small violet-purple stripes. This has finely cut bracts and leaves and is very late to flower.

'Nero' This variety, which has large sloe-black flowers with a steely sheen and green eye, was selected by Roger Poulett, who has also distributed its seedlings.

Graham's seedling has nodding, narrow-petalled flowers in deep reddish-purple.

'Paul Voelcker' A double with lime green flowers and rich crimson young foliage. A seedling from 'Dido' raised by Ruth Voelcker of West Meon in Hampshire and introduced by Blackthorn Nursery

'Ruth Voelcker' Another double seedling from 'Dido' raised by Ruth Voelcker and introduced by Blackthorn Nursery. It is similar to 'Paul Voelcker' though rather smaller at 4–8in (10–20cm), and the petals are lime green with a fine red-brown rim. The young foliage is bronze-tinted.

SEED STRAINS

'Montenegran Doubles' Double-flowered seedlings of 'Dido' and 'Aeneas', in the typical colour range of *H. torquatus*. Raised at Washfield Nursery.

'Torquatus Hybrids' A group of seedlings raised by Eric Smith of The Plantsmen nursery from a cross between *H. torquatus* and a form of *H. orientalis* subsp. *abchasicus*. The rounded flowers

were outward-facing and came in pinkish purples, with pale interiors and at least a few speckles.

'Torquatus Hybrids' A very variable group of hybrids, the result of crosses between 'Pluto' and three forms of *H. torquatus*. The resultant flowers come in pink and purple shades, some with green or paler insides and either green or purple nectaries. Raised

and introduced by Blackthorn Nursery.

'Wolverton Hybrids' A range of double-flowered forms derived from intercrossing 'Dido', 'Paul Voelcker' and 'Ruth Voelcker' to give green, primrose or green-flushed purple flowers on short stems. Raised and introduced by Blackthorn Nursery.

HELLEBORUS VESICARIUS
Helleborus vesicarius Aucher

This species is a one-off; you would hardly even know it was a hellebore. It likes to be dried off in summer like a bulb, the fat seed pods roll around like tumbleweeds, and in leaf it looks more like a buttercup. Only the flower seems vaguely like a hellebore.

This is a summer-dormant plant 18in (45cm) high which starts into growth in November and produces fat stems with shiny, rather fleshy leaves both at the base and on the stems; they look like succulent buttercup leaves. The bracts are similar but are a pale yellow-green in colour. The flowers open from February to April and look very like those of *H. foetidus*, green inside and out with a chocolate-brown or purple band towards the tip of each petal.

The fruits are unique among hellebores, for as they mature they become highly inflated and eventually reach 3in (7.5cm) in length. They are green at first then change to a bleached brown

shade; the stems then collapse and break off and the wind blows the whole fruit away.

H. vesicarius grows only on open or scrubby hillsides in a small area straddling the border between southern Turkey and northern Syria, where the hot dry summers encourage other summer dormant plants like *Arum dioscoridis*, *Corydalis solida*, *Crocus ancyrensis*, *Crocus biflorus*, *Cyclamen pseudibericum*, *Galanthus fosteri*, *Hyacinthus orientalis* subsp. *orientalis*, *Fritillaria alfredae* subsp. *glaucoviridis*, *Iris histrio*, *Ranunculus asiaticus* and *Scilla ingridae*.

Behaving as it does, rather like a Mediterranean bulb, it demands similar treatment. When the foliage dies back at the end of June it must be dried off, though not baked. As it breaks into growth in November it needs a little frost protection to prevent damage to that juicy foliage; a cold frame or cold greenhouse is enough. It is best grown in pots of equal parts of loam, peat and grit or alternatively in a bulb frame, where it should be mulched with dry leaves or dry bracken to give added protection from harsh weather.

Helleborus vesicarius
Actual diameter 10in (25cm)

long toms as they start to grow at the beginning of their second year.

In a frame this species can be grown with any other plants, mainly bulbs, which enjoy similar conditions. These include *Crocus biflorus*, cyclamen, fritillarias, *Geranium tuberosum* and *Narcissus fernandesii*.

HELLEBORUS VIRIDIS
GREEN HELLEBORE

Helleborus viridis Linnaeus

The green hellebore, *H. viridis*, may have just about the widest distribution of them all, but in most of its forms it is also one of the least showy, in spite of having consistently the darkest green flowers of all.

There are two subspecies:

Helleborus viridis subsp. *viridis*
Helleborus viridis subsp. *occidentalis* (Reut.) Schiffner

Both are deciduous, with green or sometimes purple-tinted young foliage. The mature leaves are divided into five to seven main segments, with the outer two again divided to give a total of up to twenty lance-shaped, sharply toothed divisions. The flowers are 1–2in (2.5–5cm) across and are usually dark green, although plants with yellow-green flowers are occasionally found.

In subsp. *viridis* the foliage is slightly downy

This species seems to produce but little seed; even when hand-pollinated, results are unpredictable, although the chances of success are increased if different plants are crossed.

As you might expect, the seedlings of this plant are as unusual as the rest of it. In their first year seedlings produce nothing more than two seed leaves and a pea-sized resting bud together with a few fleshy roots. Then the plant takes a rest before the next autumn, when true leaves appear and growth continues; it pays, therefore, to space-sow seeds 2in (5cm) apart, allow seedlings to produce seed leaves and then die down, and prick them out into 4–5in (10–12.5cm)

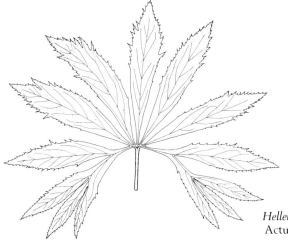

Helleborus viridis subsp. *viridis*
Actual diameter 12in (30cm)

Helleborus viridis subsp. *occidentalis* growing wild in Cambridgeshire with dog's mercury and lesser celandine. Some of the young leaves are purple-tinted

underneath when young and the mature leaves are strongly pedate with finely toothed leaf edges. By contrast, in subsp. *occidentalis* the young leaves are smooth below, the mature foliage is less noticeably pedate and the leaflets are edged with coarse teeth.

These two subspecies are also separated geographically. In Switzerland, southern Germany, Austria, northern Italy and south-east France subsp. *viridis* is found growing on the edge of woodlands and in nearby meadows. The British plant is subsp. *occidentalis*, which also occurs in western Germany, Belgium, France and Spain and is said to be naturalised in New England. This too is mainly a plant of deciduous woods, usually on limy soil, although it is also sometimes found in the open. Many of the apparently wild British plants are actually garden escapes.

Four slightly unusual forms have been found in Britain. One has red veins in the flowers; another, sometimes known as forma *maculatus*,

has red blotches at the base of the petals; a third has red styles instead of the usual green, and a fourth has dark flower stems and red-tipped nectaries.

Among the plants with which it grows in Britain are *Anemone nemorosa*, *Aquilegia vulgaris*, *Arum maculatum*, *Atropa belladonna*, *Clematis vitalba*, *Daphne laureola*, *Dryopteris dilatata*, *Lamium galeobdolon*, *Helleborus foetidus*, *Hyacinthoides non-scripta*, *Paris quadrifolia*, *Primula vulgaris* and *Silene dioica*.

In gardens this rather slow-growing species is best grown in light shade in an alkaline, humus-rich soil. It is tolerant of heavy clay soil and deep shade, but in both situations will usually grow even more slowly and flower poorly. This demure species requires suitably quiet neighbours such as × *Heucherella* 'Rosalie', *Chrysoplenium davidianum*, or a snowdrop such as the double yellow 'Lady Elphinstone'.

There is just one named cultivar:
'Pailhès' This is a form of subsp. *occidentalis* with the leaves covered in cream streaks. It was found in the Pyrenees by Leon Doyen.

7

HYBRIDS IN THE WILD AND IN GARDENS

Hybridisation is a mixed blessing. Chance hybrids in the wild have undoubtedly increased the problems encountered by botanists while studying the species, yet it is through planned hybridisation that so many wonderful garden plants have been developed. Chance crosses in the garden more often than not produce plants of less interest than either parent.

In the wild, hybrids occur between a number of species where colonies are sufficiently close to one another. It is in Yugoslavia where most wild hybrids occur, and here *H. multifidus* crosses with *H. torquatus*, *H. odorus* with *H. cyclophyllus* and *H. torquatus* with *H. odorus*; this causes problems when studying plants in the wild. Elsewhere there have also been two reports of a wild hybrid between the unlikely parents of *H. foetidus* and *H. viridis*.

Most of the hellebores grown in gardens are hybrids involving the subspecies of *H. orientalis*. These have been crossed with *H. cyclophyllus* and *H. odorus* to give yellows, *H. multifidus* subsp. *bocconei* has been used to develop green-flowered hybrids, and crosses with *H. torquatus* in its many forms have produced deep purple, 'blue', dove grey and smoky forms together with a few doubles.

The species in the *Helleborastrum* group (the stemless species) will all cross with each other, although many of the hybrids that could be created would not be improvements on their parents.

Wherever *H. argutifolius* and *H. lividus* are grown together, hybrids, known as *H.* × *sternii*, occur and two good strains have been de-

veloped. More surprisingly, *H. niger* has been successfully crossed with both these species and their hybrid to produce some fine garden plants. The cross between *H. niger* and *H. argutifolius* is known as *H.* × *nigercors*, but for many years the other two have been without valid botanical names, because the names by which they have become known are not valid under the International Code of Botanical Nomenclature. Brian Mathew has clarified the situation by giving

A division of the original *Helleborus* × *nigercors* 'Alabaster' which was named at Washfield in 1968

them valid names, so the hybrid between *H. niger* and *H. lividus*, known colloquially "H. × nigriliv", is correctly called *H. × ballardiae*, while the hybrid between *H. niger* and *H. × sternii*, which became known as "*H. × nigristern*", is now correctly called *H. × ericsmithii*.

Hybrids between *H. niger* and *H. orientalis* are regularly reported but usually turn out to be pinkish forms of one or other species; a genuine hybrid is unknown. Hybrids between *H. foetidus* and *H. argutifolius* were made at Durham University in 1960 but were not considered garden-worthy.

HELLEBORUS × HYBRIDUS
Helleborus × hybridus Voss

ORIENTALIS HYBRIDS

When this name was first coined in 1894, it was intended to cover all hybrids involving *H. orientalis*. But it is not a name which has found much favour with either botanists or gardeners; perhaps its scope is simply too wide, and we ourselves rarely use it, preferring the more colloquial term Orientalis Hybrids. So although we agree that *H. × hybridus* is perhaps appropriate for use in purely botanical contexts, for gardeners we are sure that the term Orientalis Hybrids is more helpful.

HELLEBORUS × NIGERCORS
Helleborus × nigercors J.T. Wall

A splendid, if unlikely, hybrid of *H. niger*, this time with *H. argutifolius*. This cross was first made by J. H. Stooke in 1931, good forms were raised by E. B. Anderson and Hilda Davenport-Jones, and more recently Elizabeth and now Blackthorn Nursery have distributed many plants. This hybrid combines all the qualities of its parents into a fine garden plant.

The most robust of the hybrids with *H. niger*, *H. × nigercors* produces flowers both on tall leafy stems and on shorter stems at the sides, giving a very long period of flower. Flowers are also produced in large numbers, as many as thirty-four on one stem. They are 3–4in (7.5–10cm) across,

white, slightly creamy or even green in colour, and most flowers develop a central green stripe on each petal. The flowers age to green and then remain attractive for many weeks. They are the best of all hellebores for cutting. The mature leaves are dull green and are divided in three neatly toothed segments.

This is a tough plant which thrives in full sun or in partial shade but is at its best in a rich soil. It soon makes a clump 3–4ft (90cm–1.2m) across, and the leaves may need thinning to reveal the flowers and help prevent black spot attack. Plants can be divided in August but are best left to make big clumps.

The bold leaves look good with irises or grasses, and allowing bulbs like *Crocus tommasinianus* to naturalise in the clump is very effective. Other good neighbours would be *Brunnera macrophylla* 'Variegata' and *Heuchera* 'Palace Purple'.

There are a number of cultivars:

'**Alabaster**' Raised by Hilda Davenport-Jones using *H. niger* 'Potter's Wheel' as seed parent and named by Elizabeth, 'Alabaster' was awarded an Award of Merit in 1971 and described as having 3½in (9cm) creamy white flowers shading to paler green in the centre and ageing to a yellower green.

'**Beatrix**' Similar to 'Hawkhurst' and Mr Stooke's plant, with 2½in (6.5cm) white flowers tinged with green. Raised by E. B. Anderson.

'**Blackthorn Strain**' A fairly uniform seed strain, raised by making the cross each year. The flowers are sometimes pure white, but more often greenish-white ageing to green, and there may be a green stripe running down the centre of each petal. Introduced by Blackthorn Nursery.

'**Hawkhurst**' In 1960, writing in the *RHS Journal*, raiser Hilda Davenport-Jones says that 'Hawkhurst' has 'the stout stems and flower heads of *H. argutifolius* but the pure white flowers of *H. niger* though much flushed with green. The leaves are large, deep green and very handsome.'

HELLEBORUS × STERNII
Helleborus × sternii Turrill

As botanists have sometimes classified *H. argutifolius* and *H. lividus* as variants of the same species, it is to be expected that they will cross with each other. The result is a very variable hybrid which in most cases makes a good garden plant for both flowers and foliage. In some areas of the United States it can only be grown as a foliage plant, for the fierce winters kill all the top growth.

All plants with blood of both parents come under this name, and they are a very mixed bunch. They take features from the tall, green-leaved, green-flowered and perfectly hardy *H. argutifolius* and the short, veined-leafed, pinkish-flowered and tender *H. lividus* in unpredictable proportions, although the more a plant resembles a particular parent in one feature, the more likely it is to exhibit other features of the same parent.

Nurserymen T. Hilling and Co. were the first to exhibit this plant at the RHS in February 1947, followed a couple of years later by Sir Frederick Stern, after whom it is named.

Helleborus × sternii is easy to grow, self-seeding happily in many gardens and succeeding best in full sun, with reasonable drainage. Tall forms may need support. Dwarf, pink-tinted plants are likely to be the least hardy. This plant looks well with *Euphorbia characias*, rosemaries, cistus and lavenders, along with muscari, crocus and fritillarias in Mediterranean-style plantings.

There are just two cultivars:

'Boughton Beauty Strain' Originally, this name covered plants closer to *H. argutifolius* though less tall, with greyer and more strongly veined foliage, pink stems and pink backs to the leaves. However, over the years many inferior plants and one or two in much darker colours have carried this name. So it pays to see the plants before you buy. Introduced by Valerie Finnis (Lady Scott) and originating from seed sent to her by Ken Aslet, formerly Superintendent of Alpines at Wisley.

'Blackthorn Strain' In recent years Robin White has introduced this beautiful strain, which is dwarf and carefully selected for its purple stems, pronounced silvery grey, marbled foliage, and pink-flushed green flowers. Some plants are as short as 12in (30cm) with exceptionally smoky foliage.

HELLEBORUS × BALLARDIAE
Helleborus × ballardiae B. Mathew

This sterile garden hybrid between *H. niger* and *H. lividus* was previously known colloquially as "*H. × nigriliv*", but *H. × ballardiae* is now its correct name, acknowledging the work of Helen Ballard in being the first person to make this cross. In spite of the fact that many of these hybrids make lovely plants, they are seen much less often than the other hybrids of *H. niger*, partly because *H. lividus* is less widely grown and also because it is not fully hardy.

This is a distinctive plant combining the leaf shape and pedate divisions of *H. niger* with the blue-green colour and silvery veins of *H. lividus*. Short stems carry three or four flowers which are usually between the two parents in shape, size and colour. In colour they can be brownish- or purplish-pink, darker outside than within, or the pink buds may open to pink-backed flowers which are white with green streaks within.

Helen Ballard raised the first plants in the early 1970s, using *H. niger* as the seed parent, and exhibited two at the RHS in January 1973 under the names 'December Dawn' and 'Midwinter'. Soon after Eric Smith made the same cross, but plants are now hard to come by.

This plant is probably hardy only in the south of England, but it makes a superb alpine house or conservatory plant. It appreciates a rich, well-drained position in full sun, or a deep pot of John Innes Number 2 compost. Black spot can be very troublesome, so regular spraying is advisable. In the garden it associates well with spring bulbs like the lilac-flowered *Crocus corsicus*, *Iris histrioides* 'Major', *Muscari botryoides* or *Narcissus bulbocodium* subsp. *citrinus*.

(*Left*): A plant of *Helleborus* × *ballardiae* raised by John Fielding and flowering in his garden in London

A plant of *Helleborus* × *ericsmithii* raised by Robin White and flowering in Graham's garden

HELLEBORUS × ERICSMITHII

Helleborus × *ericsmithii* B. Mathew

This hybrid of *H. niger* with *H.* × *sternii* is a fine garden plant and is now being more widely grown. Known since its introduction in 1972 as "*H.* × nigristern", it is now correctly known as *H.* × *ericsmithii*. It is the most variable of the three *H. niger* hybrids, but at its best it incorporates the hardiness and flower size of *H. niger*, the hardiness of *H. argutifolius* and the leaf and flower colour of *H. lividus*.

The foliage combines in varying amounts the three divisions of *H.* × *sternii*, the dark green colour and pedate structure of *H. niger* with the silvery veining of *H. lividus* and the spiny margin of *H. argutifolius*. Plants eventually reach about 12in (30cm). The flowers may be pale pink inside or even white and darker outside; the precise colouring varies from plant to plant. Often, the backs of the petals have a green tint and there may be a green stripe running up the centre of each petal. The flowers darken as they age.

This cross was first made by Eric Smith in the 1960s, and plants were listed by The Plantsmen between 1972 and 1975. They have rarely been available until recently, when they have been successfully revived by Robin White of Blackthorn Nursery.

This plant is less tough than *H.* × *nigercors* but is hardier than *H.* × *ballardiae* and is a fine garden plant for good soil in at least some sun. Removing the old foliage in the autumn combined with regular spraying should reduce the risk of black spot attack. This plant makes a good front-of-the-border specimen set against a stone path, and good neighbours would include *Cyclamen coum* and *C. hederifolium*, *Anemone blanda* 'White Splendour', *Cardamine quinquefolia*, *Galanthus elwesii* and *Muscari latifolium*.

OTHER HYBRIDS

There are two other names which exist for hybrid hellebores but neither is much used. *Helleborus* × *feyderi* Schniffner covers only hybrids between *H. orientalis* subsp. *abchasicus* and *H. orientalis* subsp. *guttatus*. *Helleborus* × *jourdanii* Pages was used to cover a hybrid between *H. foetidus* and *H. viridis* found in 1914.

8

BREEDING HELLEBORES

When it comes to plant breeding, gardeners tend to be cautious. Some prefer to let nature take its course and feel that hybridising is a little too much like playing God. But although some delightful seedlings will undoubtedly turn up by chance in most gardens where hellebores are grown, a great many unremarkable ones will also appear. Yet even a small degree of intervention by the gardener can result in a greater proportion of good seedlings.

Others are under the misapprehension that plant breeding is highly technical and beyond the scope of the mere gardener. In fact more patience is required than technical expertise. And the excitement of seeing your own seedlings flower for the first time and picking out those with better shapes and better colours makes the three-year wait worthwhile. For there is always an element of unpredictability to heighten that thrill of anticipation.

At its most basic, it is possible to gain a little more control over the quality of your seedlings by planting specimens of different colours widely apart in the garden so that the bees are less likely to mix up the pollen. But to be more certain of flowers with a better shape, stronger stems, clearer colours and perhaps new colours or new colour combinations, the only way is carefully to select the plants which supply the pollen and those which will carry the seed and then cross them by hand.

FIRST THOUGHTS

There is, as a rule, a three-year period from the pollination of a hellebore to seeing the resultant seedlings flower. So in order to have new plants to assess and work on every year it is convenient to have three plots on which to grow your seedlings; this also helps you to be realistic about the number of seedlings to raise.

Most gardeners are short of space and can grow only a few rows of seedlings each year, so it is important to plan the space available to fit in with the three-year cycle. Practicalities demand that you decide how much space to allocate to your seedlings then divide the plot into three. Individual beds should not consist of more than four or five rows, otherwise it becomes impossible to look closely at the flowers without standing on the beds and so compacting the soil unnecessarily. Given that the seedlings must be planted out 10–12in (25–30cm) apart, you will be able to work out how many seedlings you have space for each year.

At least a dozen seedlings of each cross should be grown, but to ensure that the full range of variability is seen, twenty or more should be grown if possible. Extras can be passed to enthusiastic friends to grow on – provided they bring flowers back for you to assess and promise to return the pick of the litter. Conversely, some crosses may yield only a few seeds and then it pays to grow them all. If you make too many crosses you will have space to raise only a few seedlings from each one. It is important to make decisions in good time, as it is easy to yield to temptation when the hellebores are all in flower and make too many crosses.

The general rule is that good-quality plants which are vigorous, healthy and with flowers of good shape and colour will make the best parents. The mother plant, or seed parent, should be chosen for strong growth and well-shaped flowers. Look for round overlapping petals and avoid narrow, starry, pointed petals –

although this is a matter of personal preference. The father, or pollen parent, should be chosen for colour and shape, perhaps for new or improved colour or larger flower size. If you have room, try to make each cross both ways as some plants are much better mothers than others. The crucial thing to remember is that good parents produce good seedlings.

If the aim is to produce a definite colour such as primrose yellow, starting completely from scratch adds unnecessary years to the process. Elizabeth started her yellows with a noticeably yellow form of *H. odorus* as mother and a strong *H. orientalis* with good, round cream flowers as pollen parent. From the seedlings she selected one to breed from. It had small but perfectly rounded flowers approaching yellow but with a lot of green in them. The others were either too green or were creamy-white.

This good seedling was then selfed (fertilised with its own pollen) and the resulting seedlings assessed. There was still a high percentage of greens and creams, but two were selected with the clearest yellow colouring. These two were then crossed with each other, choosing the plant with the best flower shape as the seed parent. The seedlings produced a large percentage of plants with primrose-yellow flowers of clear colour and good shape. But this was a long process – remember, it takes three years from pollination to flowering each time.

If you would like to aim for a stronger yellow, you can cut out three generations, i.e. nine or ten years, by buying a good pure-bred plant as a mother plant for your breeding programme. Ask if the plant is pure-bred or open-pollinated before buying it, though not every nurseryman will be able to tell you. A chance seedling which happens to combine the right qualities to good effect will give you highly unpredictable offspring. It is especially important with the clear and spotted whites to obtain pure-bred plants from which to breed. If a white is bred from a pink you will get pinks and pink-flushed whites in future generations, as quite a percentage of whites tend to turn up in the pinks, both clear and spotted.

The quickest and best way to increase good breeding plants is to self a good pure-bred plant, then you have the choice of crossing the best seedlings with each other or with the mother plant. Rigorous selection can then continue in subsequent generations, coupled always with crossing the best with the best. But too much selfing will eventually lead to weakening of the strain.

MAKING CROSSES

It is important to start making your choices as early as possible in the flowering season to give the maximum time to do the actual crossing; weather and other distractions can reduce the number of days available for pollination.

When the chosen buds on the mother plant are just about to open, pick a fully open flower off the chosen father, making sure there are plenty of stamens on it which have not yet shed their pollen. Mature stamens will drop off as the flower gets older. Pick the individual flower with about 1in (2.5cm) of stem, take it indoors, and float it face-up in a bowl of water. Do this the day before you intend to pollinate, as the pollen will be shed the next day, becoming noticeably fluffy as it is freed from the anthers. It is then ready to use. Taking the flower indoors is a precaution against chilly weather preventing the flow of pollen on outdoor plants, and it also helps prevent contamination from foreign pollen left by bees on open anthers.

It pays to pollinate at least three to five buds to maximise the chance of a successful seed set; the chosen flowers should, if possible, be on different stems in case of accidents from cats, dogs, gales, black spot or some similar calamity. You will need certain items of equipment to do the job properly:

Tweezers The best have wide ends rather than sharp points. Those with pointed tips are apt to be too harsh on delicate stamens, and the broad tips make it easier to grip them.
Wool Each pollinated flower will need to be marked in some way. It is not possible to use anything heavy or likely to chafe, as hellebore

stems are notoriously easily bruised and this leads to inevitable blackening and collapse of the flower stalk. Coloured wools, loosely tied, make identification easy; two or three ply is best. A 4–5in (10–12.5cm) length is easy to tie and can be cut in quantity by winding round a conveniently sized card and then cutting with scissors. Different colours can be used for different crosses making it easier when seed-collecting. Jewellers' tags can be used successfully in the greenhouse, and the details of the cross can be written on. Outside, the weather tends to wash the writing away by seed collection time.

Labels It is very important to label as you go. Record the parents and the date of the pollination and what the different wool colours actually mean. When you collect the seed, collect the labels too and they can then be used for the seed pots.

Pencil An HB lead pencil is more long-lasting than any special marking pen.

Kneeler For personal comfort and well-being!

Board A wooden board to rest your kneeler on is a help if the soil is wet; it prevents you making depressions in the lawn and damaging the edges.

Hood A hood is particularly useful to prevent bees and other insects gaining access to a particular flower or plant. This is vital when pollinating the flowers of species plants to ensure that the seed is true. A frame can be made of galvanised wire or lightweight timber and covered with old net curtain, and this is placed over the whole plant to keep out the bees. Be sure to secure the base of the netting to the ground with staples made of galvanised wire, and when you remove the hood for hand-pollinating shoo away any inquisitive bees.

HOW TO MAKE A CROSS

It is important to keep the pollen flowers separate when out in the garden making crosses, or the pollen may become mixed. First use your wool to mark your chosen bud, which should be just about to open. At this stage, although the stigma is ready to receive pollen, the anthers in the flower remain relatively undeveloped so there is little chance of self-pollination; the nectaries too are unripe, so bees are unlikely to be attracted. Open the bud gently, holding back the petals. If only a little pollen is to be stretched to pollinate several buds, use tweezers and pick off one or more stamens with their pollen. Paint the pollen on to the stigmas, making sure all are well covered; there may be anything from three to eight or nine. If you have plenty of flowers on the pollen parent you can fold back the petals and use the flower as a paintbrush. This will give you a good cover of pollen but you may need to pick another flower to take inside for the following day.

Some people prefer to use a small artists' paintbrush for all pollinating, transferring the pollen on to the bristles then painting it on to the stigma. The big disadvantage of this method is that you need a separate paintbrush for each pollen parent, as wiping it clean will not guarantee that all pollen is removed. It will inevitably become contaminated and lead to loss of control over your crosses. So, if you must use a paintbrush, remember to have one for each pollen parent and to keep it separate and labelled – either keep each in its own polythene bag or, if pollinating indoors, each brush can be stuck in the appropriate pot. Alternatively, pollen can be killed by dipping the brush in methylated spirits, which soon evaporates leaving the brush ready to use again.

A cap from a black Biro ballpoint pen can also be used; this is rubbed on either jumper or

Family trees of four seed strains developed by Elizabeth Strangman.
Picotees: The picotee strain is still being developed. (1), 'Violetta', was raised by putting pollen from a pink-edged white on a pure white, (2) is the result of selfing 'Violetta', and (3) is the result of crossing 'Violetta' with a pure white.
Yellows: A seedling of the yellow-green form of *H. odorus* (4) was the start of the strain and led to the choice of these two new mother plants, (5) for its good yellow colour and (6) for its good rounded shape.
Darks: 'Pluto' (7) was crossed with the old darkest purple (8) to give 'Little Black' (9); this was back-crossed on to the old darkest purple to give 'Queen of the Night' (10), which was itself crossed with a slaty blue seedling (11) to give the slaty blue strain (12)

trousers and the static electricity will then pick up pollen when the pen top is touched against the anthers. The pollen is then gently rubbed on to the sticky stigmas. This is very easy but there is always the danger of damaging the stigma.

After pollinating, gently ease the petals back into place to reduce the chance of the bees getting into the bud before your pollen has taken. Write the label and stick it in close to the plant. For the best chance of success, repeat the pollination on three successive days. Many wise old gardeners used to recommend that these 'arranged marriages' took place at 12 noon – the optimum time for success in their long experience – and this remains good advice, as the pollen should be flowing well.

For more certain success you can emasculate the mother flower, that is remove the stamens from the flower to prevent possible self-pollination. This is very fiddly; it requires good strong thumbnails and a steady hand, as it is all too easy to damage the stigmas or bruise the neck of the flower. This should not be necessary with the Orientalis Hybrids. If the three days' pollinating are accomplished before the pollen is mature and before the bud is open, the pollen painted on by the pollinator will beat the bees and the mother plant's own pollen down the style to the ovaries.

Compared with the Orientalis Hybrids, *Helleborus niger* and *H. argutifolius* are rather different. When making crosses involving these species the mother flowers should always be emasculated, and it also pays to pick off any open flowers which are shedding pollen on the mother plant at the time of pollinating.

If you have the facilities, there is no reason why mother plants should not be potted and brought under glass for pollination. This certainly makes life a great deal easier for the pollinator, although it would be wise to lift and pot plants in late summer when root growth is beginning rather than shortly before flowering when the ground may well be frozen or waterlogged. Breeding from potted plants means that rainy days cease to be no-go days, and with the added sophistication of electric light, or even a

hanging lantern, evening pollination would be a pleasure.

Pick off any unpollinated flowers towards the end of April; this will ensure that all the seed on the mother plant is for collection and that there is no possibility of it getting mixed with open-pollinated seed. Before the capsules open, smooth out the soil under your mother plants so that if by some chance seed is spilled on to the ground before or during collection, there are no cracks down which it can slip. For details of seed cleaning and storage see page 35.

CASE HISTORIES

Before suggesting some directions for breeding in the future, it is interesting to contrast the ways in which Helen Ballard and Elizabeth have developed their yellow hybrids.

Helen Ballard began with a plant of wild *H. odorus*, which she collected in 1965 near Bohinj in northern Yugoslavia. It had green, rounded flowers 3in (7.5cm) across, and Mrs Ballard was struck by the luminous gold of the green flowers when the sun was behind them. She crossed it with an early-flowering white plant formerly known as *H. olympicus*, which also had rounded flowers. The resultant seedlings were very pale primrose and not very vigorous. These were crossed with a white Orientalis Hybrid, itself the result of crossing 'Hillier's White' with the original *H. olympicus*, and the best two seedlings crossed with each other.

At this point Mrs Ballard noticed a loss of vigour and a susceptibility to botrytis, so she outbred again, using a cream seedling. This produced robust and upright plants, one of which was named 'Citron' and was shown at the RHS in 1980 – fifteen years after her Yugoslavian trip. Other lines eventually produced flowers of a deeper colour, and Mrs Ballard has since worked on improving their stamina and habit. As especially good seedlings have appeared these have been named, and plants have been available from her intermittently, other yellows being sold simply as seedlings.

Elizabeth started off by crossing a very good

yellow-green form of *H. odorus*, obtained from The Plantsmen, with a creamy-coloured, wild-collected form of *H. orientalis* from the garden of Hilda Davenport-Jones. The result, in 1971, was one really good plant and this was selfed. The best of the resulting seedlings were intercrossed and this continues. The strain is still evolving and improving, although in essence it is a small-flowered strain with rounded, intensely yellow flowers. No individual plants have been named, but seedlings are sold every year as primrose-coloured hybrids.

The 1971 plant carried spotting and the spotted ones have been selected and crossed separately to develop a spotted yellow strain.

Crosses were also made using the creamy yellow 'Sirius', one of Eric Smith's cultivars, but although this gave larger flowers they were badly shaped. These are also being improved to give a strain with larger, more primrose-coloured flowers, but the shape has still not improved sufficiently.

IDEAS FOR ORIENTALIS HYBRIDS

It is far easier to have plenty of ideas than to choose which are most likely to be successful! Given that your second and third year's pollinations will have to be done before your first ones have flowered, it makes sense to choose three different themes, one for each year.

Some of the species, i.e. *H. torquatus, H. purpurascens* and especially *H. multifidus* subsp. *hercegovinus*, have lovely finely divided foliage or young leaves coloured deep purple. These could be crossed with plants carrying flowers of good colour and substance to develop high-quality flowering plants with attractive foliage. The dove grey colouring found in some forms of *H. torquatus* would look glorious on a larger flower, and this too could be a target.

Elizabeth is working on picotees in different colour combinations, and there is room for scope here. There is also still a need for really good spotted forms, from freckled all over to heavily spotted flowers and those in which the spots are fused to give to painted marks.

Elizabeth has developed strains with yellow and green flowers spotted with red, and Helen Ballard has developed a slate grey clone with dark spots, 'Mystery'.

Spots appear to be dominant, and so once bred into a strain they are very difficult, if not impossible, to breed out. Spots show a disconcerting instability; a perfectly spotted young plant kept back for future breeding is capable of uneven spotting the following year. But there is still scope for good spotted types or flowers with a painted ring in the centre.

Horizontally held blooms are also a challenge as they do not seem to be constant, varying from year to year and as the flower ages. This feature seems to be linked to the length of the individual flower stalk rather than its rigidity. Some people are very keen on outward- or upward-facing flowers, but the nodding, open, bell-shaped flowers of the hellebore have evolved to shed excess rain, so it is doubtful if the flowers would survive the British weather – they would fill with water. And anyway, where is the mystery in a flower with no secrets?

There are also opportunities for flowers with veining in contrasting colours, like butterflies' wings; flowers with coloured nectaries are a possibility too. There is even room for improvement in some individual colours, especially the bright ruby reds; and flowers which are one colour on the outside and another on the inside would be quite an achievement. Anemone-centred flowers could be refined, while dwarfer, large-flowered varieties with smaller foliage might also be very popular. There is scope for developing good doubles in a complete colour range.

IDEAS FOR OTHER GROUPS AND SPECIES

The only way to ensure that species breed true is to hand-pollinate. Unless your species plant is isolated from other hellebores, the chances are that you will get mongrels every time. The easiest method is to hood the whole plant and pollinate by hand. It is possible to hood individual flowers with bags made from nylon cur-

80

tain netting, but they tend to chafe the stems behind the flower or damage the flower itself – the flower dies and you get no seed.

Although most species will cross with others, there are exceptions and restrictions. *H. argutifolius* will cross with *H. lividus* to give *H. × sternii*, and once you have the first two in the garden you will soon find all three intercrossing to give a wide variety of intermediate forms; some will be good, many bad. Strangely, the very different *H. niger* will cross with any plants of this group to give often very attractive offspring, but these are infertile so cannot themselves be inter-crossed.

H. niger is the ideal mother plant, having a large flower on a strong stem. When trying for *H. × nigercors*, that is *H. niger* × *H. argutifolius*, *H. niger* is easier to use as mother than *H. argutifolius* as the latter folds its stigmas down very neatly in bud. This makes it difficult to find them and to avoid damage when emasculating.

Pollinate three days in succession as with the Orientalis Hybrids, but do not expect a high percentage of hybrids. The seedlings with *argutifolius* blood will germinate before Christmas, the *niger* type seedlings in January and February.

Ideas for this group might be to use pink forms of *H. niger* with *H. lividus* to increase the amount of pink in the hybrids. At present many variants of *H. × sternii* are found in gardens but only a few good strains are available, and even these are inclined to be variable. There is scope here for strains with specific leaf shapes and patterns, shorter growth habit and green to smoky purple colouring.

H. niger has occasionally been reported as crossing with other species. National Collection holder Jeremy Wood obtained a seedling from intentionally crossing *H. niger* with *H. viridis*, but the result was a very weak plant. Occasionally hybrids between *H. niger* and *H. orientalis* are reported, but no true hybrids have so far been verified. Repeating this cross is a waste of time.

Hybrids between *H. argutifolius* and *H. foetidus* were raised in the early 1960s and brought to flowering, and there may possibly be

scope here, perhaps using 'Wester Flisk' and some of darker forms of *H. × sternii*. Natural hybrids between *H. foetidus* and *H. viridis* have been reported, and this cross too might be worth repeating in cultivation.

In general the chances of these more unlikely crosses producing gardenworthy plants are remote, and with plenty of opportunities among species which we know will hybridise, it seems far more sensible to apply a little imagination and insight to these than to struggle with other crosses, where getting them to take at all is an almost insurmountable problem.

For one group of species hybridises readily: all the species in the Helleborastrum group will cross with each other – *H. atrorubens*, *H. cyclophyllus*, *H. dumetorum*, *H. multifidus*, *H. odorus*, *H. orientalis*, *H. purpurascens*, *H. torquatus* and *H. viridis*. Most of the garden hybrids are derived from crossing *H. orientalis* with *H. cyclophyllus*, *H. multifidus*, *H. odorus* and *H. torquatus*, but there may be more scope here. One of the most exciting possibilities is to use the species such as *H. dumetorum*, *H. purpurascens* and *H. torquatus* with the Orientalis Hybrids, aiming for large numbers of small flowers with exciting leaf forms.

DOUBLES

Undoubtedly the best chances of obtaining double seedlings come from a double selfed or crossed with another double; the fairly obvious theory is to maximise the doubling gene. As in all plant breeding, some plants make better mothers than others, giving more seeds, producing sturdier seedlings and a larger percentage of double-flowered offspring; 'Dido', one of Elizabeth's double forms of *H. torquatus* from Montenegro, is just such a one. The 'Montenegran Doubles' and the 'Wolverton Hybrids', as

Named double-flowered cultivars. A selection of double-flowered cultivars of various origins grown mainly at Washfield Nursery and Blackthorn Nursery. All but 'Marion' are derived from 'Dido'

'Westwood Hybrid'

'Westwood Hybrid'

'Westwood Hybrid'

'Westwood Hybrid'

'Party Dress Hybrid'

'Marion

'Paul Voelcker'

'Belinda'

'Ruth Voelcker'

'Montenegran Double'

'Dido'

'Aeneas'

'Montenegran Double'

'Wolverton Hybrid'

'Wolverton Hybrid'

'Wolverton Hybrid'

'Wolverton Hybrid'

well as 'Paul Voelcker' and 'Ruth Voelcker', are derived from this plant, and any of these could be the start of a race of dainty doubles in a variety of colours.

There are more double forms of *H. orientalis* grown in Germany than in the UK, including a beautifully shaped white spotted form. It should be possible to use those which are available to breed more, but stock is almost impossible to come by at present.

Doubles have also turned up at East Lambrook Manor in recent years, although these are not fully double but have two rows of petals and retain their nectaries; they have not yet reached the outside world.

ASSESSING SEEDLINGS

Eventually, three years after pollinating, two and a half years after germination, the great day will arrive and the plants will start to come into flower. A few may flower the previous spring or autumn but the flowers will probably not be typical or may abort. When they flower, ruthless selection is vital; keep only the best or your garden will soon be bursting with mediocre plants. Keep your original aim in mind and select only those which really do represent progress towards your goal.

Keep all the most promising seedlings for another year if possible, as some mature better than others. It is all too easy to let go seedlings you should have kept. These may be late starters and mature into real stars at four or five years old – but in other people's gardens. The following year you must be even more ruthless, for the space will need to be cleared for the next batch of seedlings to be planted out. Remember that although those you discard may not be your very best they are unlikely to be worthless, and they will find good homes with friends or be much appreciated at plant sales.

When assessing plants it is important to note which mother plants are throwing the best percentage of plants with well-shaped, strong-stemmed or good-coloured flowers, as this can help you avoid wasting time trying to breed from

plants which will never produce good offspring.

A really great hellebore does not necessarily make a good mother plant. Elizabeth has a particularly lovely pink with perfectly rounded flowers, a green eye and perfectly even spotting surrounded by a clear pink zone. Selfed, this produces dusky pink flowers with good spotting but they all fail to open into the perfect form of the parent. The problem is solved by using pollen from a pale flower such as a shell pink or apple-blossom pink, again with very even spotting and particularly wide open flowers. The agony is that until the first three-year cycle is complete there is no way of knowing which plants are going to lead to improvements.

DEVELOPING SEED STRAINS

Seed strains are not difficult to develop; it simply takes a long time and a good eye. Our accounts of the development of Elizabeth's various strains (pages 103–5) will point the way, but in essence, once you have found that a cross gives offspring which are not only of sufficiently high quality in colour, form and habit but are also very uniform, you have the beginnings of a strain. The same cross, between the same parents, repeated each year using the same mother plant, will give you more or less similar plants.

The strain can be improved by keeping back the very best plants in each generation, allowing them an extra year or two to mature, and then doing test crosses between them and with their parents. If the results are better than your existing strain in terms of either quality or uniformity, then the new cross can take over from the old one and you have moved one step further ahead.

NAMING

There is a tendency for far too many hellebores to be named. You will see from the list in this book that even since 1945 a very large number of cultivars have been named, but many recently named plants are actually no better and are sometimes hardly different from existing ones.

There is no point at all naming indifferent plants. Why go to the trouble of painstakingly multiplying a hellebore by division, taking many years for the plant to get around to gardeners, when it was only mediocre in the first place?

So only plants which are genuinely different and distinct should be named; Elizabeth has only named twelve in twenty-five years of hellebore breeding – but instead she has developed pure-bred seed strains which have yielded many thousands of fine plants over the years. The individual plants in each strain may not be absolutely identical, but they are 95 per cent uniform in colour, shape and constitution.

If you do have a seedling which you think is sufficiently different *and* a sufficiently dramatic improvement on existing ones, then consider naming it if you must. First of all try to confirm that it really is different from others which are already in gardens; the pictures in this book will help, and it may help to consult the experts. Then choose a name which has not been used for a hellebore before; check the list in this book and that in Brian Mathew's, which goes back to the nineteenth century. Finally, try to develop it into a seed strain so that there is more chance of your plant becoming widely available in that way.

'Queen of the Night' was one of Elizabeth's early breakthroughs, a very dark purple-flowered plant of good size and form; so it was named. But through selfing and intercrossing this has been developed into the 'Queen of the Night Strain', and so plants of this type were made widely available. But giving seed strains fancy names can cause problems, as one plant from the strain is apt to find the name attached to it and distributed as if it was a clone and no other plant was entitled to the name.

Naming of garden plants in general is something of a minefield, and hellebores cause more problems than many plants. Is there any point naming a plant which cannot be propagated in any significant numbers? And why name a plant which can easily be superseded by similar seedlings bred from it, so rendering the name either an embarrassment or simply obsolete?

You will have gathered that we advise a great deal of heart-searching and self-restraint when it comes to naming hellebores. But if you do name a plant and begin to distribute it, try and ensure that a description which mentions its distinguishing features and whether it is a clone or a seed strain is published somewhere, preferably with a photograph, so that there is always a record of the true plant.

9

THE ORIENTALIS HYBRIDS

This section features two main lists. The first is a descriptive list of named clones derived at least in part from *H. orientalis*, the second covers seed strains. Only cultivars which we can confirm have been grown or introduced since 1945 have been included, as so many older cultivars have now vanished and, anyway, these are discussed in detail in Brian Mathew's book. Readers will not find a full and detailed description of every single cultivar, as this would involve a great deal of repetition and be tedious in a book for gardeners.

In most cases the descriptions are derived from the raiser's own descriptions and our own observations. Unless otherwise stated the plants are 12–20in (30–50cm) high; growing conditions can influence height as much as the cultivar's inherent qualities.

All the cultivars in this first list are clones and should be propagated vegetatively. However, seed of many of these has been offered from time to time and it is important to remember that the resultant plants will not be identical to the parent, nor entitled to its name. Only propagation by division will ensure that the resulting plants are identical and true. And we make no apology for repeating that seed collected from named forms must not be sold or submitted to seed lists under the original clonal name. To help encourage a healthy scepticism we have marked with an asterisk * those clones from which we know seed or seedlings have been distributed using the clonal name.

A problem may still arise when self-sown seedlings germinate in mature clumps, because these can be passed on accidentally as if they were divisions when plants are split. Hellebores yield so few divisions that it is natural to preserve every piece, and in this way a seedling quite different from the parent may acquire the parent's name.

Finally, names which are in colloquial use but which are not cultivar names have been given double inverted commas (e.g. **"Atrorubens"**).

DESCRIPTIVE LIST OF NAMED CLONES

'Abel Carrière' The plant at Kew is noticeably early-flowering, with flowers 2¼–2½in (6–6.5cm) across. These are dark purple outside and in, paler between the veins especially towards the centre. The petals have pointed tips, especially the two outer ones. The filaments and styles are red, and there is a faint dusting of red spots tucked in behind the nectaries, which are green at the base, then red, then honey-coloured at the tips. An old cultivar, possibly introduced by Perrys in the 1930s and described in their catalogue as a 'uniform shade of crimson-plum, conspicuously lined crimson'.

'Agnes Brook' Slightly starry, pale pink flowers with a green haze towards the centre and faintly speckled at the base of three of the petals. Raised by Ernest Raithby and distributed by Court Farm Nursery.

'Alberich' An early-flowering plant with small blackish-purple, bell-shaped flowers each with a small pale green patch at the base of each petal; the stamens do not develop fully. This is very similar to the plant the old descriptions call "H. × torquatus". A strange plant but floriferous, it was raised by Elizabeth by crossing a form of *H. purpurascens* from the Royal Botanic Garden, Edinburgh, with true *H. torquatus* and was introduced in 1982.

'Albion Otto' In recent years Bressingham Gardens have listed a plant under this name which they describe as having white flowers and a compact habit. In 1884 Heinemann introduced a plant described as a *guttatus* type with purple spots under the name of 'Albin Otto'. It is highly unlikely that these two plants are the same.

'Alcyone' An exceptionally robust hellebore with huge, lush-green leaves and flower stems as thick as a little finger. The flowers are very large and rounded, opening almost flat. They are bronze-pink-flushed outside and greenish-cream inside, flushed with dim pink towards the edges of the petals and apple green towards the base. The green nectaries turn chrome yellow with age. Rather a dim, subtle colour, far from showy, but devastating on account of its size and stout habit. Raised by Eric Smith, selected by Amy Doncaster from seedlings at Buckshaw Gardens and introduced by them.

'Aldebaran' A very vigorous seedling from "H. atrorubens of gardens" with rounded, even flowers and a deciduous habit. Flowers bright reddish-purple inside and out, with gold nectaries. Often starts flowering in December and may be damaged by frosts, but with secondary flowers looking very bright in March. Raised by Eric Smith and introduced by Buckshaw Gardens in 1979.

'Algol' A distinctive cultivar with medium-sized flowers of good shape. They are an even crimson-rose outside and almost entirely covered inside with a zone of very dark crimson-lake markings – not spots or veining but intricate clearly defined blotches, giving an etched effect. The edges of the petals are outlined with an unmarked, narrow border of bright rose pink. Raised by Eric Smith.

'Alys Collins' Pure white with a small green eye and a few occasional tiny speckles at the base of the petals. Wide open, almost flat flowers of good shape showing the influence of Ballard blood. A new cultivar named by Court Farm Nursery, not yet introduced at the time of writing.

'Amethyst'* Smoky bluey mauve with a very dark edge, dark purple carpels and yellow nectaries. Each petal is noticeably flat rather than rounded, characteristic of a number of Helen Ballard's blues, and at least one petal on each flower has a greenish tip. The stems are red-purple and the leaves are finely cut. Raised and introduced by Helen Ballard.

'Andromeda'* Large, bowl-shaped flowers of impeccable shape, absolutely even, and with a beautiful solid texture. Uniform, rich crimson-purple outside and in, with a slight blue bloom. Bronze-tinted nectaries and bronze bracts. Similar to 'Black Knight', one of its parents, but larger. Raised by Eric Smith and introduced by Buckshaw Gardens in 1979.

'Angela Tandy' Starry in shape, with plum-coloured flowers speckled and netted darker and smokier, increasingly so towards the centre. A new cultivar from Court Farm Nursery, not introduced at the time of writing.

'Antares'* Originally raised and selected by Eric Smith as an im-provement on 'Mars'. The flowers are rather starry with pointed petals, and are an even reddish-plum inside with a polished area around the brownish nectaries; outside they are the same colour but darker. Not floriferous and tends to lose its leaves in winter, but increases well and has bronze-tinged bracts. Introduced by The Plantsmen in 1975. The plant grown by Margery Fish as 'Antares-meyeri' may be this.

'Apotheker Bogren' A very old clone, mentioned by Robinson in his *The English Flower Garden* of 1883 with a couple of others only as good forms of the red group. Medium-sized flowers which are an even reddish-purple inside and out with brown-tinged nectaries. Considered still vigorous when grown by The Plantsmen, but inferior to many of their unnamed purple seedlings.

'Apple Blossom'* Selected by Margery Fish, it was first mentioned by her in 1958 and later she described it and 'Peach Blossom' as 'what you would expect from such names'. However, it seems that her 'Apple Blossom' was distinct in having red margins to the petals.

'Apple Blossom' Free-flowering on short sturdy stems, the 2½in (6.5cm) shallow cups have beautifully rounded petals which are blush pink inside with a fine dusting of a few well-spaced freckles around the green centre, and slightly darker outside with dark veins. Raised by Beth Chatto and introduced by her in 1990. Unfortunately, this name has already been used by Margery Fish for her plant.

'Aquarius'* A very distinct, vigorous and floriferous selection from Eric Smith's 'Zodiac Strain' with extremely large, flat flowers which are rose pink outside, deepening towards the base and edges to soft crimson. The inside of the flowers is pale rose pink, flushed with green or white towards the centres of the petals and with a diffuse zone of small crimson speckles, occupying only about half the area of each petal. Introduced by Buckshaw Gardens before 1979.

'Aquila'* White inside and out, but heavily shaded primrose grading to green at the base outside and more lightly so inside; there is a primrose zone up the centres of the petals, especially as the flower ages, grading to pale green at the base. There is a small stain of maroon in the centre breaking down into rays of tiny maroon dots. The nectaries are green, becoming stained maroon at the edges as the flower ages. Raised by Jim Archibald and introduced by The Plantsmen.

'Ariel' Dissected, deciduous foliage and small, cup-shaped, outward-facing flowers. Fairly solid, dark vinous purple outside; inside palest green towards the centre, becoming increasingly flushed with purplish crimson towards the edges and with diffuse darker streaks of the same colour and a few pepperings of crimson at the base. Dark bronze, satiny nectaries. Very floriferous, forming a sheaf of upright 12in (30cm) stems, packed with flowers. Usually in flower by Christmas. A cross by Eric Smith between his *H. torquatus* and what he knew as "Colchicus Superbus", introduced by The Plantsmen in 1973.

'Aries'* A selection from Eric Smith's 'Zodiac Strain' but considered identical to 'Leo' and eventually sold as such; the name 'Aries' was dropped as too similar to 'Ariel'.

"Atrorubens"* See 'Early Purple' and also page 43.

'Ballard's Black'* This legendary plant is one of those which has caught the imagination of many gardeners. However, the true plant, propagated by division, remains elusive. See page 112.

'Banana Split' Large-flowered yellowish-cream. Raised by Henry A. Ross of Ohio and named by him in 1984.

'Belinda' A delightful double form with 2in (5cm) flowers, each made up of about twenty petals. They have dark pink backs and are greeny cream inside with a dark pink rim. A relatively dwarf plant, neater and more open than most doubles and very pretty, but shy-flowering in some gardens. 'Belinda' was selected by Elizabeth from a batch of seedlings grown from mixed, open-pollinated seed from 'Dido' and 'Aeneas', her Montenegran doubles.

'Black Knight'* An older clone, now surpassed by modern varieties. The plant grown in the 1970s had medium-sized, bowl-shaped, rather uneven flowers, uniform purple outside, flushing to black-crimson at the base. Inside the flowers were crimson-purple with a darker flush around the edges, grading to pale green at the base and with diffuse 'black' speckles towards the base and especially along the veins; the nectaries were pale green. Introduced by Barr and Son in 1926 when it was awarded an AM, and described so: 'The flowers of this hardy herbaceous lenten rose are of a very dark, purplish shade, almost black. They are borne on long stems and the whole plant is robust in habit.' Reintroduced by The Plantsmen in April 1979 but discarded a few years later in favour of 'Andromeda'.

'Blowsy'* A tall, 18in (45cm), very bright, fresh-looking plant with 3in (7.5cm), flattish, dish-shaped flowers which are yellow in bud. They open to creamy yellow, darker on the backs than on the inside and green around the pedicel. Inside, all the petals are slightly paler towards the edge with just a few faint spatterings of purple spots towards the base. The petals are noticeably wrinkled and puckered. The flowers are even in shape, mainly because of the three good rounded outer petals rather than the two inner more narrow ones. The bracts are very broad and pale, toothed all the way around, and are a fresh, bright green, offsetting the almost primrose flowers beautifully. Very striking, dramatic and distinctive. Raised and introduced by Helen Ballard.

'Blue Rook' Raised by Helen Ballard and introduced by her in 1991. Similar to 'Philip Ballard'.

'Blue Showers' Pale blue, rather drooping flowers. Raised by Helen Ballard and introduced by her in 1990.

'Blue Spray'* A dramatic plant with inky purple, 2in (5cm) flowers with a smoky haze. In bud, the flowers are a bright, very dark purple with a slight sheen, opening to a very flat-petalled flower. The flowers have a tendency to a slightly uneven shape, with one petal noticeably shorter than the other four. The petals tend to be flat and rolled inwards base to tip, some are also rolled back from side to side, giving a curious and distinctive shape. The shine on the backs of the petals remains as the flowers age. The nectaries are marmalade and honey in colour and contrast with the striking purple carpels. The bracts are rich green and slightly purple on the backs and around the teeth. The impact of the plant is greatly enhanced by the 15in (38cm) stems, which are a rich, indigo purple from soil level right up through the plant to the pedicels and the flower itself. Raised and introduced by Helen Ballard.

'Blue Wisp'* A delicate plant with a spreading habit and small flowers becoming more starry as they age. Outside they are smoky blue-purple on the back with almost black veins. Inside they are silvery blue-purple with a touch of green; basically the same colour as 'Amethyst' but a little less smoky. The petals are rather flat, rolling over from base to tip, often re-flexed side to side and also a little waved. The stems are more a reddish-brown than purple at the base, with some greening in places. Raised and introduced by Helen Ballard.

'Boocizau Hybrid'* Seed has been listed by the Hardy Plant Society Seed Exchange, but we have no information about it.

'Bowles' Yellow' An unremarkable yellowish-green-flowered plant given by Bowles to Graham Thomas and named by him. For a discussion of this plant see page 113.

'Brian Mathew'* A name in use in America, seemingly derived from a misreading of B. Mathew as a botanical authority in the name H. orientalis subsp. guttatus (A. Br. & Saur) B. Mathew, and taking it to be a cultivar name. Brian says there is no cultivar bearing his name.

'Bridesmaid' A white cultivar with very attractive pink spotting in the throat. Raised in America by Henry A. Ross of Ohio and named by him in 1984.

'Brünhilde' An old German clone with medium-sized flowers of pale cream, green-flushed towards the base inside and out. Occasionally

there are a few irregular dots of crimson inside. This has now been surpassed by modern seedlings but is still grown at Kew and was listed by nurseries in the mid 1970s.

'Brünhilde' The plant distributed under this name from Germany by Heinz Klose is different from the above, and is a finely spotted, soft pink. This may be the plant distributed in Holland as 'Brunhilda'.

'Burgundy'* Shapely, medium-sized flowers in deep purple. Raised and introduced by Helen Ballard.

'Button'* A neat, vigorous plant with almost spherical creamy yellow buds opening to very good, cup-shaped flowers, 2–2½in (5–6.5cm) across and more or less outward-facing. The flowers open very pale primrose maturing to greeny primrose, and green at the base. The fresh green stems have some red shading on the outer edge. Not to be confused with 'Yellow Button' (page 102). Raised and introduced by Helen Ballard.

'Capricornus' A selection from Eric Smith's 'Zodiac Strain' but virtually identical to 'Leo' and 'Aries', perhaps with a slightly more rounded flower.

'Carina' A very distinct cultivar with beautifully cup-shaped flowers of medium size with the petals much overlapped. The outside is slightly greenish white, heavily flushed with lilac pink, and the inside is similar but only faintly blushed; the veins are marked inside and out in rose pink. The base of the petals is stained crimson and the nectaries are bronze, giving a dark centre to the flower. Raised by Jim Archibald.

'Carlton Hall' Plants in circulation seem to vary; some have a good cupped shape while others are

starry, some extremely so. A good example, perhaps, of what happens when clones are raised from seed. At their best the flowers are large and white with a hint of green and a vigorously spotted purple blaze on each petal. Flowers on some plants are strongly green-tinted, but all are green towards the centre and on all plants the whole flower fades quickly to green. Raised by Ernest Raithby and introduced by Court Farm Nursery.

'Cassiopeia' Medium-sized flowers in pale rose pink tinged with green on the outside. Inside they are shell pink, deepening towards the edge, with a soft green base flushing up the segments at the centre and paling to cream where it merges with the pink. A very subtle and delicately coloured flower, bright but not spectacular and quite floriferous. Raised by Eric Smith, selected by Amy Doncaster from seedlings at Buckshaw Gardens and introduced by them.

'Castor' and 'Pollux' The first two clones raised by Eric Smith with the intention of developing plants with black flowers. The black-purple flowers are only medium-sized and have rather narrow sepals and dark bracts, tinged with bronze, and beetroot purple stems. These two twins sound wonderful, but have rarely been heard of since being introduced by Buckshaw Gardens in 1979.

'Celadon' Nodding 2–2½in (5–6.5cm) flowers in soft, cool, even chilly green inside and out, with darker green veins towards the base of the outside. The nectaries are green. The stems are almost red at the base but quickly becoming green and the fresh green bracts have pale veins. Raised and introduced by Elizabeth in 1978, 'Celadon' is the result of crossing H. multifidus subsp. bocconei with a pale green Orientalis Hybrid. One seedling had lovely, large, well-shaped, pale green flowers; this was selfed and one of the seedlings was selected and named 'Celadon'.

'Charlotte Bonham-Carter' Very similar to 'Cherry Doris' but with darker pale plum background. Raised by Court Farm Nursery.

'Cheerful'* A bright yellow-flowered cultivar raised by Helen Ballard.

'Cherry Doris' Flowers with pointed petals, lilac on a pink ground with deeper purple veins, all over netted and spotted pale purple; no green. Raised by Court Farm Nursery.

"Chris Brickell's early yellow"* A seedling from a plant given to Chris Brickell by E. B. Anderson. The flowers are about 2in (5cm) across, with even-sized, slightly pointed petals, and it almost invariably flowers before Christmas. Although Chris describes the colour as creamy yellow it could perhaps be called pale primrose; the backs of the petals are a slightly stronger colour.

'Citron'* Flowers 2–2½in (5–6.5cm) across, greeny yellow in bud, opening to a very pure, pale, semi-translucent primrose inside with pearly green veins and tending to a little green haze towards the base. The outside is, unusually, paler, a creamy yellow. The inner two petals are smaller and squarer than the outer three, which are broader and more rounded. The flowers are held very tight on to the bracts on short pedicels, so most flowers face almost upwards when mature. The nectaries are honey-greeny yellow, slightly golden. There is hardly any red in the plant at all except where the stems branch and at the very base. There

is no red in the buds and the bracts are fresh green with pale teeth all the way round and with pale veins. Raised and introduced by Helen Ballard.

'Cosmos'* A selection from Eric Smith's 'Constellation Strain'. Large, evenly rounded, shallowly bowl-shaped flowers of greenish-white, flushed pink outside and veined in crimson. Inside they are very pale pink, slightly green-flushed, and evenly and densely spotted with bright crimson almost to the edge of the segments. There is a bright, pale green zone at the base of the petals surrounding the green nectaries. Considered the only clone to approach 'Mira' in quality. Raised by Eric Smith and introduced by Buckshaw Gardens in 1979, it is one of their varieties which is seen in gardens more often than most. There is rumour of a plant called 'Cosmos 2' but we have not seen it.

"Cream Guttatus Form" A short, early-flowering form with cream flowers, heavily spotted with maroon inside but leaving a clear zone around the edge. Raised by Beth Chatto and introduced by her in 1990.

'Cygnus' A shorter-growing cultivar with white, starry flowers up to 4in (10cm) across, with wavy-edged petals. Vigorous and very free-flowering, this cultivar was raised by Eric Smith and given to Jerry Webb in 1980.

'Dainty White' A small-flowered, white and green cultivar introduced by Mamie Walker of Wester Flisk in Fife.

'Darley Mill' Uneven, slightly pearly pink flowers flushing to white, generally with a slight purple spotting. Raised by Ernest Raithby and introduced by Court Farm Nursery.

'Dawn'* Among the largest of all hellebore flowers at 3¾in (9.5cm) across. The flowers are purple-tinted pink with darker veins in bud, opening almost flat with a little burnt bronze around the pedicel. Inside they are pale silvery pink around the edge, then dusky pink with dark veins, green nectaries and purple carpels. Very rounded and neat in bud, with rounded petals and big rounded flowers. The three outer petals tend to be larger and more rounded, the inner are smaller and almost square. The flowers are rather a silvery pink on the backs as they age, with dark pink veins, then ageing further to an unfortunate coppery colour outside and coppery green within. The 16in (50cm) stems are reddish towards the base, thinning to pink at the top. Raised and introduced by Helen Ballard.

'Debutante' Medium-sized flowers in a mixture of pale, medium and rich pink. Raised by Henry A. Ross of Ohio and named by him in 1989.

'Dick Crandon'* Flowers 3in (7.5cm) across, the back of each flower pink at the sides and tips and green at the base; white with dark pink veins in between. They are altogether paler inside, with the outer two petals larger and greener, and with honey-coloured nectaries. The rather arching stems are 10–12in (25–30cm) high, red-speckled at the base, quickly changing to plain green. Raised and introduced by Helen Ballard.

'Dimity' Star-shaped flowers, pale pink with a strong green flush and one very green petal. Once grown at East Lambrook and now found in the National Collection.

'Dotty'* Pink, heavily spotted with purple. Raised and introduced by Helen Ballard.

'Dowager' A huge-flowered, deep rose pink. Raised by Henry A. Ross of Ohio and named by him in 1984.

'Dusk'* Smoky purple in bud, then opening to 3in (7.5cm) flowers which are misty purple with speckles towards the edge of the petals and with black veins. The inner three petals are black-smudged, the others rather less so. The basic ground colour is actually deep pink, paler at the tips especially on the outer three, rather broader, petals. But they are veined and speckled in almost black, the markings tending to coalesce towards the base to give that smoky look. There are also a few shimmering red veins towards the base, green nectaries with purple tips, and a green disc underneath. The stems are red towards the base then thinning out to speckles and streaks; the bracts are green with purple teeth. Raised and introduced by Helen Ballard.

"Dusky" This name has become attached to seedlings distributed by Roger Poulett, which are descendants of a seedling bought for 2½d at a village school fête! It is a large, clean, dusky pink and is quite different from 'Dusk'.

'Early Purple' The name proposed by Brian Mathew for "H. atrorubens of gardens", a well-known, dark, early-flowering form of H. orientalis subsp. abchasicus. There are at least three forms of this plant around, but the name should be applied only to the plant illustrated in Brian's book. For more details see page 111.

'Eco Autumn Purple' A pink-flowered cultivar with the unique distinction of its green foliage turning purplish-red in the autumn. Raised by Don Jacobs of Eco Gardens in Georgia, but not yet available.

'Eco Bullseye' Another Don Jacobs selection, stocks of which are still being built up. It has white outward-facing flowers, and a rich red blotch at the base of the petals thinning out into streaks and with a clear white zone around the edge. The markings are constant from year to year.

'Eco Golden Eye' The third Don Jacobs seedling to be named, the purple-veined white buds open to purple, delicately veined petals. The filaments, carpels and the bases of the nectaries are also purple, while the anthers are golden and the nectaries have green tips. This cultivar, too, is still being bulked up and is not yet available.

'Electra' This cross between 'Early Purple' and Will Ingwersen's H. torquatus has very symmetrical, rounded, evenly bowl-shaped flowers with medium-sized, overlapping petals on each stem. They hang their heads noticeably and there are up to nine flowers per stem. Outside the flowers are wine purple with a slate blue bloom, inside they are rose with blue-purple overlay, especially between the veins, giving a distinctive texture. The nectaries are yellow-green and widely spreading to give a distinct eye to the flower. Raised by Eric Smith and introduced by The Plantsmen.

'Elizabeth Coburn' Lilac pink, heavily netted with pale purple and with clear zone at the edge. Raised and introduced by Court Farm Nursery.

"Elizabeth Strangman's Pink"* Illustrated in Marlene Ahlburg's book, this appears to be a seedling of 'Pluto' with purple nectaries, to which this name has unfortunately become attached.

'Ellen Terry' A short, nineteenth-century cultivar with flowers 2½–3in (6.5–7.5cm) across. Outside they are almost reddish-purple, particularly towards the edges, and slightly veined. Inside they are almost apple-blossom, a pearly white and pink with some green veins, and a tendency to green streaks in the centre of the petals. There is an even faint speckling of spots filling roughly the basal third of each petal. The flower is rather starry in shape, with the sides of each petal folded back. Origin uncertain.

'Eric's Best' Shallow, distinctly saucer-shaped 3in (6–7.5cm) blooms with a deep beetroot red stain almost filling the petals, then running in veins towards the narrow clear pink border with a green centre. Raised by Eric Smith and given to Beth Chatto shortly before he retired from The Plantsmen. Introduced by her in 1990.

'Ernest Raithby' An especially floriferous cultivar with light purple flowers. Raised by Ernest Raithby and introduced by Court Farm Nursery.

'First Kiss' A very light blush pink. Raised by Henry A. Ross of Ohio and named by him in 1984.

'Freckleface' A short plant rather like 'Cosmos', with open 2½in (6.5cm) flowers, each white with a slight green stripe down the centre of each petal and evenly spotted in purple. Noticeably outward-facing flowers with short pedicels. Raised by Eric Smith and given to Beth Chatto shortly before he retired from The Plantsmen. Introduced by Beth Chatto in 1990.

'Fred Whitsey' Very nice cup-shaped flowers, especially when young, in a slightly creamy white with plum spots running into streaks. The flowers turn green quickly. Weak grower. Raised by Ernest Raithby and introduced by Court Farm Nursery.

'Garnet'* A tall plant about 20in (50cm) high with large flowers 3in (7.5cm) across. The flowers are basically deep purple-red, dramatically veined almost black on the backs. Inside the flowers are smoky purple towards the centre, thinning out to red with purple veins towards the edge. The petals are rather pointed, the green nectaries dark-striped with a green eye behind them and there is a little red colouring round the base of each petal. Looks mysterious in bud, then the flowers open out almost entirely flat even before the anthers start to shed their pollen. The stems are red-tinted and speckled at the base, green at the top while the bracts are fresh, bright, slightly olive green, purple on the backs. Raised and introduced by Helen Ballard.

'Gemini' A late-flowering selection from Eric Smith's 'Zodiac Strain', with very round pink flowers and a zone of dark spots towards the base. Introduced by the Buckshaw Gardens in 1979.

'Gerrard Parker'* Large but rather starry-shaped flowers, in pink with the dark spots gathered at the base into a large, solid zone then breaking up into spots with a clear blushed white zone around the edge. The backs are purple-pink. Originated with E. A. Bowles and named after his friend who was a local art master.

'Gertrude Raithby' White with a pink flush, fairly evenly spotted with bright purple. Pointed petals. Raised by Ernest Raithby and introduced by Court Farm Nursery.

'Gladys Burrow' Small flowers in a rather muddy pinky white, netted all over with bright purple. Raised

and introduced by Court Farm Nursery.

'Grace Hood' A cultivar raised by Sergei Nolbandov and grown by The Plantsmen but not thought to be very distinguished. Probably now lost to cultivation, the dozen plants behind the label bearing this name at the Cambridge Botanic Garden are all different.

'Graigueconna' A variegated cultivar with a light creamy speckling and streaking to the leaves and bracts and with creamy yellow flowers. This plant turned up in a batch of seedlings raised by Rosemary Brown and is named after her garden in County Wicklow.

'Greencups'* Strikingly rounded flowers making a neat, hemispherical shape. The individual flowers are 2in (5cm) across and green, with a touch of the puckering seen more clearly in 'Blowsy'; the veins have a slightly olive tinge, especially at the base. The green buds are slightly red-tinted when young, but this soon disappears. The stems are slightly red at the base on one side, the bracts very broad and very finely toothed. This is a striking plant, but very similar to 'Parrot'. Raised and introduced by Helen Ballard.

'Greenland'* A greeny white, rather starry-flowered plant grown by Mrs Fish, seedlings of which were widely distributed.

'Gremlin' A medium-flowered yellowish-green. Raised by Henry A. Ross of Ohio and named by him in 1984.

'Günther Jürgl' One of three full doubles in this group grown in the UK. The flowers are noticeably outward-facing, 2in (5cm) across. The backs of the outer petals are mainly green with pink streaks, the

front of the outer petals green with purple spots. The inner petals are very narrow at the base, but paddle-shaped, then slightly wavy and very pale pink, evenly speckled purple-pink. Altogether there are about twenty-two petals. The plant is short, the leaves are very dark but small, and the bracts are also small and rather irregularly divided, altogether small. This is a good garden plant, fast-growing and free-flowering. Raised in Germany by Günther Jürgl and sometimes known as 'Jürgl's Double'.

'Hades' Slate blue with a network of fine speckles. Raised and introduced by Helen Ballard.

'Hazel Key' Starry flowers, the petals do not overlap. Even pink in colour, green in the centre, then white fading to pink at the edge. Raised and introduced by Court Farm Nursery.

'Hazy Dawn' A short cultivar reaching only 6–7in (15–18cm), the flowers are pale purple with dark purple spots and fading to green on two or three petals. Originally from Perrys, and reminiscent of 'Hercules'.

'Hecate' An upright, vigorous plant with deep purple stippled flowers. Raised and introduced by Helen Ballard.

'Heartsease' An early, small-flowered cultivar with pink flowers just over 2in (5cm) across, veined inside and out with darker pink and fading in colour towards the edges of the petals. The flowers are starry in shape, and as they age the petals have a tendency to roll their edges backwards, eventually forming a U shape. A seedling selected by Alan Bloom at Bressingham in 1953, available intermittently since then.

'Helena' A very vigorous and floriferous plant with good foliage and lush bracts, selected in 1981 by Jim Archibald. It has pure white flowers, shading to green at the base both inside and out, and is speckled inside at the base, radiating in broken streaks of maroon occupying about one-third of the petal length.

'Helen Ballard'* Vivid green, outward looking flowers. Raised and introduced by Helen Ballard.

'Hercules' A large-flowered, vigorous and robust plant with nodding flowers which are noticeably flat, wide open and well-proportioned. Outside the flowers are rose-purple, deeper towards the base. Inside they are an even soft rose, very slightly paling and taking on a green tinge towards the centre, and evenly speckled all over with rose-purple. The speckling is slightly more dense towards the base and more diffuse towards the edge. A selection from Eric Smith's 'Constellation Strain', introduced by Buckshaw Gardens in 1977.

The plant in the National Collection is only about 10in (25cm) high and pale purple, with a freckling of darker spots and with green tips to three of the petals. The flowers are not flat but more or less cup-shaped, and are just over 2in (5cm) across and uneven in shape. Perhaps a seedling.

'Hidcote Double' A blowsy double found at Hidcote Manor in Gloucestershire by Graham Thomas. It has a double row of large, purplish-pink petals giving a rather floppy effect by contrast with the neater arrangement of petals in 'Günther Jürgl' and 'Snow Queen'.

'Hyades' A spectacular plant, tall and robust, with large, shallowly bowl-shaped flowers. Outside they are an even greenish white with the internal spotting showing through; the inside is cream tinged with green. The petals are evenly and heavily spotted with dull crimson and the spots, though very dense, are clearly defined and leave a clear, narrow cream margin of just a few millimetres. At the base is a large, pale, bright green zone with no spotting, giving the flower a distinct appearance. Selected by Eric Smith from his 'Guttatus Strain' and introduced by The Plantsmen in 1975.

'Ian Raithby' Smallish flowers with very wavy petals, lilac pink netted inside with bright plum. Raised by Ernest Raithby and introduced by Court Farm Nursery.

'Indigo' A short but upright plant with deep 'blue' flowers. Raised and introduced by Helen Ballard.

'Ingot' A yellow-flowered cultivar, raised and introduced by Helen Ballard.

'Jebb's White' An old cultivar of unknown origin with cup-shaped flowers about 2in (5cm) across. The flowers are white, unspotted, and outward-facing in their later stages, with broad but pointed petals. The nectaries are greeny yellow. This plant grows in the National Collection held by Jeremy Wood, who gave it this name.

'Joan Bridges' A warm purplish-red with glossy backs to the petals. Raised and introduced by Helen Ballard.

'John Cross' A late-flowering cultivar with pale plum flowers, deeper in bud, with slightly green edges to the petals and honey-coloured nectaries. Raised by Ernest Raithby and introduced by Court Farm Nursery.

'John Jeremy Kaye' A cultivar with rich raspberry-coloured flowers raised by Reginald Kaye and said to flower twice a year.

'John Raithby' Pinky lilac with dense even netting inside and slightly veined backs. The petals are almost hooked. Raised by Ernest Raithby and introduced by Court Farm Nursery.

'Julie McMurtry' Very similar to 'Elizabeth Coburn', slightly brighter pink and slightly wavier petals. Raised by Court Farm Nursery.

"Kochii"* The name given to a number of small-flowered, early forms, often with noticeably long pedicels and usually creamy or almost white in colour. They seem to originate from a number of sources.

'Lady Bonham Carter' Pink, netted in dusky wine. Raised by Ernest Raithby and introduced by Court Farm Nursery.

'Laura' An upright, large-flowered cultivar described as light red. Raised and introduced by Helen Ballard.

'Lavinia Ward' Greeny cream with purple veins, a purple splash at the base and a clear zone at the edge. The backs are veined and painted. Seems slightly variable. Raised and introduced by Court Farm Nursery.

'Leo' 'Leo', 'Aries' and 'Capricornus' are virtually identical selections from Eric Smith's 'Zodiac Strain'. All three are vigorous, large-flowered clones with nodding flowers and are bright, soft rose pink outside. Inside they are an even, pale rose pink with a zone of dense crimson spots evenly distributed but running together at the base and leaving a clear pink edge of about a quarter of the length of the petal. 'Leo' was introduced by The Plantsmen in 1975.

'Libra' A selection from Eric Smith's 'Zodiac Strain', with regular, rounded, cup-shaped flowers. They are an even soft rose pink outside while inside they are very pale rose pink just shaded green towards the base and centre, the palest pink ground colour of any of the 'Zodiac' clones. The inside is speckled deep rose, with fine, elongated dots forming a large even zone almost reaching the edge of the petals but with a clear speckle-free zone of about 3mm. The anthers are cream and the nectaries are yellow-green. Introduced by Buckshaw Gardens in 1979.

'Lime Ice' White outside and light lime green inside. Raised by Henry A. Ross of Ohio and named by him in 1984.

'Limelight' Peachy-tinged buds open to nodding, cup-shaped, $2\frac{1}{2}$in (6.5cm) flowers which are limy cream inside and outside. Two petals are pale yellow, the others are cream. The bracts are tinted red. Raised by Beth Chatto and introduced by her in 1990.

'Little Black'* Very uniform deep purple flowers 2–3in (5–7.5cm) across, nodding at first but partially lifted by the time the stamens fall. Generally very even in shape, partially rounded but not cup-shaped. The nectaries are purple at the tips and green at the base, hiding a green zone at the base of the petals. The carpels are purple. The bracts are purple-edged and slightly toothed. Raised by Elizabeth, this is a hybrid between Eric Smith's 'Pluto' and a selected seedling from her original darkest purple strain. Introduced in 1971 and occasionally known, wrongly, as 'Baby Black'.

'Luteus Maximus' A weak plant only 8in (20cm) tall, with yellowy green buds opening to noticeably outward-facing flowers. When open the flowers are basically yellowish cream, but just $1\frac{3}{4}$in (4.5cm) across and with green tints in and out; yellow nectaries. The outer petals are broad and slightly rounded, the inner broadly elliptical, but the flower is not starry. An undistinguished plant, highly susceptible to black spot which may account for the general weakness. This may be the same as, or a descendant of, the plant sent to Bowles from Glasnevin as 'Luteus Grandiflorus'.

'Lynne'* A spreading plant about 8in (20cm) high with flowers 3in (7.5cm) across, very even in shape, and pale primrose or almost cream in colour; they are paler at the edge and greener at the base. The stems are green with a few dark speckles at the base, and the green bracts are unusually large. Described by its raiser, Helen Ballard, in her catalogue as 'a shower of white cups, faintly speckled', we have seen only very pale primrose flowers with no speckles.

'Mardi Gras' A white-flowered cultivar with a large deep red blotch. Raised by Henry A. Ross of Ohio and named by him in 1984.

'Margaret Mathew' Picked out by Brian Mathew's wife Margaret from seedlings derived from the best of his large-flowered, finely spotted pale forms, and carrying her name. The large flowers have slightly waved petals. The two outer petals are a little pointed, slightly less heavily spotted and with a faint green central stripe; the three inner petals are exquisitely and evenly spotted in red over all except at the very edge. Selected in 1967 but not distributed.

'Margery's Double' Pink-flowered double with dark spots found in an old nursery bed at East Lambrook Manor in 1990. It has longer petals, and more of them, than in East Lambrook's other double, 'Tom's Double'.

'Mars' One of Eric Smith's earlier hybrids with rather pointed, bloomy, wine purple flowers and extraordinarily red-looking inside. A poor grower and eventually replaced by The Plantsmen with 'Antares'.

'Mars' Described by its raiser, Henry A. Ross of Ohio, as 'a very large, deep, brilliant burgundy-red with very little fading. Same size as 'Dowager' only a deeper, richer red compared to the rose-red of 'Dowager'. Not as deep in colour as 'Sorcerer' but a much larger flower and of a brighter red.' Named by Henry A. Ross in 1989. Unfortunately this name is invalid, having been used over fifteen years earlier for Eric Smith's plant which was regularly distributed before it was withdrawn.

'Mary Petit' White with a creamy green flushing and a large green central area on the back. Inside, three petals are cream and spotted, two petals are green and less spotted. Raised by Ernest Raithby and introduced to cultivation by Court Farm Nursery.

'Maureen Key' White, unevenly flushed in green. Raised by Court Farm Nursery.

'Mercury'* A very good, large-flowered, vigorous and floriferous white with slightly waved edges to the petals. The flowers are a solid colour with little green inside or out, just a trace of very pale green inside and out at the base of the petals. There is an almost imperceptible dusting of minute crimson dots at the base. Also known, wrongly, as 'Mercurius'. Raised by Eric Smith and introduced by Buckshaw Gardens in 1977.

'Richard Key'   'Victoria Raithby'   'John Raithby'

'Fred Whitsey'   'Alys Collins'   'Mary Petit'

Plants appear at 3/4 life size

'Miranda'* An early-flowering selection from a cross between Eric Smith's *H. torquatus* and what he knew as "Colchicus Superbus", with rounded, globular flowers and larger, lusher bracts than others of this type. Outside, the flowers are an even, dark, rich red-purple; inside they are off-white, faintly green-tinged and not streaked but with a red-purple flush round the edges of the petals and veins picked out in the same colour. There is a fairly dense and clearly defined area of crimson-purple spotting at the base of the petals. The nectaries are green. Introduced by The Plantsmen in 1974.

'Mrs Lambert' Described in the Perrys catalogue when they intro-

Named cultivars from Court Farm Nursery. This selection includes named cultivars raised by Ernest Raithby and by Court Farm Nursery. Flowers provided by Court Farm Nursery.

duced it in the 1930s as 'a very beautiful mid-season cultivar; large open flowers, rosy-white, heavily lined, blotched and spotted crimson purple'. Plants in cultivation in the 1970s seemed to fit this description.

'Mystery' Nodding, rather flat flowers in a pale slate colour with large dark spots. Raised and introduced by Helen Ballard.

'Nancy Ballard'* White flowers, faintly speckled with pink. Raised and introduced by Helen Ballard.

'Neptune' An exceptional, slow-growing, rather dwarf clone with very rounded flowers which are blackish and bloomed with blue outside and sea green inside. Raised by Eric Smith by crossing Ingwersen's *H. torquatus* and what he knew as "Colchicus Superbus" and reckoned to be the closest of this group to the *H. torquatus* parent. Introduced by The Plantsmen before 1975.

'Nocturne' Flowers strongly cup-shaped, not opening flat and re-maining about 2in (5cm) across.

Black-purple buds open to flowers which are smoky purple in and out, with small red veins at the bottom of each petal behind the honey-green nectaries which are tipped in bright red. The petals are rather flat, especially as they age, but when young are a very nice bold shape. The stems are noticeably red at the base, thinning out to red streaks higher up. The bracts are dramatically and impressively blue-green on the top and purple underneath, with dark veins. A very pretty plant, especially with its dark bracts. Raised and introduced by Helen Ballard.

'Oberon' A selection from Eric Smith's 'Torquatus Hybrids', with small rounded flowers. Outside the flowers are dark purple, inside they are pale greenish-white flushed with vinous purple and with many dark streaks of the same colour; there are also a few almost imperceptible speckles at the base. The overall look is less red than the others of this type and the flowers seem bluer in tone, more a lavender-purple than the reddish tone of 'Miranda'. The nectaries are bronze. Introduced by The Plantsmen in 1975.

'Old Ugly'* A dwarf plant with small cupped flowers, a second generation hybrid of *H. viridis*. A strange and mysterious mixture, the petals are deep green outside while inside they are deep green with darkest blood red spots. These are fused to give an almost solid painted mark over two-thirds of the inside of the petal but leaving a clear green zone at the edge of each petal. The result of a cross by Elizabeth between an *H. viridis* hybrid and a white spotted Orientalis Hybrid in 1969 and introduced in 1972.

'Orion'* A vigorous plant, rather arching in growth, with flowers up to 3in (7.5cm) across, with very evenly-shaped pointed petals. These are cream outside with a faint pinkish flush, the outer two petals slightly green. Inside, the flowers are creamy white. The nectaries are green with dark purple tips and there is a triangular, purple, veiny haze at the base of the petals peeping from behind the nectaries. Large leafy bracts. Raised by Eric Smith and introduced by Buckshaw Gardens in 1979.

'Pamina' This was a happy mistake which arose in a batch of Elizabeth's hand-pollinated primrose seedlings and is obviously the result of a bee introducing some pink pollen. The 3in (7.5cm) flowers are a subtle shade of pinkish apricot on the backs of the petals and creamy pale apricot on the inside with slightly darker veining. There is a small, even speckling of maroon-red spots at the base of each petal. The nectaries are green. Raised in 1984, introduced in 1987.

'Parrot'* Distinctive crumpled green buds open to small, 2¼in (6cm) flowers which are a little flatter than those of 'Greencups'. The individual flowers are on long pedicels, tending to hang down, and a good 'Golden Delicious' colour. They almost have a pleasant scent, but not quite. The honey-green nectaries are noticeably long and golden at the base. The stems have a little red haze towards the base but not much. Large broad bracts. Raised and introduced by Helen Ballard, who describes it as a 'brilliant golden green'.

'Patchwork'* Curiously hairy, slightly purplish-black buds like tiny peas open to 1½in (4cm) flowers which face the ground. The backs of the flowers are silvery blue with black veins, partly overlaid with shiny bronze. Inside the flowers are smoky blue with a touch of green and striking purple veining, bright green nectaries and purple styles. The markings inside make this a captivating plant in spite of the small pointed petals. This is a weak grower, only 9in (23cm) high, perhaps because of its susceptibility to black spot. Raised and introduced by Helen Ballard.

'Paul Mathew' Picked out by Brian Mathew's son Paul from seedlings derived from white-flowered plants with larger blotches towards the centre. The flowers are slightly uneven with some green in three of the petals, and all have solid maroon, speckled-edged blotches at the base. Named in 1987 and not distributed, although its pollen has contributed to some developments in spotted types.

'Pearl' A tall plant reaching 17in (42cm), with large flowers 3–3½in (7.5–9cm) across. The flowers have a deep cup, becoming flattish and outward-facing. They are initially pale pink with a faint spotting and streaking in the throat, then becoming even paler pearly pink; there is a little green streaking. The petals are broad and pointed, the nectaries are greeny yellow. A seedling raised by National Collection holder Jeremy Wood.

'Pebworth White' White with a greeny and creamy flush and a few tiny spots at the base of the petals. Starry shape with very pointed petals. Raised by Ernest Raithby and introduced by Court Farm Nursery.

'Peggy Ballard'* An upright cultivar with 3in (7.5cm) flowers. They are shining, deep, reddish-pink on the backs with dark veins and deep dusky pink within. Raised and introduced by Helen Ballard.

'Petsamo' Very starry flowers with narrow, almost elliptical petals which are also rather waved. The petals are white inside and out, with a prominent green centre and a few faint reddish spots at the base. The two outer petals are especially green. Looks good from a distance, less good close to. An old cultivar of unknown origin.

'Philip Ballard'* Small, 2in (5cm) flowers which are dark smoky blue on the backs and inside are slightly more purplish with a noticeable faint tracery of red veins; green nectaries and purple carpels. Slightly open, arching, branching habit, with stems which are green at the base, becoming increasingly red speckled up to the first branch, and then almost completely purple. The bracts are dark green, although purple on the backs when young, the foliage is finely cut and almost black when young. Raised and introduced by Helen Ballard and named after her husband.

'Philip Wilson'* A vigorous and floriferous cultivar with dark-veined, pink buds opening to 2½in (6.5cm) flowers made up of two broad rounded outer petals and three smaller inner petals. Outside they are silvery pink with purple veins, inside the flowers are silvery white with a pink haze, especially at the base of each petal around the green eye. There is just a little speckling in the green eye, then a sudden change to pearly pink and heavier spotting. The markings are smoky purple in colour and tending to dashes rather than spots. There is an absolutely clear zone around the edge where the pearly veins become more striking. The whole flower ages to a slightly coppery, pinky green on the outside, green inside, which is not a good match with the younger flowers. When the anthers and nectaries have dropped, the green central eye with its haze

of small spots becomes very prominent. The 18in (45cm) stems are red at the base, rapidly losing their colour higher up. The bracts are bright fresh green, but with some pink tinting to the teeth and when young. Raised and introduced by Helen Ballard.

'Phylly'* Yellow in bud, opening to 2½in (6.5cm) flowers which are pale yellow, almost cream, outside and inside the same shade, changing suddenly to a green zone at base. Like 'Blowsy', there is a little crinkling to the petals and there is a tendency for a large bract to cup the flower, but the bracts are so big that they tend to detract. A vigorous plant with strongly outward-growing stems which are reddish towards the base, but soon lose their colour higher up, and there is no red at all in the top half of the plant. Raised by Helen Ballard and introduced by her in 1988.

'Pink Chintz'* Pink in bud, opening to 3½in (9cm) flowers with rather broad, pointed petals. Outside the flowers are white with a tinge of apricot and a strong patterning of purple veins, some petals having a slightly greenish centre. Inside the flowers are similar but altogether paler and with more of a pink flush; there is a green centre with darker veins, separated from the rest of the flower by a pearly off-white zone. A distinctive but very weak plant grown by Margery Fish at East Lambrook Manor and still in the garden there but which has only flowered once in the last five years. Although known as 'Pink Chintz', Mrs Fish labelled her plant 'Old Chintz' and her label remains with the plant.

"Pink Guttatus Form" Nodding flowers with deep pink backs, hooded in dark purple. Inside the flowers are deep pink, evenly spotted with dusky purple, though denser towards the centre and

with a clear pearly pink zone around the edge of the flower. Raised by Beth Chatto and introduced by her in 1990.

'Pleiades' An unusually dwarf plant, well under 12in (30cm), with short wiry stems carrying medium-sized, rounded, cup-shaped flowers which are pure white with a green tinge around the base, more obvious on the outside. The spotting is not heavy, but there are many clearly defined crimson dots giving it a very neat and delicate look and the two green petals often seen in *guttatus* types have been almost eliminated. A selection from Eric Smith's 'Guttatus Strain'. Introduced by The Plantsmen in 1974.

"Plum Stippled Form" Nodding flowers which are basically pale pink but heavily and evenly spotted purple, and with slightly pointed petals. Raised by Beth Chatto and introduced by her in 1990.

'Pluto'* A fairly dwarf plant reaching 10–12in (25–30cm) in height with flowers about 2in (5cm) across; the flowers open fairly flat, less cup-shaped than many in this group. The outside of the flowers is dull, dark, wine purple with a blue-grey bloom, while inside they are paler, basically a pale green obscured with a bloomy, slate purple flush darkening towards the edges of the petals. The anthers are cream and made especially outstanding by the ring of rich, chestnut brown nectaries. A striking plant whose flowers face outward, especially as they mature. The bracts are purple-edged, and the young foliage is shiny purple. Raised by Eric Smith using pollen from *H. torquatus* on a plant he knew as "Colchicus Superbus" and very close to the *H. torquatus* parent. Introduced by The Plantsmen in 1971. See page 62.

'Polaris'* A very tall, stout, large-flowered white, flushed green outside in a marked fashion, and with distinctive cup-shaped, pendant flowers. Selected by Amy Doncaster from seedlings at Buckshaw Gardens and introduced by Buckshaw Gardens in 1977.

'Pollux' see 'Castor', page 87.

'Primrose'* A pale yellow cultivar raised by Peter Chappell.

'Prince Rupert'* One of the best known of the older hellebores and grown by Margery Fish at East Lambrook Manor. Awarded an AM in 1927 and described at the time as creamy white with crimson spots. For more details see page 135.

'Princess Margaret'* Basically pink with darker streaks on the back, pearly white inside with a scattering of purple spots over most of the surface of each petal. Green towards the edge. Rather uneven, sometimes with six petals, some of which are rounded while others are longer, narrower and more pointed. A short plant, only 7in (18cm) high, but with 3in (7.5cm) flowers; quite pretty but now superseded. Selected by Margery Fish and still growing at East Lambrook Manor.

'Purity' A glowing pure white. Raised by Henry A. Ross of Ohio and named by him in 1989.

'Queen of the Night' The flowers are over 2–3in (5–7.5cm) across but slightly uneven in size, nodding, deep purple, slightly lustrous on the backs of the outer two or three, smokier on the inner two or three. Inside the flowers are matt purple, with the nectaries honey-green at the base but two-thirds purple. The stems are 10in (25cm) high and purple at the base. Raised by Elizabeth Strangman in 1975 by crossing 'Little Black' with a plant of her original selected darkest purple strain.

'Queen of the North' Green buds open to 2in (5cm) flowers, white on the outside with green veins and green around the edge. Inside they are almost white but with one very green petal and just a few purple spots right towards the base around the green nectaries. There always seems to be one especially green petal. Probably introduced by Barr in the late nineteenth century.

'Red Star' One of Eric Smith's later red-flowered hybrids, but a poor grower with rather spidery flowers.

'Red Wine Dob' Cup-shaped flower with slightly wavy edges, basically white fading to pink around the edges of the petals and with such a dense red central spotting that the spots almost merge into a heavy blotch. The two outer petals are less heavily marked. Raised by Cliff Smith in Australia.

'Rembrandt' Buds dusky red, smoky purple at the base, opening to 2½in (6.5cm) flowers, shining pink-purple on the back and a burnt or singed shade around the pedicel; there is also a white edge all around the flowers. On the inside, the ground colour is pale pearly pink, heavily veined and speckled, and dark dusky purple with a certain smokiness towards the base. The two outer petals are less heavily speckled but with more smokiness. The flowers are not shiny in bud but do become shiny on the back as they mature. Older flowers are very shiny and eventually become a strange greeny copper shade. The stems are red-purple at the base, continuing right up the plant but becoming streaky towards the top. The bracts are dull green, purple-backed when young, eventually becoming green and purple-veined top and bottom; the bracts offset the flowers well. Raised and introduced by Helen Ballard.

'Richard Key' Pale smoky plum. Raised by Court Farm Nursery.

'Roger Davis' Large wavy flowers with a starry shape, unevenly netted with lilac pink, and a creamy green at the tips of three petals. Raised by Court Farm Nursery.

'Rosa'* Pale matt purple flowers just over 2in (6cm) across with dark veins, white at the tips on the inside. The 10in (25cm) stems are very densely speckled red at the base, thinning out to green. The bracts are purple at first, fading to red-tinted green, mostly divided into five and reminiscent of miniature basal leaves. Raised and introduced by Helen Ballard.

'Rosina Cross' Large starry flowers with a lilac pink background, deeper-veined on the back. Inside, the flowers are evenly spotted almost all over, some less densely than others with a partially clear edge zone. Raised by Court Farm Nursery.

'Rossini' Flowers purplish-red on the backs before opening to pale pink, veined with dark purplish-red and with a burnt bronze area around the pedicel. Inside, the 3in (7.5cm) flowers are red, perhaps better described as a dark purplish-pink, with a smoky haze towards the centre and a zone of red at the

---

Plants raised by Elizabeth Strangman. This group comprises some of Elizabeth's named cultivars, plants used as mothers for her seed strains, individuals recently retained for incorporation into her breeding programme and two recently introduced German doubles

'Susanna'

Pink Mother

Torquatus
Hybrid

'Celadon'

'Pamina'

'Old Ugly' seedling

White Spotted
Mother

'Queen
of the Night'

'Violetta'

Yellow
with Red Star

'Günther Jürgl'

Pink Spotted

'Snow Queen'

Plants appear at ½ life size

edge of each petal and behind the green nectaries. There are reddish streaks in the stems rather than spots, the bracts are dark green with little purple teeth around the edge and are bronzey purple on the backs. Seems very susceptible to black spot. Raised and introduced by Helen Ballard.

'Rubens'* Reddish pink-purple buds with almost black veins open to 3in (7.5cm) flowers with the backs becoming paler and silvery. Inside they are slightly smoky pink-purple with dark smoky veins. The nectaries are green with a little purple both inside the tube and on the outside of the nectaries. A strong-growing plant, reddish towards the base of the stems, bracts green with purple veins below and bronze teeth. Raised and introduced by Helen Ballard.

'Ruby' Medium-sized, cup-shaped flowers, in a very rich deep ruby, said by its raiser to be drab when planted by itself due to its deep colouring. Raised by Henry A. Ross of Ohio and named by him in 1989.

'Sarah Ballard'* Pale clear cream. Raised and introduced by Helen Ballard.

'Saturn' Wonderful flowers, just over 2in (6cm) across, and the most uniform smoky blue-purple of them all. In effect, it is pale purple in colour then very heavily veined and speckled in smoky black, the same inside and out. The green nectaries have purple streaks and a little red starring right at the base, peeping out from behind the nectaries. Stems are red at the base, thinning out to red speckles towards the top; the bracts tend to be purple on the backs until they open out and mature when they become dull green with purple veins beneath. Raised and introduced by Helen Ballard.

'Scorpio' The shallowly bowl-shaped flowers are a fairly even pink outside, then shell pink when newly opened, deepening to soft rose pink with age, and veined in crimson. Inside they are blushed white at first, later deepening to palest rose pink. There are crimson speckles running along the veins, merging together into streaks and coalescing into a fairly dense mass at the base occupying about half the petal length. A distinctive flower, with lines of dots radiating from the base. The nectaries are greenish-yellow and the ground colour much paler than that of other 'Zodiac' clones, with streaks rather than spots. A large-flowered selection from Eric Smith's 'Zodiac Strain', introduced by Buckshaw Gardens in 1979.

'Selene' A very vigorous deciduous plant with large, outward-facing flowers on very stout stems. The flowers are perfect in shape, shallowly bowl-shaped with rounded petals, absolutely even and with a heavy, solid texture. The colour is yellower than 'Sirius' with a chartreuse flush at the base, a lovely limy yellow shade. A seedling from *H. cyclophyllus* selected by Jim Archibald in 1976. Jim suggests that it could be a hybrid between the best of his Yugoslavian *H. cyclophyllus* and 'Sirius'.

'Sirius'* A spectacular and very vigorous plant 16–18in (40–45cm) high, with thick stout stems carrying very large, flat, outward-facing, wide open flowers 3–3¾in (7.5–9.5cm) across with slightly wavy-edged petals surrounded by a ruff of large bright green bracts. The flowers are pale primrose tinged with green towards the centre, less so inside than out. The nectaries are green and the flowers have a slight sweet scent. Raised by Eric Smith and introduced by The Plantsmen in 1974.

'Slate Hybrids'* A number of good well-shaped colour forms were developed through careful hand-pollination by Professor George Slate, a botanist at the Geneva Station of Cornell University. Open-pollinated seed of these plants, either as a mixture or in separate colours, has been submitted to various seed exchanges since about 1970, currently by Nina Lambert.

'Snow Queen' A fully double cultivar reaching 11–15in (28–38cm) in height with the flowers held at an angle of 45 degrees to the stems. The flowers are made up of between eighteen and twenty-four petals; each flower is green in bud fading to cream at the edges, and the outer five petals tend to open first while the remaining petals are still in a rosebud formation. The outer petals of mature flowers are broad and waved, and creamy white shading to green at the base. The inner petals, are less broad, and narrow noticeably at the base. They are white in colour, with just a touch of cream, though green with darker green veins at the base and with a hazy green central zone. The sides of the individual petals are reflexed and they are also curved forwards from base to tip. Each petal has just a very few narrow purple streaks around the point at which the petals narrow at the base. The overall effect of these details is of a white wavy flower. Introduced from Germany in 1990.

'Sorcerer' A very dark black-purple with a plum-like bloom. Raised by Henry A. Ross of Ohio and named by him in 1984.

'Southern Belle' Large flowers of a very distinct lavender colour on tall stems. Raised by Henry A. Ross of Ohio and named by him in 1984.

'Spotty Vanda' Pink with a distinct

green central stripe, the outer two petals greener than the inner three. The whole flower is covered with purple dashes and spots except for a narrow clear rim. Raised by Cliff Smith in Australia.

'Sunny'* Yellow buds, green at the base, open to rather flat 2¼in (6cm) flowers which tend to face the ground. They are very pale cream in colour inside and out, paler than 'Phylly', and tending to green towards the base of the flower on the inside and with a distinct rich green zone around the pedicel on the outside. The flowers have a definite though faint green haze with a faint green stripe in the three outer petals. The petals are rather wavy and the flowers have a catty smell. Apart from on the backs of the hairy emerging leaves, there is absolutely no red in the plant at all. Green stems and large green bracts. Raised and introduced by Helen Ballard.

'Susanna' A striking picotee and veined type with flowers just under 2in (4–5cm) across. They are deep pink with dark veins and speckles on the outside while inside they are white, green at the base, pinking towards the edge, with very fine dark purple veining, a purple picotee edge and purple nectaries. Raised by Elizabeth Strangman in 1990 and derived from crossing one of two brothers of 'Little Black', which was paler on the back and pale inside with dark nectaries, with "H. atrorubens of gardens". The result was seedlings which were early-flowering and a better colour than "H. atrorubens". The best early-flowering one was pale purple on the back and creamy inside with rosy nectaries, and this was selfed and 'Susanna' selected from the resultant seedlings.

'Sylvia'* A strong-growing, deli-cate, pure white with a green eye. Raised and introduced by Helen Ballard.

'Taurus'* An early-flowered selection from Eric Smith's 'Zodiac Strain' with the outside of the large flowers soft rose pink, tinged green. Inside the flowers are a very pale pink, with a large zone of big crimson spots near the edges of the petals but denser and running together at the base. One of the best Zodiac types, introduced by Buckshaw Gardens in 1977.

'Titania' Originally this name was given by The Plantsmen to a small, extra dark, blue-purple-flowered hybrid of Will Ingwersen's H. torquatus, but when the stock died out the name was transferred in 1980 to a plant raised by Jim Archibald. This is a very dwarf deciduous plant flowering first at about 6in (15cm), with rounded, slightly downward-facing, cup-shaped flowers. The outside of the flowers is fairly evenly covered with minute reddish dots, giving a misty, mushroom-coloured effect. Inside the flower is unmarked creamy greeny yellow, almost pale primrose, just edged with mushroom. The nectaries are pale green.

'Tommie' A shorter-growing, small-flowered, dark blue cultivar. Raised and introduced by Helen Ballard.

'Tom's Double' This seedling was found by Tom Wild in the White Garden at East Lambrook Manor in 1989. There are two rows of plum-coloured petals and the plant is altogether smaller than most hybrids.

'Tom Wilson'* A tall, very striking plant with an arching habit and the flowers on unusually long pedicels. The buds are slightly shiny purple with black veins, opening with rather less of a shine. Inside the flowers are bluish-purple, almost smoky silvery charcoal, speckled and streaked with black smoke and with a few sharp red veins towards the base. The flat petals are mainly rolled base-to-tip inwards, some rolled backwards side-to-side too. The nectaries are green with a little purple tint, the carpels are a striking purple. The stems are dense purple at the bottom, densely purple-spotted higher up, eventually green with purplish streaks at the top of the plant. The bracts are big and green with darker purple veins on the back. The whole plant arches outwards from the ground at an angle. One of the most dramatic and impressive of all hellebores, taller, but less vigorous than 'Blue Spray'. Raised and introduced by Helen Ballard.

"× torquatus" × 'Ballard's Black' Said to be a less devastating clone than one might imagine but still very distinct. Surprisingly large and vigorous, with finely cut leaves and drooping flowers, plum-like in colour and impression. Introduced by The Plantsmen in 1975.

'Trotter's Spotted'* Pure white with very rounded flowers, very evenly spotted with large dark purple spots. Raised by Dick Trotter and introduced by his daughter Elizabeth Parker-Jervis.

'Upstart' A tall, very upright plant with shaded pink flowers with rounded petals making a perfect circular flower. Raised and introduced by Helen Ballard.

'Ursula Key-Davis' Lilac pink with purple veining and speckling on the outside; smoky inside, painted dark red, with a pale lilac rim. Raised by Court Farm Nursery.

'Ushba'* A strong-growing cultivar reaching 15–18in (38–45cm) with fat creamy yellow buds. The

100

2½in (6.5cm) pure white flowers nod at first and then rise up to an outward-facing position as the pedicels are quite short. The flowers are absolutely pure white with pearly veins, then shading to green at the centre, and ageing to cream and eventually green. There are three broad outer petals and two narrower inside petals. Some flowers, especially the older ones, have just a few red specks on the petals – a couple of dozen dots scattered over the bottom half or third of each petal. This feature varies – some flowers show virtually no sign, on some it is more pronounced. The fat stems are densely red-speckled at the base, thinning to green by the first stem leaf. The bracts are small and neat, green with pale veins, and are red-tinted on the backs. Raised and introduced by Helen Ballard and one of the most widely distributed of her varieties. One of the first varieties to be micropropagated, but the resultant plants are not all identical to the parent. Also listed as 'Usba'.

'Venus' One of Eric Smith's older hybrids, with small, rounded, cup-shaped flowers of perfect shape. These are an even greenish-white outside and creamy white inside, flushing to pale green towards the base and centre, and cream around the edges. There are many tiny crimson speckles on the greener zone, especially in lines along the veins. The nectaries are bright green. This is probably a cross between a *guttatus* type and *H. viridis*, from which the very neat habit may come, but it is not vigorous. Introduced by The Plantsmen in 1975.

'Victoria Raithby' Zones of pink, white and green on each petal with a few spots at the base; darker veining on the backs. Raised by Ernest Raithby and introduced by Court Farm Nursery.

'Violetta' The flowers are just over

2½–3in (6.5–7.5cm), mostly nodding at first, becoming slightly raised later, and are carried on tall stems up to 22in (55cm) high. Outside they are green around the pedicel then white with purple veins; the outer two petals have no purple veins at the tip, only at the edges, the inner three are white and more evenly purple veined with a purple picotee. Inside the flowers are white with a slight picotee haze and purple veins, and the two outer petals are flushed green. The stems are red at the base, thinning to speckling then green at the top. The bracts are only very slightly toothed and the foliage is distinctively rounded.

The first of Elizabeth's new picotees, a flower from a white-flowered plant in Amy Doncaster's garden with a suspicion of a wine-coloured edge was used to pollinate a pure white and the one good seedling was named 'Violetta'. When selfed it gives white flowers with a pinky purple picotee edge and veining on the inside of the petals plus a dark eye, but also a proportion of pink-flowered plants. Raised by Elizabeth in 1984.

'Virgo' Fine white-flowered clone selected by Amy Doncaster from seedlings at Buckshaw Gardens.

'Vulcan' Ruby in bud, opening to rather floppy, fragile 3in (7.5cm) flowers. The basic ground colour is pale pink, heavily veined and hazed with dark purplish-pink and densely smoky towards the base of the flower. Rather shiny on the back, with a burnt, bronze zone around the pedicel. The stems are flushed red towards the base. Raised and introduced by Helen Ballard.

'White Ladies'* A noticeably slender and delicate plant with nodding 2in (5cm) pure white flowers with just a faint dusting of spots at the base of three of the petals. Rather starry in shape, with prominent green nectaries. The bracts have purple veins. Small flowers but very pretty in a mass. Selected by Margery Fish and still growing at East Lambrook.

'White Swan' One of the most spectacular of the older cultivars and still vigorous. The buds are green, opening to 3½in (9cm) flowers which are white with green veins on the backs then green around the pedicel. Inside the flowers are pure white with a faint green stripe up the centre of the outer two petals, and just a faint dusting of purple spots peeping out from behind the nectaries on the three inner petals. The petals are slightly wavy, the inner two tending to be longer and more elliptical in shape, the others broader and more rounded. The flowers tend to face the ground, not because the pedicels are long but because the stems seem soft and arch outwards strongly. The bracts are a very bright, fresh green.

'William' Grey-purple with black veins in bud. The open flowers, just over 2in (5cm) across, are grey lilac-purple with black veins on the outside; inside they are similar, with a strong network of dark veins, pale green nectaries and purple carpels. An area of lilac grey edges the flowers where the veins do not quite reach, and there is also a darker, bluer line round the very edge of each individual petal. Raised and introduced by Helen Ballard.

Seedlings raised by Elizabeth Strangman. These flowers come from plants which are typical of the various hand-pollinated strains raised for sale at Washfield Nursery and demonstrate that you do not need to buy named cultivars to be sure of good quality plants

appear at 2/5 life size

'Winter Cheer' A small-flowered, early cultivar reaching 9–12in (23–30cm) which is pink outside, darker at the base. Inside it is white, shaded and veined pink on all but the edges of the petals, and green at the base. There are a few red spots mostly along veins at the base of three petals, with very few on the other two. The flowers are almost cylindrical with slightly flared tips, eventually opening wavy but not pointed. A seedling selected by Alan Bloom at Bressingham in 1953 and available intermittently since then.

'Woodcock' The large 3in (7.5cm) flowers are bright purplish pink on the backs, darker towards the base. Inside the flowers are white at the base behind green nectaries with a dusty veining of pink; there is a touch of green towards the tips. The flowers open rather rounded and bold, eventually becoming almost flat. An old cultivar, still grown at Kew but of uncertain origin.

'Yellow Button' Small, neat yellow flowers. Raised and introduced by Helen Ballard.

The following cultivars were grown in the 1950s and 1960s but are probably now extinct.
'Archer Hind' Spotted pink
'Aurora' Pink
'Castile' Pink
'Circe'
'Citrinus' Yellowish

'Coombe Fishacre Purple' Purple
'Domino' *H. orientalis* subsp. *abchasicus* × *H. orientalis* subsp. *guttatus*
'Festival' *H. orientalis* subsp. *abchasicus* × *H. orientalis* subsp. *guttatus*
'Georgina Nightingale' Shell pink
'Gloria' Spotted pink
'Harlequin' Blotched pink; "*H. guttatus*" × "*H. abchasicus* var. *venosus*"
'Hillier's White' White
'Hyperion' Spotted
'Lynton' Spotted
'Macbeth' Dark purple
'Margaret Briggs' Spotted
'Nancy Smith' Velvety purple
'Peach Blossom'* Pink
'Picotee'
'St Margaret'
'Snow White' White

The following cultivars were raised and named by Eric Smith but never catalogued, although a very few plants may have been distributed. Seed of those marked * has been distributed.
'Arcturus'
'Corvus' *Black-maroon
'Draco'* Blotched rose
'Ganymede'
'Mira' Dusted white
'Pegasus'
'Perseus'
'Praesepe' Streaked ivory
'Saturn'
'Uranus'
'Vega'

The following cultivars have been

raised or selected, and named, by Jim Archibald but never offered for sale, although a very few plants may have been distributed.
'Inca' Black-purple
'Katinka' Speckled ivory
'Rosalinda' Dusky rose
'Zuleika' Speckled white

The following cultivars are circulating in Germany or Holland but as far as we know have not yet reached other countries.
'Albert Weinreich'* Dark red
'Altrosa I'* Old rose
'Cattleya'
'Frühlingsfreude' Spotted white
'Frühlingsrose' Smoky purple
'Frühlingsschale' Spotted pink
'Galathe'* Pearly white
'Gelbe Auslese'
'Gewitternacht' Red-black
'Gewitterwolke'* Dark red
'Gruner Bernstein'*
'Heidirose'* Pink
'Kameliendame'* Creamy pink
'Letzter Walzer'* Spotted red
'Luna'* Yellow
'Mitternacht-Blues'* Almost black
'Monika'
'Nachtimmel' Spotted 'blue'
'Pink Mountain' Pink
'Pippi Langstrumpf'* Spotted white
'Roter Cancan'* Red
'Salome'* Bluey red
'Schwarzes Gold' Red-black
'Schwarzer Kreis'* Picoteed white
'Ursula Theim'* White
'Veronica Klose'* Picoteed cream
'Violet Ballard' Violet
'Yellow Ballard' Yellow

DESCRIPTIVE LIST OF NAMED SEED STRAINS

Over the years a number of seed strains have become available and these are described here. The individual plants in these strains will not be identical but should be close to each other in height and general habit, flower size and colour; particular patterns of spotting are the most difficult characteris-tics to fix. The general features of a strain may remain similar for some years or may be upgraded regularly by the addition of improved seedlings to the breeding stock, so that the strain is constantly evolving.

Seed strains are produced either by crossing two carefully chosen parents to give the required result or by harvesting seed from a number of selected pure-bred plants, grown together in isolation.

In some cases plants for sale are produced by selecting a number of almost identical seed-raised plants and then propagating them all by division and selling them as one strain.

WASHFIELD NURSERY

These strains have all been developed by Elizabeth and are the result of meticulous hand-pollination of carefully selected parent plants with specific aims in mind and all continually upgraded by the addition of improved parents.

'Appleblossom Strain' These have three outer petals darker than the inner two, sometimes with a few pretty spots towards the middle. This is very difficult to breed true, but even if they all come the right colour they tend to have rather a slender stem. Crosses with a strong-stemmed pure pink result in the loss of the apple-blossom colour.

'Apricot Strain' An apricot strain based on 'Pamina' is being developed but still has several generations to go before it breeds true to colour.

'Darkest Purple Strain' The original dark purple strain with large imperial purple flowers with a plum bloom. Now superseded by the 'Queen of the Night Strain'.

'Green Strain' This is simply 'Celadon' pollinated by another dark hybrid of *H. multifidus* subsp. *bocconei* to give good green seedlings which vary from very pale green like frosted white to pure deep green; all are well shaped.

'Green Spotted Strain' This strain consists simply of the result of crossing 'Old Ugly' with 'Celadon'. The aim is for a few spots, just a little delicate crimson spotting towards the middle of the flower, but this strain also includes more heavily spotted flowers with a definite green zone around the edge of each petal.

'Picotee Strain' This strain is still in the early stages. The colour is coming well, with a dark edge to the white petals, some with dark veining inside and a painted ring in the middle. But the flowers are still rather bell-shaped. It will take another ten years to get it right.

'Pink and Raspberry Strains' These started by crossing a lilac-pink seedling with a pale plum seedling. The pinkest seedlings were intercrossed and a well-shaped, pure pink given by Mrs Maxted was also used. Originally a pink strain which has been split into pale and bright raspberry pinks.

'Pink Spotted Strain' Developed from Hilda Davenport-Jones's original plant, which was pretty but a lilac pink. The aim is for a clear pink, though some are a brighter raspberry pink. The original had long weak pedicels but this fault is now eliminated. The plants now have very even spotting and a clear zone round the edge.

'Primrose Strain' This was started off by crossing a very good yellow-green form of *H. odorus* obtained from The Plantsmen with a creamy-coloured wild-collected form of *H. orientalis* from Hilda Davenport-Jones's garden. The result was one really good plant in 1971 and this was selfed. The best of the resultant seedlings were intercrossed; the strain is still evolving and improving. This is a small-flowered strain with rounded, intensely primrose-yellow flowers.

'Primrose Spotted Strain' The 1971 plant carried spotting, and the spotted ones have been selected and crossed separately to develop a yellow spotted strain. This has primrose-coloured flowers with varying degrees of crimson-red spotting but always with a clear primrose zone around the edge of the petals.

'Queen of the Night Strain' This strain was developed by selfing the original 'Queen of the Night', selecting the best five of the very similar resulting seedlings and intercrossing them to give plants for sale. The strain is constantly being improved, in particular by the elimination of plum-coloured plants, only about 1 in 100 of which now appear.

Plants are generally deep purple with a bloom inside and out. They have inherited the rounded shape of 'Pluto', and 90–95 per cent have also inherited his dark nectaries, with the remainder green with a little purple tint. Medium height, about half have dark young leaves.

'Slaty Blue Strain' The flowers are the colour of wet slate with a pale bloom, paler and bluer inside, often with distinct dark bracts and flower stems. The flowers retain their colour long after pollination and also develop coloured carpels. This strain derives from a plant received as a gift from Helen Ballard, which was selfed and the best seedlings crossed with 'Queen of the Night'.

'White Strain' This strain was created by crossing together the two whitest-flowered plants from Hilda Davenport-Jones's garden. The best seedling was very strong and free-flowering, and this was crossed with a white received from Mrs Ballard in the early 1970s. One genuinely outstanding plant was produced, and this plant is selfed to give seedlings of a very even pure white which are very early-flowering. Good bold foliage.

'White Spotted Strain' This is simply a matter of crossing the best with the best of each generation so the strain is constantly evolving. The spots are maroon-purple, not red-purple as in the spotted greens and yellows. The aim is for clear spotting with a definite white zone round the edge of the petals; it is difficult to get heavy clean spotting on a pure white background.

THE PLANTSMEN

These strains were developed by Eric Smith for The Plantsmen nursery where he worked with Jim Archibald until the nursery was succeeded by Buckshaw Gardens, where Jim Archibald continued to sell these strains.

'Constellation Strain' A strain from which some of their best named forms were selected. Described as having 'pink flowers, sometimes faintly shaded green, evenly and heavily speckled maroon-purple to give an orchid-like effect'.

'Cream Strain' Creamy white flowers often delicately green-flushed. It seems that what were sold were seedlings which fitted this description rather than true-bred seedlings from a particular plant or cross.

'Galaxy Strain' Medium-sized, rather pointed flowers, white outside, lightly tinted rose and markedly green, especially towards the base and with rose veining. The inside is white with a slight rose blush shading to pale green in the centres and at the bases of the petals. The whole inside is evenly peppered all over with rose-crimson dots. The nectaries are bright green. Raised by Eric Smith and introduced by The Plantsmen. The plants sold were divisions of three seedlings raised by Eric Smith which were sufficiently identical to pass as one. Introduced in 1974 but eventually discarded in favour of the better shaped 'Cosmos'.

'Green Strain' A variable mixture made up of selected seedlings from H. odorus, H. cyclophyllus and H. viridis, all with solid green cups. Introduced in 1975.

'Midnight Sky Strain' Deep, rich purple flowers, overlaid with a bloom and heavy speckling of even darker purple. One of the earlier strains, first listed in 1968.

'Zodiac Strain' Pink ground colour; a clear margin at the edge of the petals surrounds a striking zone of deep maroon-purple spots. Introduced in 1968, many good clones were selected from this strain.

BALLARD STRAINS

Unnamed seedlings of Helen Ballard's have come into circulation in three main ways. Collections of seedlings labelled for colour have been offered in her catalogue. Secondly customers of hers who ordered named cultivars were sent similar unnamed seedlings, labelled as such, when the named form was sold out. This has continued for many years and enabled gardeners to grow some fine plants.

In more recent years Rushfield's Nursery have also been listing Helen Ballard's seedlings under the following colour groups: Blue-black; Cream; Dark Purple; Dusky Purple; Deep Pink; Pale Pink; Speckled Pink; Clear Pink; Red; White; White (spotted); Yellow. These are small divisions of selected seedlings.

BLACKTHORN NURSERIES

Robin White of Blackthorn Nurseries has developed a series of Orientalis Hybrid strains in a good range of shades, but as well as his hybrids between various forms of H. torquatus (see page 66) has also worked on doubles and anemone-centred forms. These are not pure-breeding uniform lines but the result of intercrossing a number of different plants to produce a range of offspring, giving gardeners the opportunity to choose the forms they prefer.

As well as single-flowered strains in a good range of colours he has introduced the following:

'Party Dress Hybrids' A range of dwarf, fully double plants each with about fifteen petals, mainly in veiny pinks and often with a rather smoky haze.

'Westwood Hybrids' A group of hybrids raised by Robin White from 'Dido', which had crossed with an Orientalis Hybrid. They are named after the garden where the first one arose. The resulting plants, mainly in smoky pink and red shades, have small, erect flowers 1–2in (2.5–5cm) across, with enlarged nectaries mostly the same colour as the petals, giving a semi-double or anemone-centred effect. The degree of enlargement of the nectaries varies from only very slightly enlarged to long and tubular. These are the first anemone-centred plants to be commercially available.

BRESSINGHAM GARDENS

"Orientalis × Frühlingsfreude" Described as 'Beautiful pink-speckled hand-pollinated seedlings . . . (45–60cm)'. Graham's plant is early-flowering, with 2in (5cm) flowers which are green-flushed and veined dark and pale claret outside; inside they are pale claret pink with occasional hazy green zones and darker veins. Green eye and nectaries. Raised by Alan Bloom and introduced by Bressingham Gardens in spring 1991.

"Orientalis × Guttatus" Described as 'Hand-pollinated seedlings of a fine form with white, ruby-speckled flowers. . .(45–60cm)'. Graham's plant is watery pink outside with purple shading and veins; inside the flowers are dull, pink-veined rather darker. There are no spots. Raised by Alan Bloom and introduced by Bressingham Gardens in spring 1991.

Seedlings raised by Helen Ballard. This selection of Helen Ballard's unnamed seedlings is typical of those plants she has supplied when named cultivars have not been available. Flowers provided from her garden by Helen Ballard

10

CASE HISTORIES

A number of plants are the subject of misconceptions or have origins which are too detailed to include in our A–Z descriptive list. We discuss them here.

HELLEBORUS FOETIDUS
'Wester Flisk'

The origin of this plant has always been something of a mystery – why should such a distinct red-stemmed form turn up on the east coast of Scotland, such a long way outside its natural range?

Mrs Mamie Walker discovered this form when she moved to Wester Flisk, an old Scottish rectory near Newburgh on the south side of the Firth of Tay in Fife, in the early 1970s. She passed it on to Helen Ballard, who exhibited it at the RHS in 1980 when 'the committee felt that this plant was typical of the red-stemmed variants of the species' and did not give it an award. It is now widely available. 'Wester Flisk' comes more or less true from seed if grown in isolation from other forms, but even so any poorly coloured plants are best discarded. If other forms occur in the garden, hand-crossing will be necessary to maintain well-coloured forms.

Mrs Walker, who at one time sent cut hellebores to Covent Garden on the train from Perth, has noticed that in wet seasons the colour is less well developed than in dry ones. As well as passing plants to other enthusiasts she has continued to select them rigorously, discarding any poor forms in order to maintain the qualities she most admires, especially the continuation of the colour from the main stem to the leaf petioles and into the flowering head.

Until now the reasons for the occurrence of such a distinct form in this particular garden have been a mystery. This is an area of the country where the stinking hellebore only occurs occasionally in the wild; even then it is not considered truly native, but rather as a garden escape.

However, in the last century the rectory at Wester Flisk was occupied by the Rev. Dr John Fleming, Professor of Natural Philosophy at Aberdeen University and later of Natural Sciences at Queen's College, Edinburgh. He lived at Wester Flisk from 1811 to 1832, and although his main interest was geology, botany was also among his enthusiasms. Whether or not the Professor had a special interest in the flora of Spain we have not been able to discover, but Richard Nutt tells us that he has seen forms of *H. foetidus* similar to 'Wester Flisk' growing in north-east Spain. It seems possible that it came to the rectory via the professor and possibly the botanic garden at Aberdeen or Edinburgh.

There is further evidence of the hand of a keen plantsman at Wester Flisk – Mamie Walker tells us that double-headed snowdrops occur in the nearby woods.

HELLEBORUS NIGER
'Potter's Wheel'

A great deal of mystique and confusion surrounds this plant, and as it was introduced by Elizabeth's predecessor at Washfield we have taken pains to discover its true history. This we have been able to do following inspection of correspondence between Hilda Davenport-Jones and Major G. H. Tristram, retained at Washfield since the 1950s.

'Potter's Wheel' is especially interesting, as a crucial factor governing the degree of enthusiasm for the plant has been whether or not any given plant was 'of good pedigree'. Since we have been given a number of quite different histories of the plant and since there is at least one almost universal misconception, ideas of what constitutes a good pedigree vary. This is the true story.

Major Tristram served as an officer in the Royal Artillery and while stationed in the Potteries during the Second World War rented a small house at Bucknall. A seedling of *H. niger* appeared spontaneously in a newly planted bed of hybrid tea roses in the front garden of the house, in spite of the fact that there were no hellebores in the garden or growing nearby. The major removed the plant to his home at Dallington in Sussex before it flowered, and when it did flower it proved to be of the usual *niger* type.

A self-sown seedling of this plant was given to Hilda Davenport-Jones, whose nursery was only about ten miles away across the border into Kent, and this proved to be an exceptionally large-flowered plant. However, Miss Davenport-Jones realised how long it would take to propagate saleable quantities of this plant by division, so by rigorous selection she developed a large-flowered, true-breeding seed strain. This strain was named 'Potter's Wheel', and when given its Award of Merit at the RHS Show at Vincent Square on 18 February 1958 a basket of seven individual plants was shown to demonstrate the uniformity of the strain.

There never was one 'true plant'; all the plants which originally went into circulation from Washfield Nursery were seedlings of the 'Potter's Wheel' strain and this was maintained at Washfield by continuing selection.

It will be clear from this account that stories of the plant originating with other eminent gardeners such as Margery Fish, Norman Haddon, Lewis Palmer or E. B. Anderson are incorrect. These fine plantspeople probably acquired plants from Washfield and then distributed their own seedlings. These would often have been distributed before they flowered and therefore without being assessed for trueness to type.

There was an account given in the Bulletin of the Alpine Garden Society in 1982 by Major Tristram's grandson which we must now conclude to be inaccurate. This account describes a seedling occurring in Sussex, the major potting up the plant and taking it to the Potteries when he was posted there, then naming it 'Potter's Wheel' and billeting it with a gardening friend as the war became more serious.

During the 1970s and 1980s the name 'Potter's Wheel' became attached to a variety of inferior forms of *H. niger* as seedlings were sold and given away. For unless flowers are hand-pollinated and only those which retain the characteristics of the strain are distributed, the name becomes attached to seedlings of unknown parentage and uncertain quality.

It is interesting to notice the difference between divisions of a plant of 'Potter's Wheel' known to have been sold by Miss Davenport-Jones and seedlings raised from these same plants; the seedlings we inspected had smaller flowers and were more starry in shape. Plants sold as 'Potter's Wheel' must, after all, conform to the original standard, so it is worth repeating the features which make 'Potter's Wheel' so distinct. A description of the plants which received the award was published in the RHS Journal, and in addition to referring to the glossy, dark green leaves it goes on: 'The immense flowers measure from 4 to 5 inches across, with broad glistening white, overlapping sepals, the bases of which, together with the nectaries, are a deep, clear green. The pleasant colour effect is admirably set off by the cluster of golden stamens in the centre of the flower. The 9-inch stems on which the flowers are carried are erect and sturdy and serve to lift them, clean and unsullied, above the splashes of winter rain.'

Miss Davenport-Jones also left some notes on the plant in which she mentions that the flower stems often reached over a foot in height. 'The pure white broad overlapping petals,' she wrote, 'produce a perfectly round bloom – hence the name 'Potter's Wheel'. And the texture of the petal is firm with plenty of substance, an important point in a plant flowering in January and February.'

(*Left*): *Helleborus foetidus* 'Wester Flisk' growing in the garden of the rectory at Wester Flisk. Forms with a stronger red tinting have been selected since its original introduction

(*Above*): 'Potter's Wheel', the finest form of *H. niger*, raised by Hilda Davenport-Jones at Washfield Nursery

HELLEBORUS NIGER
'St Brigid'

This cultivar was discovered in a garden in Kildare, Ireland, in about 1850 and named by Francis Burbidge, then Curator of the Trinity College Botanic Garden in Dublin, after the author Mrs Lawrenson who used 'Saint Brigid' as her pseudonym. The main feature of this plant was that the dark green foliage grew taller than the flowers and so protected them from the weather.

More recently Anne Watson, who runs a small nursery in Yorkshire, was given a plant by an Irish gardener who had grown it for many years. He felt that its most distinctive feature was its long flowering period, new flowers opening for about a month longer than is the case with other cultivars. After growing it for some years, Anne Watson confirms this view.

The plant she grows has large deep glossy green leaves on long stems but they are often so heavy that they lie flat on the ground. The flowers are up to 3½in (8cm) across, on stems about 9in (23cm) tall which are flushed brownish-purple. They are white in colour with a little green at the base inside and out, slightly darker on the inside, and one or two of the petals have a little pinky brown flushing on the outside. The carpels are greenish-yellow and the nectaries lime green.

HELLEBORUS NIGER
'White Magic'

This strain originates in New Zealand and was originally raised by Mrs Pat Stuart of Wanaka, Central Otago. A friend of hers, hoping to raise a pink form of *H. niger*, crossed *H. niger* with a deep wine-coloured form of *H. orientalis*. Mrs Stuart was given a small handful of seedlings which, as well as yielding colours varying from pale pink to deep wine, produced one very large-flowered white which she returned to her friend. Unfortunately he lost the plant, but Mrs Stuart rescued three self-sown seedlings from where the plant had been and after selecting for ten years developed a true breeding strain.

'White Magic' was listed by the New Zealand-based wholesale nursery Duncan and Davies in 1986 as deriving from a cross between *H. niger* and *H. orientalis*, the dark foliage and clear white flowers backed with blush pink being mentioned as special features.

As far as we are aware there has been no recorded hybrid between these two species, and whatever happened in Mrs Stuart's or her friend's garden, the plants of 'White Magic' now available in this country show no trace of *orientalis* blood. As grown in Britain this variety is known for its small, dark, rounded foliage, the exceptional number of flowers it produces, and their tendency to turn pink as they age. While we are forced to discount the possibility that this strain is derived from crossing *H. niger* and *H. orientalis*, it is testimony to the value of rigorous selection by Mrs Stuart over a number of years in making improvements to her original plants. While we do not doubt that hybridising the two species was attempted, we suspect that the cross did not take and that the flowers on the plant of *H. niger* were fertilised with their own pollen.

HELLEBORUS TORQUATUS
'Dido' and 'Aeneas'

These two double-flowered plants were found by Elizabeth in 1971 in a particularly large and varied colony of *H. torquatus* in Montenegro in Yugoslavia. Only two plants with double flowers were found, the doubling being the result of the nectaries developing as petals; both were large and venerable clumps from which single noses were collected. Over the years they have shown definite characteristics of their own. 'Aeneas' is perhaps the more beautiful, as much as anything for the wonderful range of greens in the opening buds. But there is no doubt that 'Dido' is proving to be the more vigorous garden plant and is also proving a successful mother plant. 'Dido' gained an AM when shown in 1984.

All the small doubles raised so far are related to 'Dido' either as offspring or as second-generation hybrids – these include Elizabeth's own 'Montenegran Doubles' and Robin White's 'Wolverton Hybrids'. All inherit her grace; they could not be described as large and frilly but are small and graceful as befits the species.

HELLEBORUS
"ATRORUBENS OF GARDENS"

For many years a widely grown, very early-flowering, purple-flowered plant was known as *H. atrorubens*. However, as it became clear that this plant had no connection with the wild species of this name, it became known as "*H. atrorubens* of gardens". More recently Brian Mathew proposed clarifying this confusing situation. He placed the plant as a form of *H. orientalis* subsp. *abchasicus* and for this familiar, winter-flowering selection he proposed the name 'Early Purple'. The plant was illustrated in his book. Unfortunately the situation does not seem to be quite that simple, for a number of different plants have been going round as "*H. atrorubens* of gardens" though clearly only one deserves the name 'Early Purple'.

We make no apology for devoting space to this plant, for not only does the specific situation regarding this familiar plant need explanation, but it is not untypical of the problems which beset the cultivated hellebores as a whole.

First, we examine the plant as it appears in literature. There is a painting of 'Early Purple' in Brian Mathew's book, and the most striking feature of this plant is that its flowers are purple fading to green on the backs and *green* within, even when the flowers first open. This makes it quite clear to which plant the name 'Early Purple' should be applied. In discussing 'Early Purple', Brian also refers to the painting of a plant from E. B. Anderson's garden in the *Botanical Magazine* in 1969, but the flowers shown in the painting are shining purple inside and out.

This plant has been known since at least the 1870s. Some of the pressed specimens of these plants at Kew are labelled "*H. colchicus*", another is labelled "*H. atrorubens = H. abchasicus*". William Robinson, writing in *The English Flower Garden* (1901), distinguishes these plants as follows: 'The finest of these red or crimson kinds is H. colchicus which is larger than any other . . .'

In the 1930s Perrys were selling a plant as "atrorubens" which they described as having 'cup-shaped flowers, rich rose plum, heavily spotted maroon'. The plant Margery Fish grew she described so: 'Early December sees the first plum-purple flowers opening at ground level without any leaves. As the stalks grow, more flowers open until there is a normal perfectly balanced plant about the turn of the year, and it will remain for a month or more.' This sounds more like *H. purpurascens*.

The plant illustrated by Graham Thomas on the cover of his *Perennial Garden Plants* (first published in 1976) must have given many gardeners an idea of what constitutes "*H. atrorubens* of gardens" but he now says that this plant is a garden hybrid. Things are confused further by the printings of various editions of the book reproducing the colour of the flower in a succession of different shades.

In the recently published *Hardy Herbaceous Perennials* by Jellito and Schacht, an illustration is captioned as *Helleborus* Hybrid 'Atrorubens' but this too is noticeably different from 'Early Purple', as there is no hint of green in the pale red flowers, which fade almost to white at the edges. It bears a greater resemblance to the painting in the *Botanical Magazine*. In the text the plant is said to be related to *H. purpurascens* and there is also an allusion to *H. baumgartenii*, an invalid name once used for a form of *H. purpurascens*. The authors conclude that the correct name for this plant is "*H.* × Atrorubens". Unfortunately the authors also maintain that *H. torquatus* is a form of *H. purpurascens*.

This same photograph is also in Marlene Ahlberg's *Hellebores* captioned *H. atrorubens*, while in the text she aligns it with *H. purpurascens* and true *H. atrorubens* together with, to a lesser extent, *H. orientalis*.

While this plant is clearly not the same as 'Early Purple', it is possible that it is descended from it; the authors of both books advocate raising the plant from seed and there is bound to be some variation in the seedlings. Marlene Ahlburg has herself named some. This plant is similar to one with red-tinted bracts grown at Orchard Nurseries (see below). The possibility that this plant may be a seedling is reinforced by the history of a plant introduced by The Plantsmen as 'Aldebran'; they describe it in their catalogue of April 1979: 'A selected seedling from H. "atrorubens" of gardens with rounded, purple flowers and deciduous habit. Very early . . .'

The plant grown by Christopher Lloyd at Great Dixter and illustrated in his *Garden Flowers from Seed* clearly falls into this group, and he refers to it simply as *H. orientalis* subsp. *abchasicus*.

To summarise, we now refer to three plants which Graham has seen in the last couple of years, plus 'Early Purple'; all have been referred to as '*H. atrorubens* of gardens'.

Plant 1 Received from Mamie Walker of Wester Flisk.
In its first year this plant seemed identical to that illustrated in Brian Mathew's book; in particular, the backs of the flowers were purple at the centre shading to green at the edge and with purple veins extending into the green zone. The inside of the flowers was also green. However, in later years the colour deepened and the amount of green lessened significantly so that it now seems identical to Plant Two. This form is the one grown at Wisley and by Elizabeth.

Plant 2 Seen at Orchard Nurseries in Lincolnshire.
The flowers are very dark purple at the base outside, then mostly pale purple with dark veins; they are the same inside but very pale at the tips. The nectaries are green, though purple at the base.

Plant 3 Seen at Orchard Nurseries in Lincolnshire but originating with Helen Ballard.
This is a shorter plant, 10–12in (25–30cm) in height. The flowers are similar to those on the other Orchard Nurseries plant, but noticeably richer and more shimmery and with the flowers more densely gathered together at the top of the stems, giving a very crowded appearance. The nectaries are honey-coloured, though reddish at the base.

Plant 4 The plant known as 'Early Purple'.
Painted by Mary Grierson from her own plant. The main features are the purple backs to the flowers, fading to green towards the edges and with purple veins, while inside the flowers are green with no veins and with green nectaries.

This is a problem which needs more study before it can be finally clarified.

HELLEBORUS
'Ballard's Black'

This is another plant which seems to retain its legendary status among some gardeners but which appears to have vanished from gardens so that we cannot now compare it with modern cultivars.

This plant was not, as often thought, raised by Ernest Ballard, Helen Ballard's father-in-law. Helen and Phillip Ballard explained to Elizabeth in 1976 that the original plant was actually bought from a Burkwood & Skipwith stand at an RHS show by Ernest Ballard, better known as the raiser of many fine Michaelmas daisies. This plant, with its very dark purple flowers, was of poor constitution and gradually grew weaker and died, but not before it had set seed. These seedlings were almost certainly sold as 'Ballard's Black' by nursery foreman Percy Picton, who eventually took over the nursery.

Margery Fish made a very pertinent comment about this plant in *Gardening in the Shade*. 'I wish the rare 'Black Knight' and 'Ballard's Black' would seed true, for these are amongst the most exciting of the hellebores and so often their seedlings are medium pink instead of a purple that should be dark as night.' However, the plant grown by Mrs Fish came as a seedling from Netta Statham, who herself received seed of the plant from E. B. Anderson! So while the original plant may have been very fine, any plants still growing alongside labels carrying the name 'Ballard's Black' are at best likely to be seedlings of a similar colour to Ernest Ballard's original plant.

HELLEBORUS
'Bowles' Yellow'

In 1921 a collection of hellebores was selected by Sir Frederick Moore, director of the botanic garden at Glasnevin in Dublin, and sent to E. A. Bowles at Myddelton House. Among these was one known at the time as *Helleborus luteus grandiflorus*. This did well at Myddelton House and in 1957 was much admired by E. B. Anderson, who said that 'when in flower, [it] stood out strikingly against a dark background of aucubas'. Twenty years after receiving the plant, Bowles wrote to Lady Moore: 'Hellebores are better than usual. The set of green forms from Glasnevin are among my favourites and I am always blessing the kind friend who collected so many and gave me of the best so generously. The butter yellow one is the one visitors prevent becoming a circular specimen. It has sown itself and one is almost as good as mamma, real butter, not marge . . .' This is quoted by Charles Nelson in his fascinating book *In an Irish Flower Garden*.

Graham Thomas then takes up the story. In the mid 1920s he worked as a student at the Cambridge University Botanic Garden when Bowles arrived with 'a yellow hellebore we now call 'Bowles' Yellow''. Mr Thomas was given a division, grew it for many years, and passed it to friends. It is illustrated on the jacket of his *Perennial Garden Plants* and in his *Complete Flower Paintings*, where it appears a good yellow with dark nectaries. However, as in the case of his painting of "*H. atrorubens* of gardens", the colour in the reproduction varies with different printings.

Strangely, divisions of the plant he has distributed now seem noticeably different from his original plant, being small, green and without the dark nectaries. In recent years plants have occasionally been distributed from Myddelton House or by Frances Perry as 'Bowles' Yellow',

but these plants are different again. They are more vigorous, larger-flowered and much richer in colour. To add to the confusion, a plant originating from Myddelton House at about the time of Bowles's death and very similar to those distributed more recently is also generally reckoned to be the true plant.

For convenience, Graham refers to his yellow plant with pale nectaries which he received from Myddelton House as 'Myddelton Yellow', and the smaller, greener-flowered one supposedly derived, by division, from Graham Thomas's original plant as 'Bowles' Yellow'.

The answer to this conundrum probably lies in Bowles's own words on the subject in that letter to Lady Moore. He referred to the plant's generosity with seedlings and the fact that visitors went away with them, and also mentions that he had already picked out a better one, in a truer yellow. It may well be that the plant known as 'Bowles' Yellow' in the 1920s was quite a different plant from that known by the same name thirty years later.

HELLEBORUS
"Mum of the Doubles"

Many of the double-flowered Orientalis Hybrids grown in British, as distinct from German, gardens originate from one particular plant. This was given to Netta Statham by Margery Fish and was the best of a generally mediocre batch raised by her from seed given to her by E. B. Anderson. This plant, which Netta Statham calls her "Mum of the Doubles", had dark purple flowers and dark flower stems and was allowed to seed around Netta Statham's garden; in the early 1970s it produced its first double and semi-double seedlings. These vary considerably in form – some are wide open with an extra layer of petals and some are more double but rather messy in form, like 'Hidcote Double'. The colours are disappointing and are mostly dirty greeny, pinky plums.

Netta Statham gave seed from her "Mum of the Doubles" to Hidcote, and it is possible that the 'Hidcote Double' is derived from this seed.

HELLEBORUS
'Pluto'

This famous plant has been the parent of many fine hybrids, and around 200 plants were distributed by The Plantsmen nursery. It is a dwarf plant, with flowers which are wine purple with a blue-grey bloom outside and pale green obscured with a bloomy, slate purple flush on the inside, and dark nectaries.

This was raised by Eric Smith before he became involved with The Plantsmen, using the form of *H. torquatus* introduced by Walter Ingwersen. Writing to Hilda Davenport-Jones on New Year's Eve 1967, Eric says he considers *H. torquatus* 'very slow to increase, unfortunately, and I think it will always be a rare and expensive plant. Though I am fairly certain it is self-sterile, one can get hybrid seed, and this does produce some quite interesting plants. Am growing on quite a number at the moment. I don't think that you have yet seen the one I call 'Pluto'. . . In this case, torquatus was the pollen parent; the other one being one I raised from seed under the rather doubtful name of 'colchicus superbus'. This was not a particularly exciting thing, but had dark purple nectaries, and . . . these have been inherited by 'Pluto'.' A few months later he writes: 'I find the latter ['Pluto'] seems to take at least two years to settle down before the flower size and colour is at its best.'

'Pluto' was introduced by The Plantsmen in 1971. 'Ariel', 'Miranda', 'Neptune' and 'Oberon' not only have similar parentage but were grown from seed from the same seed capsule.

HELLEBORUS
'Prince Rupert'

This is one of the best known of the older cultivars, described in 1927 on the occasion of its AM as follows: 'The substantial, round, nodding flowers of this variety are creamy-white in colour, densely spotted with crimson.' This is not very precise, and the description from a Perrys catalogue about ten years later only serves to confuse: 'A very beautiful variety; large, open, silver white flowers, heavily spotted rich crimson-maroon; pea green sepals.'

'Prince Rupert' was one of Mrs Fish's favourites, but in *An All the Year Garden*, she says that this cultivar was 'practically the same' as the plant she grew as *H. guttatus*. Apparently she also maintained that the presence of a sixth petal was a distinguishing feature. The plant of 'Prince Rupert' now growing at East Lambrook and still bearing Mrs Fish's label looks too good to be the original dating from 1927. The pure white flowers are over 3in (7.5cm) across; the broad petals are rounded at the tip and they are very evenly speckled purple with a tendency for the spots to run into veins; there is a clear, pure white zone around the edge. Many but not all flowers have an extra petal, usually slightly distorted, which may be an extra outer petal with no spots or a slim inner one. Either way it does not add to the beauty of the flower.

At the risk of sacrilege, we are tempted to suspect that blood from one of Eric Smith's cultivars, many of which Mrs Fish grew, has crept into the plant now growing at East Lambrook. Perhaps it is a self-sown seedling which grew up in the clump of the original plant.

11

PEOPLE
AND THEIR PLANTS

We are delighted to be able to include here (in alphabetical order) contributions from a number of eminent hellebore growers which give an insight into their enthusiasm for the plants as well as outlining their views on various aspects of hellebore botany or cultivation. We are most grateful for their co-operation. We also include here a summary of the work of Margery Fish, whose garden at East Lambrook Manor is an inspiration to so many gardeners.

HELLEBORES AT BUCKSHAW, 1964–83

by Jim Archibald

Among the first plants which Eric Smith moved to Buckshaw Gardens in Dorset during the autumn of 1964 were his hybrids between *Helleborus torquatus* and *H. orientalis*. For some years Eric had worked as propagator in the herbaceous plant department of Hillier & Sons. In the walled garden under his charge grew a purple hellebore, imposingly labelled '*H. colchicus superbus*' but undistinguished except for its bronze-coloured nectaries. This feature was sufficiently distinct to move Eric to cycle home one winter evening in the late 1950s with some flowers with which to pollinate the plant of the dark Ingwersen *H. torquatus* which he grew in the family garden in Archer's Road, Southampton. From the dozen or so seedlings, Eric gave five clonal names. 'Ariel' and 'Miranda' have rather similar, red-purple exteriors to their characteristic cup-shaped flowers but are quite different inside – the former with bronze nectaries, the latter with yellow-green ones. 'Oberon' gives a slaty, lavender-purple impression and 'Neptune', an exceptionally slow-growing clone, is the closest to the seed-parent in its very dark flowers. 'Pluto', however, adapted well to vegetative propagation and proved by far the best garden plant. While less cup-shaped than the others, the flowers, dull purple outside and pale green inside, retain the rich-brown nectaries.

The other hybrids to which Eric had given cultivar names at that time were few. 'Mercury' was his best white – a good, if not outstanding, plant without much trace of green in the flowers. Neat little 'Venus' looked like a cross between *H. viridis* subsp. *occidentalis* and *H. orientalis* subsp. *guttatus*. Eric's reds had started with 'Mars', which he later decided was rivalled by another, for which the appropriate name 'Antares' existed and was used. An even later seedling was named 'Red Star', but I am afraid that I found them all unsatisfactory·plants in everything except their colour. None was a good grower and all possessed spidery flowers. I have not retained any of them. On the other hand, 'Sirius' was outstanding among these early selections and remains a first-class plant today. Its very large, outward-facing, pale primrose flowers, surrounded by a ruff of bright green, cauline leaves, and its vigorous and floriferous character, make it a much more desirable and satisfactory garden-plant than what we grew at the time as "*H. kochii*", and has subsequently been called 'Bowles' Yellow' by Graham Stuart Thomas. This may have been an influence on 'Sirius' but I suspect that most of its characteristics were derived from another plant we grew under the name 'Brünhilde'. At that time, Eric had brought together a collection of hellebores under a wide range of cultivar names from a variety of sources.

Eric had retained a gauche boyishness into his later years and was nurtured by a coterie of elderly lady gardeners of the period: regal Margery Fish, extrovert Nancy Lindsay, discriminating Amy Doncaster and the superficially sinister Rita Maxted. Mrs Maxted, who always dressed in black and had one hooded eye, which belied the twinkle in the better one, had, in particular, taken Eric under her wing. A certain internecine animosity pervaded the relationship of these ladies, often manifesting itself in discussions as to which of them possessed 'the true' whatever-it-might-be. Inevitably, Eric found himself drawn into such matters. 'Mrs Maxted says that her 'Ballard's Black' is better than mine,' he told me once. 'I really can't see how she can say that.' The possible element of truth in her statement was made apparent some years later, when Percy Picton visited us at hellebore-time. He was a delightful man, surely one of the great plantsmen of this century, who took a great joy in his work. One particular pleasure, he told us, was to go over the beds of hellebore seedlings flowering for the first time and say, 'There's a 'Ballard's Black', and there's a 'White Ladies',' and so on. I recount such a conversation not to denigrate the great mid-century gardeners but to emphasise that their concept of how a cultivar name should be applied might have differed from the current one. I have stood next to Margery Fish as she extracted a self-sown seedling at the base of a clump, while she said, 'I must give you my

'Greenland'. Of course, as this has not flowered, we don't know whether it will be 'Greenland' or not but it usually comes true.'

Doubtless I shall not ingratiate myself to those who seek to collect plants as if they were pieces of antique furniture when I write that, after clinging to token stocks under these old cultivar names for some years, I discarded the lot. Out went 'Apotheker Bogren', 'Coombe Fishacre Purple' and 'Apple Blossom' from Margery Fish. Out went 'Prince Rupert', 'Petsamo' and 'Albion Otto', which had been acquired from the old Perry nursery at Enfield. Out went 'Ballard's Black' and 'Black Knight'. None of the plants we had under these names was anything but mediocre. I might just have kept 'Black Knight' had not his child, 'Andromeda', been superior in vigour and beauty, but even then I am aware that many, more darkly beautiful than she is, may have been produced by those raising seedlings at present. The one old name which is still with me is cream 'Brünhilde'. She may not be very special but she is a remarkably vigorous lady for her age.

Between 1967 and 1975, when Eric and I ran the retail nursery The Plantsmen together, there was an unprecedented opportunity for Eric to grow thousands of hellebore seedlings through to flowering. Unlike the hostas, where beds of dreary, unrequired, green-leaved seedlings gave me a constant problem of disposal – Eric could never countenance discarding any of his children on the rubbish heap – hellebores could easily be sorted into colours and sold as 'strains', which I have always felt could provide a more vigorous plant than divisions from a named clone, in any case. A great deal of discussion between us went into which seedlings should be retained and, in due course, these would acquire names and be propagated vegetatively. Considering the volume of seedlings raised, I am glad to say the names were not too prolific. 'Castor' and 'Pollux' were two very dark twins, which were both kept as Eric could not decide which he preferred. A subsequent seedling which I named 'Corvus' was along the same lines and better than either. 'Pleiades' and 'Hyades' had close affinities to *H. orientalis* subsp. *guttatus*. The former was a dwarf, neat plant with tidily crimson-speckled white cups, and the latter a tall, robust greenish-white heavily spotted with dull crimson, which unfortunately did not maintain its initial vigour after years of division. Two fine whites were named 'Polaris' and 'Virgo', and two dimly coloured, greenish, creamy pinks, 'Cassiopeia' and 'Alcyone', having been selected by Amy Doncaster on two of her annual visits, were dutifully retained. Her taste always inclined to the subtle and was definitely esoteric. It was the spotted and speckled forms, however, which were Eric's triumph. These were graded into 'strains' according to the ground colour and pattern of spotting: 'Midnight Sky Strain', from which no particular clone was named; 'Galaxy Strain', which doubtless was responsible for the remarkable 'Cosmos', with white bowls flushed with pink and evenly spotted all over with bright crimson; 'Constellation Strain', which yielded the stout 'Hercules', rose, speckled all over with purple; 'Zodiac Strain', pinks with a clearly defined zone of spotting, which produced some splendid plants. Eric selected 'Aries', 'Leo', 'Capricornus', 'Scorpio', 'Libra', 'Gemini', 'Taurus' and 'Aquarius' – definitely too many.

Although Eric's hybridizing was an active process and he would be very busy on a sunny day in early spring, it was also a haphazard one, as he did not emasculate flowers, clean his pollen brush or cover his crosses. The origins of his seedlings are mainly very vague. Two clones, however, involved, as the seed-parent, the plant we grew as "*H. atrorubens*", which has since been given the uninspired but very accurate name of 'Early Purple' by Brian Mathew. 'Aldebaran', a similarly early red-purple, was exceptionally prolific in its vegetative increase but was otherwise undistinguished. Eric thought very highly of the other, 'Electra', a cross with the dark *H. torquatus*, but, though it is a pleasant enough little well-shaped purple, I cannot confess to any great personal enthusiasm for this either. The little work he did away from Section Helleborastrum was both planned and rewarding. He had never succeeded in crossing *H. niger* with *H.*

argutifolius, despite annual attempts, but not to be confounded, he pollinated one of the clumps of *H. niger*, which we kept potted under glass, with *H. × sternii* pollen. This was successful and produced some fine, remarkably even hybrids. Inspired with such success, he moved on to using *H. lividus* pollen on *H. niger*. Though the vegetative increase of clones from such crosses was not worthwhile commercially, the cross between *H. niger* and *H. lividus* in particular is far from being uncommercial, as the seedlings which are going to show the hybrid characteristics mostly germinate, like *H. lividus*, in autumn and can be segregated then, leaving those which will look like plain *H. niger* to germinate later.

Though Eric's association with the other hellebore enthusiasts of the period was mainly personal and involved many visitors to Buckshaw Gardens in spring, he maintained a long correspondence with Sergei Nolbandov in Sussex. Every year a multitude of neatly inscribed seed packets would arrive, all to be sown separately in small pots by Eric. I cannot recollect any outstanding seedlings from this source, nor can I remember all the cultivar names Nolbandov had bestowed on his favourites. I do remember 'Grace Hood', mainly because she was followed by 'Grace Hood II' and then 'Grace Hood III'; I was not approving. However, this dynastic concept must have had a secret appeal to Eric, as, after he had retired from commercial nursery work in 1975, I found plants labelled 'Sirius II' and 'Sirius III'.

While Eric took all the small stocks of his newer hostas with him when he left Buckshaw, he only wanted the pots of the current year's seedlings of hellebores. This left me to consolidate and sort out the established clumps and larger stocks, a task complicated by his stratagem of splitting a clone into three when it was first selected and planting the divisions in three different parts of the nursery. Such divisions were not always named and he did not number such plants, so all that existed might be a label saying something like 'Small, extra dark, blue purple *H. torquatus* hybrid'. The Zodiac types were especially numerous, and we had substantial stocks of ten separate clones to line out in adjacent blocks. After allowing them to establish for a few years, I had no alternative but to conclude that 'Leo' and 'Aries' were the same clone and represented four of the blocks. I was never wholly satisfied that 'Capricornus' was different, and 'Taurus', while certainly distinguishable, was not really substantially distinct either. A few of the clones he had named and which existed only as a single plant or very small stocks were never located. Although I took him to the nursery at hellebore time for several years, he could never identify with assurance such clones as 'Algol', 'Arcturus', 'Vega', 'Ganymede', 'Pegasus', 'Perseus', 'Saturn' and 'Uranus'. Some selections quite simply did not lend themselves to vegetative increase. Such were 'Mira', a crimson-dusted white, 'Praesepe', a strange ivory with washed-out crimson streaks, and 'Draco', a beautiful rose pink, in which the zone of basal spots had amalgamated into a solid, soft crimson patch. These were passed to friends in the hope that their characteristics would manifest themselves in more vigorous seedlings.

While we grew and distributed a very much larger volume of hellebores after Eric left, I could not afford the luxury of retaining seedling beds from which to select clones in flower. Almost all the hellebores were sold wholesale either as young seedlings for growing-on or as budded plants in larger containers. Fortunately we had sufficiently discriminating retailing contacts, who appreciated what we were supplying, to give us reports on the quality of the latter. There was no doubt that 'Cosmos', 'Sirius' and 'Aquarius' produced outstanding seedlings. Some were doubtless better in some respects than the parents, which brings into question the value of propagating selected clones. Although our main sales were in seedlings, I did not neglect vegetative propagation and worked up stocks to several hundred of the Zodiac clones. One year we had over 200 'Pluto' available for wholesale distribution. I wonder where they all went eventually. While neither my circumstances nor my inclinations after 1975 were

conducive to naming a multitude of clones, a few were selected and propagated. Some years earlier I had prevailed on Eric to retain three seedlings in which he had no great interest but which seemed to me to possess an outstanding new characteristic. They had a pale ground colour coupled with bronze-crimson nectaries and staining at the bases of the segments. These are white 'Aquila', pink-veined 'Carina' and cream 'Orion'. 'Carina' was my favourite but 'Orion' is proving the better garden-plant. The observant might have noted that, while I felt it appropriate to retain Eric's astronomical theme in these names, I moved to the southern skies. For the few I regarded more exclusively as my own, I started using the specific names of moths of the family Saturniidae, creatures of the night with sufficient affinity to the planets to provide continuity. 'Selene' was selected as an outstanding green, something Eric had not been inclined to pursue enthusiastically, out of seedlings from some of my Balkan *H. cyclophyllus* possibly pollinated with 'Sirius'. Her initial vigour and the perfection of her lime yellow flowers have not been altogether retained over the years. It is still early to assess the long-term possibilities of black-purple 'Inca', with dull-black cauline leaves, and red-purple 'Zuleika', but mushroom pink and primrose 'Titania' is well established in our affection and proving an excellent plant here in Wales. This trio, the last of the hellebores to be named at Buckshaw, owes much to the influence of *H. torquatus* and brings us back full circle to Eric's early, inspired hybrid.

I am told there is a hellebore being distributed as 'Eric's Best'. What this might be I could not say, but I can certainly see Eric muttering with indignation at such presumption as he wanders among the clumps of *H. cyclophyllus* in the Elysian fields. He loved all his children. It would have been impossible for him to think of any as his 'best'. On the other hand, it might not be wholly inappropriate if the perpetrator of such a name followed it with 'Eric's Best II' and 'Eric's Best III'.

HELLEBORES AT OLD COUNTRY

by Helen Ballard

My interest in hellebores began in the early sixties, when I put four plants selected from the Ballard Colwall Nursery into a forlorn north-facing border which had before contained only nettles and the stump of an old pear tree. Here they were in the high shade of the house and exposed to all the north winds.

I chose the plants for their sturdy stems and substantial cup-shaped flowers. Two were red, and two white. Someone had called one white plant *H. olympicus*. It flowered profusely, often through the winter, and had a green eye.

To this number I added very few – eventually one or two short plants from Yugoslavia of a glowing green, and some purplish variants of *H. multifidus serbicus* (now called *H. torquatus*) which gave a hint of blue. I was also given a very useful plant by Mr E. B. Anderson. It had small dark droopy flowers and, no doubt, a very complicated ancestry. This took me some way along the road to a really dark hellebore.

Interested in the idea of breeding, but being no botanist, and with a very shaky knowledge of · genetics, I had to pose rules for myself. Having decided what I was aiming at, it was not enough to be on the lookout for slight variations; it was even more important to notice which of the desirable characteristics observed were transmitted to the offspring. From this came some very useful parents.

Eventually I hoped to extend the colour range of hellebores within their sombre limits – their colours were already very subtle. Sepals, nectaries, stigmas and stamens all varied, adding to the general richness of effect. This I think partly explains their fascination once one has adapted to a more muted colour range.

From my original plants I had red-, pink- and white-flowered plants. I tried to make them more upright by selection, and by crossing, to increase their hybrid vigour. (Hellebores do not generally react favourably to selfing.) I was not convinced by the advice I was given at the outset 'Cross everything with everything.' The gene pool was relatively restricted, and still is.

I achieved a yellow hellebore, primrose yellow at least, but with bluish shades I was not successful. There was a lot of grey in these. Sometimes the darker plants have a bluish bloom, but this is superficial. The real colour is demonstrated when the sun is low in early spring. Then the flower heads with the sun behind them seem to be on fire.

My husband and I spent happy hours looking for hellebores in the wild and trying to distinguish the different green species. We had a lot of help from Brian Mathew's first survey of the genus in the March 1967 number of the A.G.S. Bulletin. I was encouraged by Mr E. B. Anderson and his enthusiasm. When in Ljubljana I summoned up my courage to ring up Professor Mayer at the University and, in halting German, to ask for his advice. We were received very kindly, and as well as the information he gave us I remember some superb Turkish coffee, and a startling bowl of almost red Christmas roses, a colour they go sometimes when they are really over.

In the end the location of plants, and the conditions under which they were growing, fixed them in one's mind better than naming, especially for someone unable to describe their differences in full botanical detail. This was done in Brian Mathew's recent book.

The most thrilling experience during this search for hellebore species was seeing the Christmas rose (*H. niger*) flowering in great stretches on mountain-tops in north-west Yugoslavia. It was above the tree line, very wet but free-draining, on north-facing slopes. Equally exciting was walking up a valley in Majorca full of *H. lividus* and finding it in perfect harmony with the colours of the limestone gorge. (Magically, the same ethereal grey and red are repeated in the Majorcan paeony and cyclamen.)

'Nocturne'

'Saturn'

'Blue Spray'

'Ushba'

'Greencups'

'Tom Wilson'

'Philip Wilson'

'Blowsy'

'Phylly'

'Dawn'

'Dusk'

'Garnet'

Plants appear at ³/₅ life size

In the Caucasus we just missed seeing the coloured forms of *H. orientalis*, but we brought back some small seedlings which after two years flowered in the garden in a colourful mixture.

After my first planting of hellebores on the north side of the house, I kept on adding plants to this favourable situation until I needed another border and had the idea of an early spring border mainly of hellebores. They were underplanted with a lot of smaller things – primroses, wood anemones, snowflakes and a great variety of snowdrops – which were my husband's special study. The result was an early spring counterpart of the summer border which kept its interest for at least two months, and was always a surprise.

Of course there were always drawbacks inseparable from trying to tame a farm garden. And I well remember that one night, alerted by heavy breathing below my bedroom window, I looked out and found a broad back and hooves firmly planted on my border. Luckily nothing likes eating hellebores.

My enthusiasm must have been a trial for my family, as it was scarcely dinted by jokes. Outside the greenhouse someone put up a notice – DANGER. HELLEBORE CROSSING.

A BOTANIST'S VIEW

by Brian Mathew

If asked to pick out the memorable in my (so far!) life-long interest in hellebores, I would immediately recall my first encounter with these modest perennials at an early age while messing about in the woods near our house in Limpsfield, some forty-odd years ago. The mysterious dull purple blooms, produced so early in the year, while the trees were still leafless, intrigued me, so the plant was duly dug up (it *was* on a garden refuse dump!) and transplanted to our own garden, where it became a much-prized possession and lasted for many years, long after I had left home in search of a living in horticulture and botany.

Thereafter, wherever I went, hellebores seemed to form an interesting aside to my activities. First during an enjoyable period at the Ingwersens' nursery, when I had the threefold pleasure of working for and with Walter, Will and Paul, as well as with their splendid staff of that time under George Henley; the gentle 'old Mr Ingwersen' would sit in the office describing his travels and feeling over the plants which I took him, for he was quite blind by then, happily recalling events long past. One of these was clearly very special to him, involving Montenegro and the curious blackish *Helleborus torquatus*, a plant which was found by chance while answering the call of nature during a thunderstorm, which is one of the most Wagnerian plant-collecting stories I have heard! This was duly introduced to the nursery and, intrigued by the story, I set off in search of it to see if it was still beneath the large beech tree where he had last seen it some years earlier. It was in fact still there, after a period of some forty years, but my supposedly tender loving care soon encouraged it to depart this life! The stories imparted by this unforgettable plantsman lit a hitherto unknown touch-paper, and I was very soon set on a course to visit the Balkans in search of these fascinating plants.

The students' course at Wisley provided another delightfully painless opportunity to

---

Named cultivars raised by Helen Ballard. This selection of named cultivars raised by Helen Ballard shows the variety of good colours she has developed as well as the rounded flower forms. Flowers from plants grown at Bridgemere Nurseries

meet and learn from such eminent plantsmen-botanists as Chris Brickell and Ken Aslet. The collection of hellebores was not noteworthy, but I do remember a plant of the hybrid *H. × nigercors*, and a splendid clump of the dwarf *H. purpurascens*, although in a rather poor greenish-brown colour form, not the lovely slaty purple one.

At Wisley I was also fortunate in joining up with a splendid group of students, and the interaction with fellow enthusiasts further stimulated my love of plants, so it was not long before my ancient MG was conveying myself and David Pycraft to a relatively 'closed' Yugoslavia in search of, among other things, hellebores. I well remember travelling along country roads which were provided with armed guards at every corner, a feature not really conducive to stopping for botanical forays! These memorable trips, followed by the Bowles' Scholarship Expedition to Iran in 1963 (with Stuart Baker, David Barter and David Pycraft), and a long botanical tour of Turkey in 1965 with Margaret Briggs (now my dear wife), John and Helen Tomlinson and Paul Miles, added masses of information about hellebores in the wild, from *atrorubens* to *vesicarius*; the latter was in seed at the time and a collection was made, but it remains a very rare plant in cultivation.

My first links with Kew evolved at about this time too, as I needed to see the collections of dried material there. Another stroke of luck came in the form of Desmond Meikle, who was in charge of the European/Asiatic section of the Herbarium and who also had an interest in hellebores. His kindly guidance on classification and nomenclature was a tonic to one who was taking his first faltering steps from horticulture into taxonomy, and we had great fun drawing overlapping circles showing supposed relationships between the species!

Other noteworthy experiences in my world of hellebores included making the acquaintance of such plantsmen as E. B. Anderson, Eliot Hodgkin, Norman Hadden and Sir Frederick Stern (as in *H. × sternii*), all of whom cultivated a great range of species and hybrids and were

blessed with a great generosity so that my own collection expanded considerably during this period. The next obvious move was to try to put some of the knowledge on to paper, and this is where the real difficulties began, for there is nothing like committing oneself to print for sorting out what-you-know from what-you-think-you-know! The outcome was the fairly non-committal little *Gardener's Guide to Hellebores*, published by the Alpine Garden Society in 1967.

Of course, this was not the end of my interest and I continued to study, collect and hybridise them; over the years this has brought with it the bonus of meeting up with many more enthusiasts, such as Eric Smith and Jim Archibald (The Plantsmen), Amy Doncaster, Helen Ballard, Margery Fish, Netta Statham, Primrose Warburg, Elizabeth Strangman, Richard Nutt, Will McLewin, Robin and Sue White, and Herbert and Molly Crook who undertook many plant-hunting holidays weighed down by a formidable number of my botanical requests concerning hellebores and crocuses!

Twenty years on, the booklet was badly in need of revision and, with much more information accrued, it seemed appropriate to turn it into a fully fledged book with as much colour illustration as possible. Fortune again lent a hand, this time in the form of one of our leading botanical artists, Mary Grierson, who, apart from being brilliant at her profession, happened also to love hellebores, a fact which is obvious to all who browse through the pages of *Hellebores*, the successor to the gardener's guide.

Of course, *Hellebores* is not the last word – nothing is in the world of plants – and if it were there would be no need for more than one book on each subject. My view of the taxonomy and nomenclature of the wild species is only one opinion among many, ranging from those who think that the natural variation is such that there is only a handful of species, through to those who recognise many species and variants. My own survey was intended to be an intermediate view, with a strong leaning towards practicality. In horticulturally popular plant groups I think it is important to consider the needs of the grower when it comes to providing a system of classification, even if the result is a compromise; if the system provided is too 'way out' it will almost certainly not be followed anyway! The system which allows for no overlap between the recognised 'units' results in four distinct species, *H. niger*, *H. foetidus*, *H. vesicarius* and *H. argutifolius* (if *H. lividus* is included with it). In the case of all the other European, Balkan, Turkish, Caucasian and Chinese 'species' I am fairly certain that it is possible to find overlaps in the various characters if one really sets about trying to destroy a particular system of classification; the prior name for this huge unwieldy species is Linnaeus' *H. viridis* (1753). This would include as synonyms *H. orientalis*, *H. purpurascens*, *H. atrorubens*, *H. torquatus*, *H. dumetorum*, *H. multifidus*, *H. odorus*, *H. cyclophyllus* and *H. thibetanus*. I cannot imagine that many folk would believe in or follow such a drastic course of action, least of all nurserymen and gardeners, who prefer to have a reasonably uniform entity under one particular name. It has been suggested to me that if such a classification were to be adopted under the name *H. viridis*, then for the practical purposes of communication the nurseryman could define a particular plant by its description, such as '*H. viridis*. The dwarf purple variant from Czechoslovakia with much-divided leaves'. Of course, in doing this the nurseryman has then identified it as something different and provided it with a name, this time consisting of ten words instead of one; I suggest that it is actually much more convenient to refer to it as *H. purpurascens*, even if this does occasionally overlap in its features with *H. torquatus*. The other extreme of classification does not allow for much variation in the characters, in which case it becomes necessary to recognise increasingly smaller 'units', sometimes resulting in strings of epithets such as *H. multifidus* subsp. *intermedius* var. *violascens* forma *linearifolius*. It may be a compromise, but I prefer 'my', albeit slightly fuzzy, system!

The most recent highlight in my hellebore world has been the acquisition of a packet of seeds of the Chinese *H. thibetanus*. I am glad to report that six have germinated, so maybe this elusive plant will at last be seen in gardens.

Earlier on I mentioned the hybrids *H. × nigercors* and *H. × sternii*, crosses between *H. argutifolius* and *H. niger*, and *H. argutifolius* and *H. lividus* respectively. These names are validly published under the internationally agreed Code of Botanical Nomenclature and apply to any hybrids having those parentages; individual clones within those may be selected and given cultivar names, for example *H. × nigercors* 'Alabaster' and *H. × sternii* 'Boughton Beauty'. Other hybrid combinations between these three species have been made, but to date nomenclaturally acceptable names have not been provided. The crosses involved are *H. lividus × H. niger* and *H. niger × H. × sternii*. It is unfortunate that the names "*H. × nigristern*" and "*H. × nigriliv*" which were suggested by Eric Smith in *The Hardy Plant* (the journal of the Hardy Plant Society), Vol. 5, no.2 (1976), are invalid. Firstly, they should have been provided with Latin descriptions, with dried voucher specimens ('type specimens') deposited in a Herbarium, and, secondly, the epithets do not conform to the present Code of Nomenclature. Recommendation H.10A states that in forming epithets for species-hybrids, 'authors should avoid combining parts of the names of the parents'. Since *H. × nigercors* was published long ago, in 1934, this is a *fait accompli* and cannot be changed, but unfortunately it would be against the Code to publish "*nigriliv*" and "*nigristern*", even though as epithets they are usefully informative about the parentage.

In view of Eric Smith's great contribution to the breeding of hellebores, and the fact that he was one of the earliest, if not the first, to cross *H. niger* and *H. × sternii*, I propose the name *H. × ericsmithii* for all hybrids bearing this parentage. Helen Ballard has also raised some of the finest hellebore hybrids and one of her lines of interest has been in crossing *H. lividus* and *H. niger*, so it is appropriate to name the resulting hybrids *H. × ballardiae*. Each of these names requires a formal description.

124

H. × *ericsmithii* B. Mathew (=*H. niger* L. × *H.* × *sternii* Turrill), a *H. nigro* scapo plurifloro nec unifloro et foliis venis conspicuis argenteis ornatis distinguenda; a *H.* × *sternii* floribus maioribus et foliis plurilobis nec trilobis distinguenda. Type: Cultivated specimen deposited at the Herbarium, Royal Botanic Gardens, Kew (K).

H. × *ballardiae* B. Mathew (=*H. lividus* Aiton × *H. niger* L.), a *H. nigro* foliis margine valde et acute dentato-serratis distinguenda; a *H. livido* floribus maioribus et foliis plurilobis nec trilobis distinguenda. Type: Cultivated specimen deposited at the Herbarium, Royal Botanic Gardens, Kew (K).

The hybrids between *H. niger* and *H. lividus* are, as one might expect, stocky in their habit of growth, more like the former except that, apart from the basal leaves and flowers, there are also short stems which carry additional ones, just as one would expect of a cross between a stemless and a stemmed species. This feature shows up best in the *H.* × *nigercors* hybrids since the stemmed parent, *H. argutifolius*, has much more elongated stems than *H. lividus*. The leaves of the *H.* × *ballardiae* plants which I have seen so far are usually a deep almost bluish green with silvery veining, showing the influence of *H. lividus*, but they are divided pedately into five segments more like those of *H. niger*, and there are often a few teeth on the margins, again inherited from *niger*. Eric Smith, writing in *The Hardy Plant*, Vol.5, noted that some *niger* × *lividus* seedlings which he had raised had bluish, silverveined foliage, so it seems that this feature is fairly consistent. The flowers are more like those of *H. niger* in shape, although perhaps rather more deeply saucer-shaped than flattish, and they are much larger than those of *H. lividus* but, like the latter, there are several per head, usually three or four when the plants are growing well. Although nearly white inside with a pinkish flush on the outside when first open, they rapidly change to a purplish-pink throughout and sometimes take on a sort of gunmetal colour. Unfortunately I cannot enthuse about their value as garden plants, since they do not do at all well in our garden and I find that the only

way to keep them looking reasonably happy is to grow them in a cool greenhouse in deep pots. However, this need not necessarily be taken as a criticism of these hybrid plants, since neither of the parents do well either! *H. niger* makes little attempt to grow at all and *H. argutifolius* is always somewhat sickly, especially in cold winters. In the cool greenhouse *H. lividus* looks fine, but will seldom survive outdoors so I have long since given up trying it without protection. Needless to say, *H.* × *nigercors* fares no better, so I have not even tried the *H.* × *ericsmithii* (*niger* × *sternii*) hybrids. This is just misfortune on my part, for these can all be very fine plants and I have seen many really good specimens of *H.* × *nigercors* in various gardens, some nice *H.* × *ericsmithii* at Elizabeth's nursery, and Helen Ballard has fine pot-grown *H.* × *ballardiae*, although admittedly in a cool house for breeding purposes.

H. × *ericsmithii* is rather more variable in its appearance, which is what one would expect since *H.* × *sternii* itself varies from compact plants which resemble *H. lividus* through to those which look more like *H. argutifolius*. The appearance of any of the *niger* × *sternii* crosses will very much depend on the particular form of the latter which is chosen as a parent. Because of the three species involved it is possible to have a complete range from compact plants with few flowers per stem, and pedate five-lobed leaves, thus looking more like *H. niger*, through to taller-stemmed plants with several flowers per head and spiny-margined leaves with a tendency to be three-lobed, more closely resembling *H. argutifolius*. *H. lividus* usually makes its presence known in the form of a pinkish-purple suffusion on the outside of the flowers, and a certain amount of silvery or pale veining on the leaves.

Of the *H. niger* hybrids, *H.* × *nigercors* is probably the most striking. It is usually like a stocky *H. argutifolius* with bold foliage varying from three- to five-lobed and with spiny margins but, curiously, the teeth are even coarser than in either of the parents. The flowers are saucershaped, large and white with a tinge of green, and produced both in a terminal head like those of the Corsican hellebore, and with some extra ones on stems from the base as in *H. niger*. It is not greatly variable, but obviously there is a certain amount of variation depending upon the parents. The cultivar 'Alabaster', which had the fine *H. niger* 'Potter's Wheel' as one parent, is a particularly good form.

An interesting point raised by Eric Smith in 1970 in *The Hardy Plant* concerns the time of germination of these hybrid hellebores. He noted that the seeds of *niger* × *sternii* germinated over a long period and that those which gave rise to '*sternii*-like' seedlings came up first, in October, followed much later on in January by those which more closely resembled *H. niger*. It does seem to be a feature of the stemmed helle-bores *H. lividus* and *H. argutifolius* that their seeds tend to germinate in autumn, as do those of *H. vesicarius*, and it is likely that this is a natural response to the Mediterranean climate in which they have evolved, germinating at the onset of cooler, damper, autumnal weather in order to allow the seedlings as long as possible to establish before the next hot dry summer. The majority of hellebores are inland plants from

cold-winter areas, often in the mountains, and their seeds naturally germinate in spring after a period of cold, although in cultivation in the relatively mild climate of Britain this can be as early as December or January. In the wild *H. niger* can be seen in flower in March, and it is only when cultivated in lowland gardens that it (sometimes!) becomes the Christmas rose. It appears that *H. niger* is usually chosen as the seed parent for these crosses, and it also seems to be the rule that they are normally sterile. Although I have seen seed-pods forming, in my experience they do not get as far as producing viable seeds. This means that in order to increase the stocks the cross has to be repeated each time, although vegetative propagation by division is possible, albeit rather slowly.

H. argutifolius has been crossed with *H. foetidus* and it would therefore not be unex-pected if *H. foetidus* could be hybridised with *H. niger*. Whether this is desirable or not is quite another matter, but it would be interesting to experiment in this direction if only to find out whether it was possible!

CONFESSIONS OF A HELLEBORE ADDICT

by Will McLewin

I am not sure when my interest in hellebores changed into an obsession. When I began visiting Yugoslavia early each spring to study the species in the wild my enthusiasm was undeniably serious. Now that I have given up a career as a lecturer in mathematics and instead run a not-very-commercial nursery devoted mainly to growing and understanding them, it is clear that 'interested in hellebores' does not adequately describe my condition.

Initially, the persistent difficulties I encoun-tered with their taxonomy, both for species and hybrids, were compounded by the paucity of lit-erature and the contradictions and ambiguities in what little there was. However, these prob-

lems enticed rather than discouraged me.

I feel now, with some chagrin, that my early endeavours were largely wasted. I had not then appreciated the particular difficulties associated with the genus, and naïvely accepted far too much second-hand information from non-specialists. Integrity of labelling was largely ab-sent, innocently I have no doubt, although inno-cence in this context is a poor excuse.

There are two basic reasons, blatant sharp practice aside, for what is a persistent problem in practice. One comes from the plants them-selves, the other from the people who want them. Because hellebores grow relatively slowly and cannot be reproduced rapidly from cuttings, particular clones have to be propagated by the slow process of division. Although most plants set seed well, they hybridise freely. As a result, production of authentic named plants in commercial quantities is not possible. All this would not matter if people eager to possess a particular hellebore were keener on acquiring and enjoying the qualities in question than the name. Perhaps nothing would be as useful as everyone being much more demanding on the question of provenance.

So strong feelings about authenticity and accuracy, fuelled by regrets for lost years and influenced by a previous life as an academic mathematician, continue to be reflected in my work on hellebores. I think of species and hybrids as two separate categories, and growing and propagating them as two distinct activities.

SPECIES HELLEBORES

Species hellebores present the gardener, the botanist and everyone in between with problems. What are valid species and subspecies names? What do these names mean in terms of wild populations? How can 'stray' plants be identified? These are questions for which simple, comforting answers are not available and are unlikely to become available. This is unfortunate, because some people are discouraged and so miss out on some superb and intriguing garden plants. These uncertainties also provoke disappointment, which is often directed at the plant itself instead of at the provider or the recipient where it usually belongs. In fact, to enjoy the subtle delights of species hellebores, all that is needed is a basic appreciation of why there is a problem – and a pinch of common sense.

Difficulties arise because wild populations are always variable, often clearly and obviously variable. With caulescent species, *H. foetidus* for example, the variations within particular colonies are not usually striking and there is no doubt that all the plants are *H. foetidus*. With acaulescent species, *H. atrorubens* for example, flower colour, leaf divisions and leaf size may vary to the extent that at the very least several subspecies appear to be involved.

Although I have been visiting Yugoslavia for some time, the complexities of the acaulescent species are greatest there and I still feel in need of more experience. It is possible that a large colony of uniform, dark *H. torquatus* exists but I doubt it. There seems to me more likelihood of the name's validity being questioned, because the name and specific status for the group of plants involved is among the least satisfactory of the species.

In another ten years, say, I expect to have much more information from many more sites, together with more confidence and more insight. I also expect to feel, as I do now, that there are no simple definitions and just as many mysteries; so I do not feel that frustrated, baffled silence is appropriate. The variability in the wild seems to me to be an inherent characteristic of the genus that we just have to live with. Whether what follows from that is a cavalier, uninhibited attitude to labelling or a cautious, severe approach is a personal choice. I prefer the latter because it seems to me the only way to bring clarity to a confused situation.

Brian Mathew's classification may not be the last word on the subject, but at the very least it is an excellent starting point and his book is an invaluable reference. Any future changes in species organisation are likely to be modifications of this basic structure, so my comments on individual species follow his nomenclature.

The caulescent species, *H. argutifolius*, *H. lividus*, *H. foetidus* and the wayward *H. vesicarius*, are generally distinct, occur in separate localities and wild hybrids are unknown. The exceptions are *H. argutifolius* and *H. lividus*, which cross readily in gardens and are separated only by virtue of each growing on its own Mediterranean island. The acaulescent species are the most complicated. To start with, although the extreme varieties are unmistakable, there are many intermediate forms and they will all cross with each other with alacrity if given the opportunity.

With the extensive development of the more exotic garden hybrids, the true forms of *H. orientalis* have become no more than curiosities for the committed enthusiast. However, it seems likely that specialised fieldwork in the Caucasus would yield some surprises which might necessitate revision of the *H. orientalis* subspecies. I find it hard to believe that the well-known variations, already more substantial than those between *H. torquatus* and *H. multifidus* subsp. *multifidus* for example, would not be extended to justify further subdivisions. There is no reason other than a feeble capitulation to entrenched sloppiness for continuing to refer to the diverse and widespread garden hybrids as 'orientalis hybrids'. The yellows are mostly *H. odorus*, the purple-blacks are largely *H. torquatus*. Perpetuating this error renders *H. orientalis*, a valid and true species name, unusable.

Helleborus odorus is widespread and creates a lot of confusing colonies. Or at least, the most tempting interpretation is that tendencies in *H. atrorubens*, *H. multifidus* subsp. *istriacus*, *H. dumetorum* and probably also *H. purpurascens* in the direction of *H. odorus* are the result of *H. odorus* influence. At its best *H. odorus* is a lovely bright pale yellow, a cheering sight on grey days, but I remain sceptical about separating it from *H. cyclophyllus*. Possibly some extensive work in Greece will be convincing, but the crucial differentiating factor, free carpels, seems to be inconsistent and I have come across deviant carpels in *H. multifidus* subsp. *istriacus*, for example.

You have to admire taxonomists as they struggle with such problems on a vast scale. Perhaps if they were given the resources and status of nuclear physicists and accountants, species hellebores would be less problematic.

The various forms of *H. multifidus*: subsp. *hercegovinus* near Dubrovnik, then subsp. *multifidus*, subsp. *istriacus* and subsp. *bocconei* as you work anticlockwise round the Adriatic into Italy, all deserve to be better known as garden plants. The separation into subspecies works well and 'feels right'. I know the near neighbours subsp. *hercegovinus* and subsp. *multifidus* form relatively few sites, but all consist of substantial colonies of fairly even unambiguous plants.

The hellebore that I associate most with woodland is *H. dumetorum*. In the wild, at least in colonies I know, it has a wonderful characteristic leaf with narrow barely serrated segments and shy, rather infrequent flowers. In cultivation the leaf segments seem to broaden and it is free-flowering.

This brings us to the purple-flowered species: *H. atrorubens*, *H. torquatus* and *H. purpurascens*. Without, so far, experience of *H. purpurascens* in the wild I do not feel able to comment on it, except to express the weary conviction that most of the garden plants with the label *H. purpurascens* are in fact cultivated hybrids. I consider *H. atrorubens* to be as distinct as any species in this group, and I am growing steadily more enthusiastic about its attributes. On the other hand, although the plants that it is convenient to call *H. torquatus* are a widespread and substantial presence in the wild, this species strikes me as unsatisfactory and 'unresolved'.

Some observations are common to both species. The most important is that all the substantial colonies I have seen have flower colour ranging from totally green, usually yellowy green, through all sorts of shades and mixtures to almost totally dark indigo-violet. The inside surface of violet-coloured sepals is always greener, although photographs or over-enthusiastic reporting may disguise this, with the result that the wonderful and enticing interplay of green and violet which is truly representative of both species is largely unappreciated. Quite often the insides of the sepals are elegantly veined, in some plants strikingly so, with violet veins on a yellow-green surface.

H. atrorubens seems to be confined to a relatively small area of Slovenia and is not easy to find. Despite the colour variations, in colonies where there are no obvious signs of other species, even the few comparatively green-flowered plants are distinctly *H. atrorubens*. In contrast *H. torquatus* is widespread, albeit never common, and plants from different areas do have a different feel. In Croatia I find it hard to distinguish green-flowered *H. torquatus* from *H. multifidus* subsp. *multifidus*. Designating a plant as *H. torquatus* only because there are nearby

128

plants with violet-coloured flowers may be unavoidable but is not satisfying. Faced with a large colony of them and saying 'This one is *H. torquatus*, this one is *H. multifidus* and this one is a hybrid' is even worse.

I believe it is possible to reduce misconceptions and widespread confusion over identity and classification, and help the species become better known, by adopting a rigorous and uncompromising approach to propagation. I propagate acaulescent species plants only by division of wild collected plants or from wild seed from colonies I know, never from nursery seed. This means I can be absolutely sure of the authenticity of plants I grow and make available. Choosing representative samples from wild colonies, not just the most attractive, and growing them under uniform conditions in the nursery facilitates leisurely study and reliable insights –

though most of the time 'leisurely study' seems wildly optimistic.

HELLEBORUS × HYBRIDUS

In rather the same way that I feel there will always be unresolved mysteries with the true species, I have a feeling, more sinking than stimulating, that my work with hybrid hellebores will never seem well organised. On the whole I welcome serendipity, I positively prefer to feel that I am merely helping hellebores along their own path instead of cajoling them in directions that I select as desirable. Nevertheless there are frequent occasions when a plan would be a comfort and make it easier to decide which fantasies to abandon.

A reluctance to add to the names in circulation and then to see them appearing on ever-

---

WILL MCLEWIN'S CATEGORY CODE

BASIC COLOUR

1 green	11 medium pink
2 green/white	12 dark pink/purple-pink
3 white, ivory	13 red/crimson
4 cream	14 bright wine
5 yellow	15 purple
6 cream/green, yellow/green	16 purple-black
7 peach	17 purple-brown
8 pink/white	18 purple-blue
9 pink/white/green	19 blue-grey, mauve
10 pale pink	20 blue

SPOTTING

1 fine/dust, all over	pronounced clear border
2 medium to heavy, all over	7 central eye of colour or spots
3 sparse, fine, usually central	8 fine veins and spots in fine lines
3+ just a very few spots	9 heavy veins, webbed spots
4 medium to heavy, sparse	10 picotee, pink/purple edge
5 central zone of merged spots	11 central clear zone or – no spots
6 medium to heavy, sometimes merged,	

LEAVES AND STEMS

T	*torquatus/multifidus* influence
L	red/purple/dark early leaves
R	red (spotted) stems
M	particularly large leaves
E	particularly small

FLOWER SHAPE/SIZE

X	large
K	small
R	round
P	pointed
C	crinkled/undulating
DD	doubles

FLOWER BACK

B	notably different
B+	strongly different
V	veined
H	hooded/shadowed
W	well-coloured/bright
S	short pedicel/outward facing

NECTARIES

G	green
Y	yellow
A	amber/bronze
D	dark
F	developed

Seedlings from Will McLewin. A selection of mainly spotted seedlings raised by Will McLewin

Plants appear at 3/5 life size

divergent seedlings influences my work with hybrids. Another influence is a lack of interest in clonally propagating particular named hybrids when I have essentially similar but better unnamed plants in my trial beds. As my interest and delight in the subtle charms of the true species has grown, I have lost enthusiasm for developments which seem to me unnatural. Blowsy doubles, like dahlias gone wrong, you can keep.

The pleasure I get from close examination of the flowers is probably why I have concentrated more on developing different types of spotting and less on pure, deeper colours. Flowers with internal spotting seem to me to have more character and to offer a greater range of observation; from overall effect to minute details. The possibilities seem endless: all-over fine spots, a central eye of heavy spots, a neat unspotted border and so on. I am still surprised to find descriptions limited to spotted or not. Recent exciting developments include what I call webbed, spots in distinct lines, and the opposite of a central eye of spots, namely a central clear zone on an otherwise spotted flower.

Evenness of colour and overlapping sepals seem to me desirable so I encourage these qualities, indeed I regard them as necessary qualities in a good hybrid. Perfectly round flowers do not do a lot for me but I welcome them when they occur. I also like what I call hooding, the colour change on the backs of the fully opened sepals marking an earlier position. Like everyone else I am still working towards genuine blues, but I am pleased to find myself not all that bothered about success in that and similar directions; distinctive species plants excite me more.

The next stage of hybrid development seems to me to be a critical one, for it could easily turn into the sea of vanities where camellias and roses float: a seemingly endless list of names, many representing barely distinguishable plants alongside increasingly bizarre 'novelties'. If we could all avoid believing that a plant suddenly becomes more desirable because someone has called it 'Ambrosian Dawn' it would help.

While I am certainly not promising never to name hybrids, my inclination is to describe basic categories using a numerical code for colour and spotting type with an alphabetical features list. In its present form the code uses twenty colours and twelve spotting types. I enjoy being able to write 10/6/DXP instead of 'large, pointed, pale pink flowers with heavy spotting merged together in the centre with a clear border, dark nectaries and exceptionally large leaves'!

HELLEBORES AT BLACKTHORN NURSERY

by Robin and Sue White

It is not easy to say what makes one like hellebores rather than dahlias. I tend to prefer simple flowers, although my enthusiasm for epimediums and daphnes does not really fit. Perhaps the time of the year they appear, braving an English spring, when one is hungry for things to get going in the garden, has a lot to do with it. If hellebores flowered in June they might not have the same appeal.

When my wife Sue and I started our own nursery in 1974, I was aware of hellebores' potential, as I had come across some comparatively good ones in the early 1960s at a nursery where I was training. Not knowing of Elizabeth and not being able to afford the prices of Helen Ballard, I found it very difficult to start building up a collection.

I feel very grateful to Peter Chappell of Spinners, who was generous with seed from his plants and who was the first person to retail our *H. × sternii* 'Blackthorn Strain' and *H. niger* 'Potter's Wheel Strain'.

SPECIES

At Blackthorn we try to grow as many wild species as we can obtain true, and the seed parents are isolated as much as possible to prevent crossing. Of the species available we feel our form of *H. odorus* from Corfu is a very worthwhile garden plant. It is often in flower before Christmas, producing fragrant acid green flowers on long stems. These look dreadful after frost but soon recover. The worst enemy is strong winds.

We have built up a small collection of forms of *H. torquatus* and by hand-crossing these together and adding blood from 'Pluto' have produced a range of small-flowered hybrids. We have also developed our 'Wolverton Hybrids', derived by inter-crossing 'Dido', 'Paul Voelcker' and 'Ruth Voelcker'; these are short and early-flowering with small double flowers in green, primrose or green flushed purple.

Our 'Westwood Hybrids' also involve *H. torquatus*, this time 'Dido' crossed with *H. orientalis* hybrids, resulting in plants with small, erect flowers in pinks and reds, with enlarged nectaries the colour of the petals.

Early January 1992 saw the first flowering of a new colour group of semi-double *H. torquatus* hybrids. So far they range in colour from very pale to deep pink, some with paler insides, and also purple-bronze. Some flower at 6–8in (15–20cm), a few at up to 12in (30cm), and the young foliage is often dark crimson. We have decided to call this group *H. torquatus* 'Party Dress Hybrids'.

A purple 'Wolverton Hybrid' differs from a purple 'Party Dress Hybrid' in having a pale green inner surface to its sepals and petals. 'Party Dress Hybrids' are the next generation on from the 'Westwood Hybrids', the latter having enlarged, coloured nectaries, but not fully petaloid.

HELLEBORUS NIGER AND ITS HYBRIDS

There is a lot of argument about 'Potter's Wheel'. Our plants are derived from a plant bought by Peter Chappell from Hilda Davenport-Jones, and that is the best pedigree you will find. We have recently acquired four divisions of another plant also bought from Miss Davenport-Jones and will be introducing these into our breeding programme. 'White Magic' has a curious history (see page 110), but we find its dark stems carry very large quantities of flowers. Plants of both these strains are produced from seed collected from isolated groups of parent plants.

Our 'Blackthorn Strain' is produced by using 'Louis Cobbett' as a seed parent, hand-pollinated by 'White Magic'. Although the colour varies slightly, it generally has pink buds opening almost white with a good green eye surrounding the anthers. As the flowers age they turn pink. Because of its mixed parentage, seedlings from 'Blackthorn Strain' are variable.

Plants resulting from crossing *H. niger* with *H. argutifolius* and *H. × sternii* generally display F1 hybrid vigour. While it is possible to reproduce these plants from division, it is hardly a commercial proposition and the resulting plants may take several years to settle down. Also, over a number of years a clone continually reproduced by division will decline in vigour. My aim has been to produce individual crosses, each one genetically unique, which will be free from disease and establish quickly when planted out. Although more than one person has claimed to have seed on their plants, I have never heard of any seedlings resulting and therefore assume that all crosses are infertile.

H. × nigercors plants show little variation with green leaves and flower stems, while the petals may be pure white, but are more often greenish-white, ageing green. Occasionally, a green band of colour runs down the centre of each white petal, giving a beautiful star effect.

The cross between *H. niger* and *H. × sternii*, which we will continue to call *H. × nigristern*, is a more variable plant but its stems are dark, its foliage shows the influence of *H. lividus* and the flowers age well, remaining extremely attractive until at least May or June. Flower arrangers go crazy over them.

I have produced a few plants from crossing *H.*

H. × ericsmithii

H. × nigercors

H. × ballardiae

H. niger 'Potter's Wheel'

H. niger
'White Magic'

Plants appear at 2/5 life size

H. niger
'Blackthorn Strain'

H. niger
'Louis Cobbett'

H. × sternii
'Blackthorn Strain'

niger and *H. lividus* and will continue to do so. There must be a query over hardiness, however, although it makes a lovely pot plant for a cool room or conservatory.

We have produced our own strain of *H. × sternii* since the early 1980s. Some forms of *H. × sternii* grow in excess of 3ft (90cm); they become top-heavy and flop over, particularly once the flowers develop. In general, these more vigorous plants have less colour in their stems and flowers, as they favour *H. argutifolius*. We have tried to make our 'Blackthorn Strain' shorter in habit with dark crimson stems, silver or marbled foliage and pink-flushed flowers. It is produced from an isolated group of stock plants. Unfortunately many people imagine the plant requires shade, which has the effect of drawing it up and reducing all coloration.

These plants will set seed and mostly produce worthwhile plants, but to keep the strain true to type, coarse vigorous plants should be removed.

From a commercial nurseryman's point of view, producing named forms from division is not attractive. Also, the customer can end up paying a lot of money for a poor-quality plant. It has therefore been my aim to produce a range of plain and spotted colours as two-year-old flowering plants from seed. Every year I get a few really good plants which I keep as seed stock in place of my worst stock plants, so I should, in theory, be improving the overall quality of plants produced.

As for the future, who knows? One thing I would like to do is breed the dark nectaries of 'Pluto' into the semi-doubles. I believe that once micropropagation has been perfected the two hardy *niger* crosses will be the most popular garden hellebores and that they will also be widely grown for commercial cut flower production.

MARGERY FISH AND HELLEBORES AT EAST LAMBROOK

Mrs Fish tells in forthright terms that her efforts to achieve as long a season as possible in her garden received no encouragement whatsoever from her husband Walter. Mr Fish wanted his brave show when the sun was shining and that was when he wished to enjoy his garden.

After his death in 1947 Mrs Fish rapidly embarked on her own plans for the planting of the garden at East Lambrook. Hellebores were already established in the small front garden and were quickly split and moved throughout the main garden areas. She purchased and was given

many of the very best forms available in the early 1950s. She had an early complaint about *H. orientalis* hybrids because they tended to produce 'shabby and scabby' foliage. The leaves got so untidy and marked, well before the flowers had finished, that she soon had no compunction about cutting them all off. Today most of the old leaves are cut off during the winter before flowering commences. The effect is well worthwhile and the plants do not seem to mind at all.

Flowers for the table were always important to Mrs Fish, and she found that the only way to succeed with the Lenten rose was to slit the stem up to the first leaves. They would then last for a long time indoors. If they looked dejected when first picked she would put them in hot water up to their necks. This did the trick!

Hellebores were an early success at East Lam-

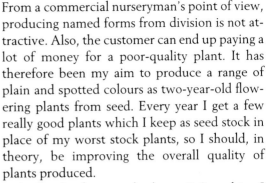

H. niger and its hybrids. Examples of the strains of *H. niger* and hybrids of *H. niger* with *H. argutifolius* and *H. × sternii* developed by Robin White of Blackthorn Nursery

brook because the heavy almost solid clay was just what the plants seemed to relish. So many other plants were lost early on because they just could not tolerate the wet clay during the long winter months. As the texture of the soil improved this became less of a problem. The Christmas rose, *H. niger*, never seemed to thrive naturally at Lambrook, perhaps because during the summer months the heavy clay dried out too much for it.

Mrs Fish, as always, persevered, and successfully grew a number of named forms, some in the troughs which surround the Malthouse on the east side and which can be kept watered and fed throughout the drier periods. There still remains what is believed to be *H. niger* 'Eva'. This is a most impressive plant, having a pure white flower all of 4½in (11cm) in diameter, but unlike 'Potter's Wheel' the ends of the petals are more pointed so do not produce the circle or wheel effect. Mrs Fish describes the plant as finer than 'Potter's Wheel' and the best form she knew. She obtained it from Harrogate. A split from the original plant taken in 1985 has flowered for the first time in 1992! *H.* 'Potter's Wheel' has disappeared from the garden, and a small piece of Mrs Fish's original plant given back to the garden has not survived either. A pink-flushed form known as 'Ladhams', after the late B. Ladhams, was regarded by Mrs Fish as a particularly good form but is now lost. Other forms of *H. niger* mentioned were subsp. *macranthus* var. *altifolius*, 'St Brigid', 'St Margaret', 'Maximus' and 'Dr Louis Cobbett'. There are slides of 'Potter's Wheel' and 'Dr Louis Cobbett' which are definitive. Where are all these plants today?

In Mrs Fish's 1965–6 plant list she offers *H. niger* 'Eva' for five shillings and 'Potter's Wheel' for four shillings! Regrettably there are no descriptions of the plants. In the same list there are a number of 'Named varieties' but with no descriptions. Of those mentioned the following are still in the garden: *abchasicus*, *abchasicus* 'Pale Form', 'Apple Blossom', *atrorubens*, 'Ballard's Black Hybrid', 'Greenland', *guttatus* 'Hybrid', *guttatus* 'Green', *guttatus* 'Pink', 'Picotee', 'Pink

Chintz', 'Dwarf Purple', 'White'.

Also mentioned are 'Aurora' and 'Gloria', but there seems to be no trace of either or of anyone who knows what they were. It is possible that 'Aurora' was a named plant from Eric Smith, who was often at Lambrook swapping plants with Mrs Fish. 'Black Knight' was also listed at the same price as an alpine strawberry, two shillings. The generosity of Mrs Fish and her wish to share as widely as possible her many plants resulted in the demise of many. Maybe 'Black Knight' also fell foul to the constant splitting that took place. It is interesting to note that *H. corsicus* syn. *H. argutifolius* was priced at three shillings and sixpence. Mrs Fish grew many of the species hellebores and she had a particular liking for the stinking hellebore, *H. foetidus*. A pleasant scented form of *H. foetidus* still seeds itself in the Green Garden. It is not certain whether this is in fact the form Mrs Fish refers to as 'E. A. Bowles'. *H. foetidus* matched her requirements for a freely seeding plant that was attractive when others were waiting to come to life and then, having flowered, provided a useful architectural effect, easily associating with other plants in the carefree style for which she attracted so many devotees. The Italian form of *H. viridis*, which is taller with lighter more apple-green flowers than the British native *H. viridis* subsp. *occidentalis*, still survives in the ditch. It has made a really good showy clump, much admired but seldom named correctly! *H. cyclophyllus* grew in the triangle bed at the back of the Malthouse together with a number of other 'specials'. There still remain a number of fascinating hellebores in this bed which have baffled the most knowledgeable. Other *Helleborus* species are also now growing there and the potential for interesting progeny is awaited.

Over the past fifty years since Walter and Margery Fish started the garden at Lambrook the hellebores have performed wonderfully well to produce offspring which continue to delight and surprise. Four years ago the first 'double' was noticed. In fact it is not a true double in that it has two rows of petals, much deformed, giving an appearance of a ruff. The petal colour is dull plum and is not very attractive. However, three years ago a much more interesting 'double' appeared. This plant produced a flower which was pale and very speckled and much more double. It was moved from where it had appeared as a seedling so that an over-avaricious visitor was not tempted to give it a better home! Its new home in the garden so far has not enticed it to flower again. All those who know where it grows are patiently keeping a watchful eye on progress.

During the restoration of the garden over the past seven years a number of hellebores were found to have labels embedded in them with the unmistakable writing of Mrs Fish. There is a good clump of a clear white-flowered plant named 'White Ladies'. It is a very apt name, as the plant is at the end of a row of various hellebores and the flowers are all of the same size and height, so giving the impression of a group of ladies all talking to each other as they nod their heads, caught by the slightest breeze that disturbs them. The original plant of 'Prince Rupert' has misbehaved with its neighbours and produced an invasion of overcrowded offspring. The Prince itself is a magnificent form *H. guttatus*, with many of the flowers producing six petals. The speckled marking is the most intense of any *guttatus* form in the garden. Some of the offspring have the pink flush which Mrs Fish named as *guttatus* 'Pink', but none have the size of flower of the Prince himself. One of the problems with the overzealous promiscuity of the *orientalis* forms is that the original plant is often overwhelmed by the offspring, so that it is not always easy to decide which was the original plant. A most attractive clump named 'Princess Margaret' was found on the bank on the eastern side of the ditch. The flowers stand out from all their neighbours as they are the palest pink against the apple green of the new leaves. The inside of the flower has a centre of suffused green turning to pale pink and then darker pink on the petal edges. The inside face of the petal has a random smattering of a few intense *guttatus* markings. The plant clearly appealed to Mrs Fish, though there is no record as to from whom she obtained it. Maybe she named it herself as a selected seedling. Anyway, it survives and certainly deserves a name and a place in the garden.

'Picotee' describes a plant which has survived well in the garden. It is a small-flowered plant but has many flowering heads when mature. The edges of the petals are marked continuously with a plum colour which is both attractive and distinctive. The petal shape is similar to *H. torquatus* but has none of the blue colouring of some forms of the species. The colour is mainly pale plum, lightened considerably against an off-white background. The flowering stems are erect, holding the flowers well above the foliage. The coloured edging of the petals and their shape is passed on to many of the seedlings which appear nearby.

Mrs Fish introduced a delightful hellebore which she named 'Greenland', described in her book *A Flower for Every Day* as a very good greeny-cream form of *H. orientalis*. It was widely distributed as seedlings, carefully collected from the parent which was kept in confinement to avoid possible misbehaviour, but even so it was variable. Mrs Fish mentions having *H. olympicus* (*H. orientalis* subsp. *orientalis*) in the garden, and it is quite possible that 'Greenland' was a selected seedling of the species. There are also surviving in the Green Garden two forms of what Mrs Fish called her 'Primrose' hellebore. These are not as yellow as those currently selected, but are good. One has a dark ring of carpels and the other light green.

A new area of hellebore planting which has been most successful both for the plants and for the effect is at the foot of a length of beech hedge which runs alongside the path through the orchard. The plants have done particularly well on the eastern side of the hedge. Seedlings abound in the path if not devoured by woodlice and mice. Many of the plants are either named varieties or those found in neglected parts of the garden, and are therefore possibly some which Mrs Fish cherished. They certainly add to the pleasure given by the hellebores from Christmas to mid April, and then provide wonderfully varied foliage and ground cover throughout the re-

mainder of the year. A recent over-indulgence with manure created amazing foliage but a most disappointing show of bloom. The lesson learnt: an autumn feed of bone meal with a late spring mulch of well-rotted compost and muck seems to provide all that is required for vigorous flowering plants. Splitting at any time, even when in full bloom, seems quite in order. One of the advantages of splitting while in bloom is that the best association of colours can be more easily created. The best effects are achieved by careful grouping. Some of the very dark colours can be lost completely and never noticed – they need to be given a position where they are on their own, to be admired as individual plants. The massed planting of all the other colours is much easier to manage. One of the most satisfactory ways of admiring a hellebore is to be at or below the level of the bloom. By planting hellebores at eye level along the ditch Mrs Fish was able to work and walk in the ditch and observe the blooms very closely, and the same close scrutiny is also fully deserved by the fascinating collection of snowdrops which grow along the ditch banks among the hellebores.

It is hard to imagine the garden at Lambrook without hellebores. If the season is kind, there can be nothing so full of promise for a new year as the varied plantings of hellebores of every colour and form among the snowdrops. Clumps of pulmonaria just coming into bloom in early February and the occasional surprise of a clump of yellow aconite give the whole garden a warm and colourful feel. The more vivid colours of daffodils and other bulbs which usually herald spring too easily take the eye away from the more subtle hellebores. There can be little doubt that the hellebores at Lambrook will continue to thrive and produce offspring which will delight all those who visit and work there.

A delightful glade of hellebores, snowdrops and ferns at East Lambrook Manor in Somerset

12

THE NATIONAL COLLECTIONS

In 1978 the National Council for the Conservation of Plants and Gardens (NCCPG) was set up to co-ordinate the conservation of Britain's garden heritage. At that time there was growing concern that large numbers of good plants, still popular among gardeners, were no longer available through nurseries.

One of the measures taken by the NCCPG was to set up National Collections of plants from specific genera. The aim was to conserve stocks of threatened garden plants, to make it possible for enthusiastic gardeners to obtain a wider range of plants and to stimulate botanical, horticultural and historical studies of the plants involved. The main duties of a collection holder are to build up a diverse and representative collection, to maintain the plants in a good state of health, to propagate them where possible to ensure that the death of an individual plant does not mean the extinction of that cultivar, and to provide reasonable access for interested members of the public who may wish to see the collection.

Two National Collections of hellebores have now been established. One is in the care of the Hampshire Group of the NCCPG and the other at Hadlow College of Agriculture and Horticulture near Tonbridge in Kent.

THE NATIONAL COLLECTION IN HAMPSHIRE

by Jeremy Wood

It has been argued by some that a National Collection should be confined to cultivars and hybrids, and that the naturally occurring species are best grown in a botanic garden. Among those responsible for the hellebore collection a different view prevails, as many as possible of the species being included along with cultivars and hybrids. Quite apart from the fact that many of the species are fine garden plants in their own right (*H. argutifolius* and *H. niger* being obvious examples), it is felt that a display of cultivars would be incomplete without at the same time being able to compare them with the wild forms from which they are ultimately descended. Approximately half the collection falls into the category of *H. orientalis* hybrids in a wide range of forms and colours. Alongside these are examples of *H. orientalis* from wild-collected seed to demonstrate what that part of their ancestry was like, of *H. cyclophyllus* and *H. odorus* which have been used to impart yellow shades, and a plant of *H. torquatus*, the species from which the dark purple colour of numerous cultivars has been derived. Seedlings of *H. torquatus* from different origins have been planted in the hope that the flowers will display a wide range of colours, as do the wild forms of this species.

Another reason for including wild species of

hellebore in the collection is to provide a source from which further breeding can be carried out. In his recent book, Brian Mathew mentions various primary hybrids which are not available from commercial sources. Some of these were produced over a century ago and described by Schiffner. For historical reasons it is of interest to reproduce these hybrids, and a limited effort is going on in this direction. Certain crosses have never been successfully achieved, but may none the less still be possible. For instance, *H. niger* is said not to hybridise with species other than *H. argutifolius* and *H. lividus*, but in the Hampshire Group attempts to pollinate *H. niger* with other species such as *H. cyclophyllus* and *H. torquatus* appear to have been successful even though the progeny, to date, have little to recommend them. Of more horticultural interest are hybrids between *H. niger* and *H. lividus*, and it is possible to exploit the variation in both these species by selecting particular forms with which to make the cross. Work in this direction is continuing, and already several different forms of the hybrid have been produced.

The commercially available hybrids *H. × sternii* (*H. argutifolius × H. lividus*), *H. × nigercors* (*H. niger × H. argutifolius*) and *H. × ericsmithii* (*H. niger × H. sternii*) are important features of the collection, as they form such a striking contrast with the *H. orientalis* hybrids. In all three the leaves are just as important as the flowers, and in the case of *H. × sternii* several different forms are grown, including 'Boughton Beauty' and 'Blackthorn Strain'. Various named cultivars have been developed from *H. niger* itself, those in the collection including 'Major', 'Potter's Wheel Strain', 'Louis Cobbett', 'White Magic', and the cross between the last two known as *H. niger* 'Blackthorn Strain'. Another species from which named cultivars have been developed is *H. foetidus*, and the attractive form 'Wester Flisk' is found to come true from seed provided it is prevented from crossing with other forms of the species.

Turning to the large category of hybrids that do not have *H. niger* in their parentage, and have mostly been derived by crossing *H. orientalis* with other species, or by selecting particular forms within the species, some of Eric Smith's hellebores were among the first to be acquired for the collection and more of his hybrids have been added over the years. Those with spotted or speckled flowers, derived from *H. orientalis* subsp. *guttatus*, are always much admired by visitors. Examples are 'Capricornus', 'Cosmos', 'Galaxy Strain', 'Libra' and 'Zodiac Strain', some of which were donated by Jim Archibald, Eric Smith's partner for many years. Another fine hellebore of this type came to light recently at Hadspen, the garden to which Eric Smith moved when the partnership came to an end.

As far as is known he never named this hellebore, but it is certainly one that he bred; a division of it was kindly donated by Nori Pope, who currently looks after the garden. Among unspeckled hybrids bred by Eric Smith must be mentioned 'Sirius' and 'Pluto'. The former is a clear, pale yellow; the latter, produced by crossing one of the *H. orientalis* selections with *H. torquatus*, has flowers that are deep purple outside and mauve-green inside, making it a very choice cultivar.

Helen Ballard has been a prolific breeder of hellebores, particularly over the last decade. Among the cultivars in the collection that have formed fine, vigorous plants are 'Citron', 'Garnet', 'Nocturne', 'Rossini' and 'Ushba'. All have large, outward-facing flowers, features that Helen Ballard has been deliberately aiming for. But in addition to some of her named cultivars the collection has been gradually accumulating a range of unnamed yellow, pink, red and dark purple hybrids as a result of annual visits to the nursery.

Comparatively few of Elizabeth Strangman's cultivars have been given names, and among these the collection holds 'Alberich', 'Pamina', 'Queen of the Night' and 'Violetta'. But many of her unnamed cultivars have been acquired, mostly in shades of green, yellow, pink and dark purple.

The products of these three breeders, Eric Smith, Helen Ballard and Elizabeth Strangman, each have certain characters which distinguish

140

them from the other two, so in a sense they complement one another. However, one feature that they all tend to have in common is flowers with rounded, overlapping sepals. There is no doubt that this gives the modern hybrids a very special elegance, and breeders are likely to continue in that direction. But in a collection there is room for occasional plants that go against the general trend, and one hellebore in particular has such long, narrow sepals that its flowers are reminiscent of a clematis. Opinions as to its merits vary from the unprintable to the ecstatic, and in order to satisfy the latter, steps are being taken to raise some of its seedlings.

The older cultivars are not, as yet, well represented in the collection as they are difficult to track down. In some cases a plant acquired under a certain name has proved to be so different from the original description that it has clearly not been propagated by division, and so

the name is invalid. Old hellebores in the collection that appear to be authentic include 'Brünhilde' (cream), 'Queen of the North' (speckled white) and 'White Swan' (plain white). The late Margery Fish was, among other things, a collector of hellebores, and the present owner of East Lambrook Manor has kindly donated divisions from a number of her surviving plants, among which are 'Dimity' (mauve), 'Greenland' (white with a green stripe) and 'White Ladies' (white with faint speckling).

Seedlings from some of the better cultivars mentioned in previous sections have themselves proved to be good hellebores, different from any of the others and worthy of a place in the collection. One such has large flowers with broad sepals, initially white flushed pink with faint spotting in the throat, losing the pink flush on ageing. It has been named 'Pearl'. Others from an unnamed red cultivar show equal promise.

THE NATIONAL COLLECTION AT HADLOW COLLEGE, KENT

by Kemal Mehdi

The genus *Helleborus* has always been well represented in the College's plant collections, and its value in many garden and landscape situations has ensured its place in teaching programmes. Over the past few years there have been significant developments in amenity horticulture within the college, and the hellebore collection has been an area of increasing activity.

Staff were already keen on the genus, and aware of rising public interest in hardy herbaceous plants. Support and encouragement for more work in this direction has come from the strong and active local groups of both the Hardy Plant Society and the NCCPG, and the collection has now been accepted as a National Collection by the NCCPG to complement the existing collection in Hampshire.

The hellebores at Hadlow College are used for

a number of teaching purposes. The most obvious relates to their use in the garden and concentrates on *H. niger*, *H. argutifolius* and the Orientalis Hybrids. These are covered in terms of not only their characteristics and requirements but also their uses in planting schemes, with the emphasis on their value for ground cover and for their long season of early interest and display.

Ensuring that students have a sound knowledge of the more common plants likely to be encountered in their future careers is important.

Named cultivars from the Hampshire National Collection. This selection includes cultivars raised by Jim Archibald, Eric Smith, Margery Fish and main collection holder Jeremy Wood. Flowers provided from Jeremy's collection

'Miranda'

'Sirius'

'Pluto'

'Capricornus'

'Orion'

'Aquarius'

'Lilac Picotee'

'Jebb's White'

'Cosmos'

'Queen of the North'

'Pearl'

'Greenland'

Plants appear at ³/₅ life size

However, where the plants are concerned it is not our only aim. Equally important is that a student should develop his or her own interests, be they alpines, bulbs, shrubs or the more narrow field of a specific genus. We encourage them to recognise that a life in horticulture offers more than a simple career progression and that the plants themselves can be a source of immense pleasure and satisfaction.

The less common species and hybrids have a role to play in making up the overall range and depth of the college's plant collections, and as far as possible staff encourage students to look beyond the taught syllabus work.

Hellebores also lead themselves to the teaching of botany. The large open flowers of *H. orientalis* are a good example for teaching floral parts and structure, and they are produced in such profusion that material is always readily available in spring in sufficient quantities for the largest classes.

They are also valuable in teaching the basics of taxonomy, and using the key from the *European Garden Flora* it is relatively easy to key out the different species. In the process students not only learn how to use a key, but gain an appreciation of the relative importance of the various characteristics in plant naming and identification. In hellebores, the first step is to highlight the different growth habits of those with leafy stems and those whose leaves arise only at the base.

Genetics is not a large subject in most of our programmes, third-year Diploma students going a little beyond Mendel. As a practical exercise they determine the main characteristics of pollen and seed parents, and then examine seedlings arising from the cross. This work prompts them to consider the features of the plant, how to describe them, and involves use of the RHS colour charts. Where widely differing parents are used the resultant seedlings are very variable, but where similar line-bred parents of Washfield stock are used we have obtained surprisingly uniform results, and the exercise usefully illustrates this point.

The results of this work are cumulative, and although unlikely to advance the science of genetics, may eventually yield useful pointers for our own pursuit of relatively true breeding lines. The biggest drawback is of course the three-year lag between trying a pollination and seeing the results.

The nearness of Washfield Nursery has done much to stimulate work at Hadlow, and without advice and support from Elizabeth Strangman we would have wasted a great deal of time. It was here that we first really decided to try some hand-pollination work, as we appreciated the rewards involved in dabbling with a few crosses.

Even to think in terms of 'dabbling with a few crosses' was an early misconception. The first year of hand-pollinating was a haphazard affair; we tried a little of everything, and it was apparent that clearer goals and more focused work were needed to achieve results. Visits to Washfield and discussing the problem with Elizabeth led us to decide that we should concentrate our work on the spotted flower forms of the Orientalis Hybrids. In recent years the search for good black- and yellow-flowered forms has been successful, but there has been little new among the spotted types, except perhaps among the green-, yellow- and black-flowered forms. And although there are plants around with superbly spotted flowers, many show irregular spotting. The paler-flowered forms may also tend to a weaker constitution.

The overall aim, then, is first to produce good examples of spotted flowers across the whole range of colour forms and in the full variety of spotting patterns. These plants will then need further work to develop them into reliable strains which regularly produce high percentages of uniform seedlings.

The interior of the hellebore's cup-shaped flower offers only part of their charm, and although useful in determining the general direction of work, by no means settles the question. Given the way that the flowers nod at the ends of their stems, perhaps it is of greater importance to consider coloration on the outside of the flowers. Although we have not yet set clear goals, outer petal colour is taken into account when assessing the results of crosses.

The whole business of how the flowers are held can be the cause of heated debate. 'How much more convenient if the pedicel were shorter, and the flowers looked up at us? No more need to bend and turn each flower upwards!' The riposte is swift, and often along the lines of 'lost mystery', developing the themes of 'magical moments' and 'building excitement' when turning the flowers of new plants in seedling rows to view their hidden faces.

Then there is the matter of elegance and poise, words we naturally associate with the flowering of hellebores. It is certainly true that much of the attractiveness of the plant comes from its flowering habit, and equally true that examining the first flowers of seedling plants is an exciting experience. So perhaps a strain of plants with upturned flowers is not such a good idea.

But it is not a matter of either nodding or upturned flowers; what is wrong with having plants with upturned flowers in addition to those with nodding flowers? In fact, we have seen red/maroon-flowered plants with this habit, but know of no one working on them, and have no plans to go in this direction ourselves.

Flower size and shape are closely tied in to the garden value of the plant when in flower. Those with larger, heavily pendulous flowers have the most scope for rich spotting patterns and suit the compulsive turner. Most of our work is on these types.

The opposite of these plants are those with flowers of a lighter substance. These are often direct or closely related hybrids with *H. torquatus*. Plants like 'Pluto', 'Patchwork' and 'Little Black' have great presence when sympathetically placed in the front of a bed or border. They rely on their poise and dainty habit and have no need for richly coloured and spotted interiors. In the interests of focusing our work, we have reluctantly decided not to work on species hybrids; life presents some hard choices.

Flowering season is another area of interest we have added to our aims. Most of the Orientalis Hybrids are tantalisingly slow to get into their full flowering state. This is partly because they quite naturally stand still during the cold frosty weather that is usual early in the year. It is equally a perception borne of impatience on the part of the over-eager enthusiast. Nevertheless, there are plants which regularly have their normal flowering season around Christmas, and we are at present trying to select suitable parent plants.

The need to retain plant health and vigour is of obvious importance. Hybrids are usually more vigorous than their parents, and this has proved to be the case. But we have noticed that many of the spotted forms and some of the lighter pinks can suffer from a blackening and rotting of the flowers and bracts. Perhaps this is the underlying cause of our suspicions that the paler-flowered forms may have a weaker constitution than darker-flowered plants. The problem is at its worst early in the season, when the flowers are still in the fully closed bud stage. Needless to say, the damage follows through and disfigures the plant when in full flower. Of course one can administer regular applications of fungicides, and this unpleasant chore is a necessary evil on specialist nurseries, and with collections. It may not be a necessity for many gardeners, who have fewer plants, and would not normally have to bother with brewing up protective potions.

One solution would be to choose seedlings from dark-flowered forms like 'Queen of the Night Strain' which have none of these problems; but who enjoys self-denial? I want both. We have made no progress to date, but continue to discard plants regularly which are not A1 fit.

Foliage quality is also accorded great importance, although we do not reject plants which have only average foliage effect. Leaf size and shape vary greatly, and the same is true of texture. Some plants have a truly massive umbrella of leaf, and many of the best have a very polished shine to the leaf surface. At present our selection criteria are directed at the obvious, interest being centred on emphasising the architectural qualities of the plant.

The collection at Hadlow is very strong in its

range and in numbers of Orientalis Hybrid seedlings, few of which will receive names. Numbers of named cultivars from the past are increasing and will continue to do so as stock becomes available. These plants are at present mainly those of three breeders – Eric Smith, Helen Ballard and Elizabeth Strangman. Older cultivars are harder to track down and there has been little progress to date.

Species are perhaps one of the most interesting aspects of the collection. As well as having great charm, they have the added attraction of a diversity of forms. The species collection is increasing and in many cases we know the geographical area in which the plant was collected; few, however, have collector's numbers.

The bulk of the collection is at present kept in a very private area of the College grounds where access is restricted. As these plants grow to a suitable size they will be split and a second plant will go into the teaching areas. The College is not open to the general public on a daily basis, but it is likely that in the future, when there are sufficient duplicate plants out in the grounds, the College may run a Collection Open Day. At the time of writing other ideas that would result in wider access to viewing these and other plants are under discussion.

In summary, the hellebores at Hadlow stimulate a lot of interest in the collection both within the College and from visitors. Work on the collection is viewed as a long-term project, from which rise some useful spin-offs for teaching programmes. Perhaps the most exciting aspect is the large numbers of good plants which are becoming available for general garden and landscape plantings in the College grounds.

Seedlings from the Hadlow National Collection. This selection of mainly spotted seedlings raised at Hadlow College shows the range that is possible within this group

13

HELLEBORES IN AMERICA

We are conscious of the fact that parts of this book may seem parochial to our American readers, but in order to tell the story of these plants we have had to discuss the ideas and the plants of many British gardeners and botanists. We also realise that many British gardening books published in the United States pay but little heed to the American experience, or in doing so, dilute their comment to the extent that it is of little use on either side of the Atlantic.

In order to cover the American scene more specifically we therefore decided to devote a chapter entirely to hellebore-growing in the States; but at once we were faced with a problem – neither of us has even been there, let alone grown hellebores there! So this chapter is compiled with the help of a number of experienced hellebore-growers to whom we are most grateful for their generosity in sharing their experiences with us.

Like so many plants grown widely in Britain, hellebores seem particularly at home in the Pacific north-west, and it is in this area that the widest range is grown, although there are also good growers and good collections in the northeast.

Few wild species have yet become widely grown in the States, although there seems no reason why they should not be successful. Among the hybrids few British clones are grown, and although Henry A. Ross of Gardenview Horticultural Park in Strongsville, Ohio, has named a number of cultivars, these have not yet become widely distributed.

NAMES

In a way, it is a relief to discover that the misapprehensions of American gardeners are no different from those of the British when it comes to hellebore names. Neither in Britain nor the States are gardeners as keen as they might be to bring order to the nomenclature of garden plants. However, perhaps American gardeners have more reason to be less than up to date, as most of the horticultural and botanical research on this group has been done in the UK and other parts of Europe.

So first, to clear up a few misconceptions, *H. argutifolius* is still often known, incorrectly, as *H. corsicus* or *H. lividus corsicus*; *H. × baueri* is an invalid name for *H. × sternii*. The plant grown as *H. atrorubens* never seems to be the wild species of this name but, as in Britain, a form of *H. orientalis* subsp. *abchasicus*.

The term Orientalis Hybrids is used less often than *H. × hybridus*, but we disagree with the view of Henry Ross that the botanical concept of *H. orientalis* should be broken down and the many forms given individual status as species. The three subspecies *(orientalis, abchasicus and guttatus)* seem to us to cover the three main botanical groups, while the botanical name *H. × hybridus* and the more colloquial phrase Orientalis Hybrids covers hybrids between these subspecies and other species such as *H. odorus, H. cyclophyllus, H. viridis* and *H. torquatus*.

Forms of *H. orientalis* such as var. *albus* and var. *atropurpureus* are used more often in the States than in the UK, but have no botanical status and serve only to confuse. *H. multifidus* var. *viridis* does not exist, and the plant referred to is probably subsp. *bocconei*. 'Ballard's Black' and 'Pluto' are sometimes said to be derived from *H. purpurascens*, whereas *H. torquatus* is the plant involved. *H. × intermedius* usually refers to *H. torquatus*, which is a species in its own right and not a form or synonym of *H. purpurascens* as is sometimes quoted. The name 'Brian Mathew' has appeared in ARGS seed lists but Brian assures us there is no such plant.

The mistaken idea that *H. niger* 'White Magic' is a hybrid between *H. niger* and *H. orientalis* originated in New Zealand and is discussed on page 110; 'White Magic' is simply a selected seed strain.

HELLEBORE BREEDING

Henry Ross is one of the few people in the States to have done any serious selection work, and he has named thirteen cultivars; these have not yet been released, as vegetative propagation is such a slow process. His cultivars are: 'Banana Split', 'Bridesmaid', 'Debutante', 'Dowager', 'First Kiss', 'Gremlin', 'Lime Ice', 'Mardi Gras', 'Mars', 'Purity', 'Ruby', 'Sorcerer' and 'Southern Belle'. More details will be found in the descriptive section beginning on page 84.

Unfortunately the name 'Mars' was applied to a quite different plant in 1973 so is not valid.

Until his death in 1990, Kevin Nicolay of Seattle, Washington, worked on developing large black-flowered forms and also big buttery yellows. He used a wide range of material originating with Elizabeth, Helen Ballard, Eric Smith and various other sources. His plants are now being evaluated by a number of Washington State gardeners such as Peter Ray of Puget Garden Resources, Vashon Island, and also Glenn Withey and Charles Price who have Kevin's original plants. As an example, Ann Lovejoy of Bainbridge Island grows a lovely plant with big cupped bells almost 4in (10cm) across, with a lovely substance, in midnight purple brushed black outside and the same inside with a matt bloom. Kevin also worked on hyb-

ridising *H. foetidus*, crossing 'Miss Jekyll' with 'Wester Flisk'.

Don Jacobs of Eco Gardens, Decatur, Georgia, is building stocks of plants which are true to colour by dividing established clumps of his best colour forms and adding his best seedlings. His colours range through yellow, various pinks and white (spotted and unspotted) and with a variety of flower forms from rounded and cup-shaped to more undulate. He is also selecting a few especially good forms for naming, and has so far named 'Eco Bullseye', 'Eco Golden Eye' and the unique purple-leaved 'Eco Autumn Purple'.

We have also come across the 'Millet Hybrids' which are available from Lamb Nurseries in Spokane, Washington, and the 'Slate Hybrids' developed by George Slate of Cornell University, seed of which has been distributed through the ARGS seed exchange for over twenty years, most recently by Nina Lambert of Ithaca, New York. John Elsley of Wayside Gardens is building up stocks of some good forms.

HELLEBORUS × HYBRIDUS

This is the most widely grown group of hellebores, not only in the Pacific north-west but also in the south-east, mid-west, mid-Atlantic and New England regions. They seem able to withstand a good variety of climatic conditions.

In general, few named forms are available, although some nurseries sort seedlings to colour; many smaller nurseries pot up and sell seedlings which have germinated under mature stock plants, but these will give unpredictable results. Although most colours are to be found in gardens, pure colours are rare, with deep reds and yellows especially scarce. Divisions of especially good plants are occasionally available but command high prices. Sam Jones of Piccadilly Farm, near Bishop, Georgia, produces around 50,000 plants a year of *H. × hybridus* in a wide variety of colours from a quarter of an acre of stock plants, though only a few hundred larger plants for callers are colour-sorted.

There seems a greater appreciation of the foliage of all hellebores in the States than in

Britain. In particular, gardeners in the Pacific north-west are always looking for good foliage plants that will provide ground cover and contrasting leaf shapes around the ubiquitous rhododendrons and will grow in the woodland edge conditions and look natural. All hellebores fit the bill perfectly.

An exciting development in foliage hellebores has been the selection of 'Eco Autumn Purple' by Don Jacobs of Eco Gardens. This is a unique plant whose leaves develop strong purple-red colouring in winter.

In the Pacific north-west, shade is necessary in most areas. The cool wet springs would be expected to foster plenty of black spot but its occurrence seems rather patchy. In Evie Douglas's garden in Snohomish, Washington, her plants thrive and flower well in three-quarters shade and she has no problem with black spot. Flowering lasts from about March to May, often sparked off by a sudden warm spell in February. In some gardens self-sown seedlings are so prolific that they are weeded out in handfuls.

Summers can be dry in this area, with the majority of the rain falling in winter and spring, and fungus is a real problem for some Seattle gardeners. Ann Lovejoy reports that in her cool climate hellebore seed sometimes rots before ripening. She mulches very thoroughly to conserve summer moisture, using compost or manure then shredded bark or chopped straw over everything to keep down weeds. Janette Waltemath of Portland, Oregon, reports the need to water once a week in hot, dry weather. Botrytis is troublesome for her, and she alleviates the problem with a dusting of fungicide in early winter.

On the east coast *H.* × *hybridus* is probably the easiest hellebore to grow, but here too summer shade is generally necessary. Wayne Winterrowd of Readsboro, Vermont (zone 4 with a winter minimum of $-20°F$), grows them in the more sheltered parts of the garden and gives winter protection with conifer branches. He also grows them in pots along with *H. niger* and *H. foetidus*. Caroline Burgess, of Stonecrop at Cold Spring, New York (zone 5b), reports that her

plants have proven tough enough to survive winter temperatures, usually about $-5°F$ to $-10°F$ and occasionally lower, without a protective cover now that the garden is becoming well sheltered. The foliage is best removed completely at the end of winter, as it is usually badly battered. Mulching to conserve water is advisable, and in prolonged dry spells the plants will need a thorough watering to keep them growing well, especially if in severe competition with tree roots. Black spot seems to be only a minor problem on *H.* × *hybridus* – slugs seem to cause more damage.

Nina Lambert reports that in spite of winter temperatures sometimes as cold as $-30°F$, varmints are the worst problem. In winters of deep snow the mice bed in the clumps, chewing nests in the centre; mothballs are used as a deterrent. On top of that, she says that hellebores are 'like candy to the deer', so she suspends hotel-size bars of Cashmere Bouquet soap from $2\frac{1}{2}$ft (45cm) high stakes to keep them away! As she says: 'By spring we have white balls on the ground, and white rectangles above, and inquiries about our 'interesting garden labels' from confused neighbours, joggers and passing motorists,' Slugs, she also reports, seem to demolish entire crops of self-sown seedlings overnight.

Flowering is usually March to May, depending on the season, although the plant known as "*atrorubens*" has been known to flower in January in northern Connecticut (zone 5/6), where the mean temperature for that month is $-9°F$. Judy Glattstein of Wilton, Connecticut (zone 6), grows her plants shaded by white oaks on sandy soil with lots of compost. They are watered in hot spells, given a feed in spring, and mulched with shredded oak leaves in early summer to keep them cool and conserve moisture.

Further south, in Virginia (zone 8), Pamela Harper of Seaford reports that these plants are among the top ten perennials, thriving in the hot humid summers, with only January a genuinely dormant season. The only problem appears to be that they self-sow so abundantly that they almost become weeds. Here they prefer either high, thick shade or beds facing north or east with no afternoon sun.

In California *H.* × *hybridus* also seems to do quite well, although *H. argutifolius* is reckoned the best hellebore for the south west.

HELLEBORUS NIGER

This seems an altogether more unpredictable plant, as it is in Britain, and less easy to please than *H.* × *hybridus*, although it grows well for Noble Bashor in Salem, Oregon. It is available from a few nurseries, though generally the quality seems rather variable and a number of gardeners report on the low survival rate following division of plants. 'White Magic' is listed by Klehm Nursery of South Barrington, Illinois.

'Potter's Wheel' is grown, although it is doubtful if it compares with the original strain, while Charles O. Cresson of Hedgleigh Spring in Swarthmore, Pennsylvania, has plants showing a tendency to doubling, with shorter petals developing from the nectaries. These sound rather like 'Pixie' (page 56).

In the Pacific north-west *H. niger* does not thrive on the lighter soils, and seems to need more sun than *H.* × *hybridus*. The winters can hit the flowers hard as they open in January and February; perhaps the general mildness leaves them susceptible to cold snaps. It generally self-sows much less enthusiastically than *H.* × *hybridus*, and the slugs love it.

In Charles Cresson's garden it thrives in acid conditions, is long-lived, and self-sows more freely than in many other gardens. Sprays of benomyl prevent black spot, but this seems altogether a fussier plant and less tolerant of drought than *H.* × *hybridus*.

On the east coast *H. niger* is the hardiest hellebore of all and grows well even in zone 3. Where the winter temperature drops below 10°F all the foliage can be lost, and even in less severe conditions it may be so damaged as to demand its removal.

Further south, in Virginia, *H. niger* is slow and there are suggestions that it may be improved with Epsom salts. It dislikes the hot summers

and needs more careful placing and a richer soil than other species.

To the west, at Decatur, Georgia, Don Jacobs finds it does well and that it appreciates an occasional top dressing of crushed dolomite. Allan M. Armitage of the University of Georgia, at Athens, also recommends the use of lime, although Sam Jones of Piccadilly Farm not far away at Bishop says gardeners should not be encouraged to plant it in his area as it does not thrive!

In California, especially in the south, *H. niger* is poor; the absence of a real winter and the hot summers just do not suit it.

HELLEBORUS ARGUTIFOLIUS,
H. LIVIDUS and H. × STERNII

The plants in this group are altogether less hardy and less often grown. *H. argutifolius* is the most widely grown, but in colder zones it often behaves as a herbaceous perennial. The overwintering flowering stem is killed by frost, but the rootstock happily sends up fresh stems in spring; the plant is much appreciated as a foliage plant. Naturally, *H. lividus* is much less hardy and much less widely grown, but its possibilities as a greenhouse or conservatory plant seem to have been overlooked; however, Judy Glattstein of Wilton, Connecticut, grows *H.* × *sternii* successfully as an alpine house plant. Although a number of people grow *H.* × *sternii*, some of the forms seen are disappointingly close to *H. argutifolius*.

Charles Cresson has been experimenting with hardier strains of *H. argutifolius*, and one from Montrose Nursery seems especially tough. It seems this is a line that could usefully be developed; perhaps selections could also be made of hardy but well-coloured forms of *H.* × *sternii*.

On the west coast *H. argutifolius* thrives best in full shade; the edges of the leaves are crisped in full sun, and as a result plants grow to over 3ft (90cm) and need staking. Even here, overwintering flowering shoots may be killed if the temperature drops below 10°F. Flowering is in February and March and the plants self-sow enthusiastically. *H. lividus* is not often grown, while *H.* × *sternii* does well in partial shade.

While the flowering shoots of *H. argutifolius* may be killed in the east, and the plants even killed outright in zones 4 and 5, local shelter from buildings and an overhead tree canopy can provide sufficient protection to carry them through. Improved hardy forms would be a great boon – the tender form from Siskiyou Rare Plant Nursery was killed outright even in a mild winter in zone 6/7. This plant is sometimes grown in the protection of a greenhouse in colder zones, either in the greenhouse border or in large pots. Staking is again necessary, otherwise the stems collapse.

In San Francisco *H. argutifolius* is drought-tolerant once established and is generally reckoned the best hellebore for that part of the world, but *H.* × *sternii* and *H. lividus* should do well and it might be worth trying *H.* × *ballardiae* and *H.* × *ericsmithii* if plants were available.

HELLEBORUS FOETIDUS

This is a widely grown and well-liked plant, second only to *H.* × *hybridus* in popularity, and red-stemmed forms deriving from 'Wester Flisk' are especially sought after. Like *H. argutifolius*, plants are often short-lived; in areas with warm summer temperatures and high humidity this is a particular problem. Their first and second year's flowering can be their most effective, although they usually leave behind sufficient seedlings to act as replacements. Again, they are much appreciated as foliage plants.

Once the temperature in the west drops to 10°F the plants really suffer, and Evie Douglas feels they would thrive best in full sun and a heavy soil. Blooming starts in January.

In the east, snow cover is vital to protect the plants in the depths of winter. Wayne Winterrowd of Readsboro, Vermont, covers his plants with peach baskets in snowless seasons otherwise ice forms on the branches and breaks the stems.

OTHER SPECIES

Few other species are grown yet, although *H. viridis* and one or two of Elizabeth's Montenegran doubles are to be found. Some gardeners are raising species plants from Jim Archibald's recent seed collections in Yugoslavia and Turkey. Lawrence J. Johnson of Middlebury, Indiana, writing in *The Garden*, reported that *H. cyclophyllus* had endured a series of savage winters yet never failed to flower. He also mentioned that a visitor to the public garden in his care was so taken with the first plant of *H. foetidus* to flower there that they stole it!

ACKNOWLEDGEMENTS

We would like to thank the following enthusiasts, without whom this chapter would not have been possible: Allan M. Armitage, Noble Bashor, Ann Bucher, Caroline Burgess, Elaine Baxter Cantwell, Charles O. Cresson, Evie Douglas, Judy Glattstein, Pamela Harper, Dan Heims, Don Jacobs, Sam Jones, Nina Lambert, Ann Lovejoy, Henry A. Ross, Marco Stefano, Joanne Walkovic, Janette Waltemath, Wayne Winterrowd, and in particular Sue Buckles.

14

HELLEBORES IN AUSTRALIA

by Trevor Nottle

The first arrival of hellebores in Australia is, as far as my researches go, unrecorded, or at least the record has not survived. The few lists of plants imported before the invention of the Wardian case do not include them. Following a successful trial shipment of grasses, ferns and a primrose to Melbourne and Sydney in 1834, the possibility of using Wardian cases to transport soft perennials such as hellebores across the oceans to Australia existed. Yet they seem not to have rated a mention until 1893, when they appear as a brief entry in Mrs Rolf Boldrewood's *The Flower Garden in Australia*. She appears to have been describing forms or hybrids of *H. orientalis*, as she lists 'H. *aleorubens* [sic] – purple flowers. Christmas rose has white flowers. H. *orientalis* – rose colour. H. *antiquorum* – white shaded to pink'. Maybe such quiet flowers were too old-fashioned for such a thoroughly modern writer – after all, she was well up the social ladder and knew her bedding plants and those useful for achieving sub-tropical effects. Nurserymen who imported from Europe, North America, Japan and China may not have thought it worthwhile bothering with such horticultural low-life when they could safely import more fashionable (and profitable) items such as tree peonies, newly discovered orchids, ferns and aroids, the latest camellia, rhododendron and azalea hybrids, and endless apples and pears for the burgeoning commercial orchards of the colonies. Although my survey of early colonial paintings has not been exhaustive, I have not come across any flower pieces or garden pictures that show examples of the first hellebores.

None the less hellebores did arrive, and began a modest career in cool climate 'hill station' gardens and in shady borders, from Sydney all around the southern coast to Adelaide and across the Bass Strait in Tasmania.

The oldest surviving cultivar that I know is an *orientalis* hybrid of exceptional 'blackness' that I received from Otto Fauser of Olinda in the Dandenong Ranges. His plant came from the garden of his neighbours Barbara and Phillip Gordon, and their plant came from their great-aunt who bought it from a Bayswater (Melbourne) nurseryman in about 1928. All three are skilled, knowledgeable gardeners and this plant, among many others, has been shared around by them. It is a rich dark plum purple with a lovely grey bloom overlaid. The foliage is thick and leathery and it doesn't get black spot.

David Glenn, a well-known perennial grower also at Olinda in Victoria, found a fine assortment of hellebores growing in an overgrown bungalow garden in his mountain-top town. A little detective work on his part revealed that they had been imported from England in about 1940 by a retired Indian Army man, Brigadier Officer, and that they came from his sister's garden in England. I have seen these plants in bloom and can vouch for David's high opinion of them. The form of the flowers is excellent, well-rounded and full, and the colour range very good. Having seeded about freely in the rich, well-watered mountain soil, the massed plants make a tremendous show in winter and have been one of the sources from which David has built up his own splendid selection of stock plants.

North of Melbourne lies Mount Macedon, another area where many old gardens survive from the late nineteenth century, even if sometimes seriously damaged by bush-fires. Among the many plants that have naturalised in the shady glades of European trees and tree-ferns are masses of *H. orientalis* hybrids. From a garden called Dreamthorpe I have received a plant of a hellebore with yellowish flowers. My specimen came to me from Suz Price, an inveterate collector of all kinds of good garden plants who has scoured many of the old gardens in the area for interesting things. It is a form of *H. orientalis*. Although I have seen other forms in many colours from gardens on 'The Mount', very few of them compare favourably with those grown by Brigadier Officer. Barney Hutton, Lady Law-Smith, Steven Ryan (Dicksonia Nursery) and others continue to grow and select seedlings in the district.

Somewhat further afield, near Blackwood, Tommy Garnett grows a variety of species and hybrids in his 'Garden of St Erth', one of the few private gardens in Australia open to the public on a daily basis. Nearby, in Trentham, Denis Norgate has been growing perennials commercially for more than forty years. He is a very critical selector when it comes to hellebores, and he has introduced and distributed widely some good clones, especially a fine, tall, upstanding pure white. He has offered *H. niger* for many years, and also sells *H. angustifolia* and *H. foetidus* from time to time.

Cliff Smith of Bilpin in New South Wales received world-wide attention when an article about his hellebores was published in *The Garden* (Vol. III, Part 3, March 1986), but he was not the first to supply gardeners in that State. Paul Sorensen, a noted landscape designer and contractor, included hellebores in his designs and supplied them from his nursery along with conifers, maples and rhododendrons, for which he was noted. He was also one of the first to supply and use hostas. He operated a nursery and

landscape business at Leura in the Blue Mountains west of Sydney from 1920 until his death in 1983.

It is possible that Mr Jensen of Exeter in the Southern Tablelands near Bowral was an even earlier commercial grower of hellebores. When I visited his place in 1985 he and his brother, both stone deaf and in their eighties, still sold plants from among a jungle of shrubs, trees, bulbs and vines. I went in search of a white hellebore for a friend's new garden. Having roused one of the brothers and conveyed what I wanted, I followed the old man through the overgrown and derelict nursery to a spot where a large hellebore of the required colour grew. The whole plant was dug out and sold to me for a very modest sum. Mr Jensen had operated his nursery for many, many years; how many I cannot say, for although he is part of the local garden lore no one seems to remember such details. As I recall, the two brothers succeeded to ownership of a family business, so their hellebores may pre-date those sold by Paul Sorensen. Mr Jensen and Mr Smith both conducted a mail order business as well as direct sales. Mr Smith advertised regularly in *Your Garden* and *Garden Lover* and sold hellebore plants to home gardeners throughout southern Australia. Naturally demand for his seedlings grew following his publication in *The Garden*, but so far I have not been able to locate any collectors who have plants of either 'Red Wine Dob' or 'Spotty Vanda', which were illustrated in his article. Now in his eighties, Mr Smith no longer grows hellebores much.

Among the plantsmen who have maintained interest in hellebores in New South Wales, mention must also be made of Dean Havelberg, who gardens privately at Exeter. He and his partner Douglas Smith raised many plants from seed for their own garden, among them *H. × sternii* and *H. lividus*.

In south Australia hellebores lived quietly, with few suppliers other than home gardeners who passed them over the garden fence to neighbours or sold them at church bazaars. David Thomson of Summerton was an adventurous nurseryman who began raising *H. ar-*

gutifolius and selling it through his florist's shop at Burnside. He picked a good time to introduce this and *Euphorbia wulfenii*, as floral art was immensely popular at the time – the late fifties – and these two green-flowered plants were in constant demand. The Corsican hellebore has proved itself a very reliable garden plant and remains very popular. A large bed of it under large trees in the Botanic Gardens of Adelaide demonstrates how useful it can be as a ground cover in difficult situations such as dry shade. In situations where water is well supplied and root competition is less, *H. argutifolius* will often grow well over 4ft tall and make large clumps. The most common form has out-facing flowers displayed on an open upright inflorescence, but I have seen a form with a very compact 'dome' of pendant blooms growing in the garden of Felicity Kent at Mount Barker which I thought very desirable.

Tasmanian conditions provide a good environment for *H. orientalis* and its many forms, and for *H. niger*, but the frosty and sometimes snowy winters are less kind to other species. Ken Gillanders has sent out hellebores from his Woodbank Nursery at Longley for some years. Supplies seem to vary according to what seed is available from overseas sources. Occasionally he sells plants raised from field-collected seed, and these always meet a strong demand.

More recently hellebores have been very widely grown by collectors and commercial growers in Victoria. The temperate climate suits hellebores well; it is sufficiently cold in the hill and mountain regions to grow *H. niger* well, while more tender varieties such as *H. lividus* are also reliable in most situations where frosts are slight. 'Tender' plants in Australia are usually thought to be those that cannot take the heat of an Antipodean summer; thus *H. argutifolius* is widely regarded as hardy and *H. niger* is generally thought to be difficult and tender. Many of us think *H. vesicarius* would be hardy – if only we could get it!

H. niger frustrates many who attempt to grow it, even those who try to please it by applying ice-cubes to the soil around the root zone in an attempt to imitate a hard frost and thus trigger flower production. By far the best plants I have seen are grown by Barbara and Phillip Gordon. Under a very tall old *Eucalyptus regnans* in their Olinda garden it prospers in variety. The most attractive forms are those tinged with pink on the reverse and which have flowers held at right angles to the stem. While not up to the colour intensity illustrated in a recent report by the plant hunter Will McLewin, writing in *Plant Heritage* (Vol.2 No.9), they are lovely and always give rise in me to the urge to beg some seed and try *H. niger* just one more time.

As mentioned previously, David Glenn is one of the main Australian growers of hellebores. In the main his stocks are derived from the seed strains sold by Jim and Jenny Archibald named and selected by Will McLewin, and from the plants imported by Brigadier Officer. The black Bayswater hellebore is propagated vegetatively. David's *Orientalis* hybrids range from blush through apple-blossom pink without spots to all the deeper shades, some intensely spotted, others less so. The best hold flowers at right angles to the stem. As the *orientalis* varieties are evergreen in Australian conditions, it is usual for the foliage to be cut off in early winter to tidy up the plant and to show off the flowers well. In some gardens where conditions are difficult and the plants crowded, a black spot fungal infection sometimes attacks new foliage and emerging flower buds. The most effective remedy is to improve cultivation and to remove all old and diseased leaves.

H. × sternii is a very variable plant at the best of times, and most plants in Australia tend to favour *H. argutifolius* strongly. David has been very selective in releasing seedlings, and consequently collectors are now able to acquire a form that shows affinities with *H. lividus* in more diminutive growth, foliage touched with silver along the veins and flowers beautifully stained with pink on the reverse of the petals. Rene Coffield has a small alpine nursery at Creswick in Victoria, and while visiting her daughter in England purchased several plants of *H. lividus* with a view to receiving the seeds, the cost of importing the plants being prohibitively high. Rene was one of the first to make plants of this lovely hellebore available in Australia. Craig Irving of Euroa in north-eastern Victoria grows many plants from JCA seed and was the first to mention to me that he had seedlings of the red-stemmed *H. foetidus* 'Wester Flisk'. This strain is not widespread yet, but collectors would be able to acquire it from a number of growers if they wished.

In 1988 the Ornamental Plant Collections Association was formed, along the lines of the National Council for the Conservation of Plants and Gardens in the UK. A reference collection of hellebores is maintained for the Association by Dale McDonald of Romsey, Victoria, but at the time of writing a comprehensive list of species and cultivars in the collection was not available. Mrs McDonald has one notable introduction to her credit; a variegated form of *H. argutifolius* in which the variegation appears as a mass of fine dark green spots uniformly scattered over the white leaves. I have no information about the appearance of such maculate forms anywhere else, so it may be a unique Australian development. The plant is somewhat less hardy than its plain form, and is generally grown in a shaded position away from the competitive roots of trees and shrubs. Rene Coffield has a fine specimen growing in a shade-house in her garden. It regularly flowers and sets abundant seed which comes about 80 per cent true to the variegated form. Plants are becoming available to collectors from several sources.

Aside from those already mentioned, Ted West of Upper Fern Tree Gully just outside Melbourne is a keen collector of hellebores and he, like everyone in this country, casts a wide net in order to obtain seed of the species and cultivars that he seeks. Some of the most valued plants in his collection have come from his extensive correspondence with Brian Mathew, Jim and Jenny Archibald, Ballards and members of the Hardy Plant Society.

In Adelaide, South Australia, Don Barrett and Harvey Collins grow many hellebores too. Their special pride are three seedlings of *H. vesicarius* (JCA 563.002 88/89), and they are also watching with great interest many seedlings appearing from seed obtained from Marlene Ahlberg in Germany and from various European and North American alpine and rock garden clubs. My only noteworthy success has been to establish a small colony of *H. odorus* subsp. *laxus* (JCA 562.000). Although reported as deciduous in its habitat, it remains evergreen in this garden. My plants flower well but have not yet set any seed.

One of the main reasons for the growing interest in hellebores among plant collectors is their increasing availability. Many Australian enthusiasts are convinced that as well as being attractive garden plants, many of the species could be grown here with more success than is achieved by growers who must contend with the colder conditions of European and North American winters. Given the chance, Australian gardens could become a safe haven for species currently under threat in their habitats. The impetus for this to occur is evident in the zeal with which seed sources are pursued around the world and in the growing lists of hellebores in cultivation in Australian gardens.

APPENDIX

WHERE TO SEE HELLEBORES

UNITED KINGDOM

East Lambrook Manor, South Petherton, Somerset
Great Barfield, Bradenham, Buckinghamshire
Hyde Hall, Rettenden, Essex
The Old Rectory, Burghfield, Reading, Berkshire
Royal Botanic Garden, Edinburgh
Royal Botanic Gardens, Kew
Royal Horticultural Society Garden, Wisley, Surrey
Savill Garden, Wick Lane, Englefield Green, Surrey
The NCCPG National Collection can also be visited, but strictly by appointment only. Write to Jeremy Wood at Lower House, Whiteparish, Salisbury SP5 2SL.

Please check in *The Good Gardens Guide* before travelling.

UNITED STATES OF AMERICA

Gardenview Horticultural Park, 16711 Pearl Road, Strongsville, Ohio, 44136
Wave Hill, 675 West 252 Street, Bronx, New York 10471

WHERE TO BUY HELLEBORES

UNITED KINGDOM

A fine range of hellebores is available from Elizabeth's nursery:
Washfield Nursery, Horns Road, Hawkhurst, Kent TN18 4QU

The following nurseries also specialise in hellebores:
Ashwood Nurseries, Greensforge, Kingswinford, West Midlands, DY6 0AE
Blackthorn Nurseries, Kilmeston, Alresford, Hants SO24 0NL
Phedar Nursery, Bunkers Hill, Romilay, Stockport, Cheshire SK6 3DS

The following nurseries usually have stocks of good hellebores:
Higher End Nursery, Hale, Fordingbridge, Hants SP6 2RA
Little Creek Nursery, 39 Moor Road, Banwell, Weston-super-Mare, Avon BS24 6EF
Rushfields of Ledbury, Ross Road, Ledbury, Herefordshire HR8 2LP
Unusual Plants, Beth Chatto Gardens, Elmstead Market, Colchester CO7 7DB

Please check the latest edition of *The RHS Plant Finder* for catalogue charges and opening times.

UNITED STATES OF AMERICA

Carroll Gardens, 444 East Main Street, P.O. Box, 310 Westminster, Maryland 21157
Cricklewood Nursery, 11907, Nevers Road, Snobohish, Washington 98290
Forestfarm, 990 Tetherow Road, Williams, Oregon 97544
Gardenview Horticultural Park, 16711 Pearl Road, Strongsville, Ohio, 44136
Gossler Farms Nursery, 1200 Weaver Road, Springfield, Oregon 97478
Greer Gardens, 1280 Goodpasture, Island Road, Eugene, Oregon 97401
Heronswood Nursery, 7530 NE 288th Street, Kingston, WA 98346-9502
Little River Farm Perennial Nursery, Route 1, Box 220, Middlesex, N. Carolina 27557
Piccadilly Farm, 1971 Whippoorwill Road, Bishop, Georgia 30621
Plant Delights Nursery, 9241 Sauls Road, Raleigh, NC 27603
Sunny Border, 1709 Kensington Road, PO Bx483, Kensington, CT 06037

SEEDS

Seeds, but not plants, are usually available from:
Jim and Jenny Archibald, 'Bryn Collen', Ffostrasol, Llandysul, Dyfed SA44 5SB
Chiltern Seeds, Bortree Stile, Ulverston, Cumbria LA12 7PB
North Green Seeds, 16 Wilton Lane, Little Plumstead, Norwich, Norfolk, NR13 5DL

Hellebore seed can be imported into the United States from Europe without restriction. It is usually available from:

Life-Form Replicators, P.O. Box 857, Fowlerville, Michigan 48836
Phedar Nursery, address as above
Jim & Jenny Archibald, address as above
North Green Seeds, address as above

READING ABOUT HELLEBORES

Ahlburg, Marlene, *Hellebores* (Batsford).
Mathew, Brian, *Hellebores* (Alpine Garden Society).
Philips, Roger and Rix, Martyn, *Perennials* (Pan).
Thomas, Graham Stuart, *Perennial Garden Plants* (Dent, Sagapress/Timber Press).

ACKNOWLEDGEMENTS

It is impossible to write a book like this without help, and many enthusiasts have been generous with their time and their knowledge. We wish to single out a few for particular mention:

Brian Mathew for providing the framework for all enthusiasts with his own invaluable book on hellebores, and for his advice and encouragement; Jim Archibald for information about his and Eric Smith's plants; Helen Ballard for her captivating plants, and for welcoming us to Old Country; Will McLewin for his infectious commitment, and for welcoming us to his nursery; Kemal Mehdi for showing us his newly designated National Collection; Andrew Norton for welcoming us to East Lambrook and for his invaluable help with the section on Margery Fish; Trevor Nottle for providing the chapter on 'Hellebores in Australia'; Mikinori Ogisu for information about *Helleborus thibetanus* and for photographs of the plant in its natural habitat; Chris Sanders for showing us his plants; Robin and Sue White for getting on and doing it and not just talking about it, and for welcoming us to their nursery; and Jeremy Wood for showing us his National Collection.

To those of the above who also provided flowers to be photographed and contributions to the text – again, thank you.

We have been fortunate in being able to use pictures from some fine photographers. In particular we would like to thank Roger Phillips for so generously taking the time to photograph flowers for us in his studio. We would also like to thank Valerie Finnis and John Fielding for providing us with a number of pictures. Most of the other pictures were taken by Graham, but we are also very grateful to Chris Grey-Wilson, Alan Leslie, Phil Lusby, Tim Sandall and Mikinori Ogisu. Thanks too to Frances Hibberd, who drew the lovely leaf drawings, and also to Charlotte Molesworth for her illustrations.

Many gardeners have contributed to our chapter on 'Hellebores in America', and we greatly appreciate their help; they are mentioned individually on page 150.

In addition to all those already mentioned we would like to thank the following people, all of whom have helped with the book in their different ways: Hilary Bird for the index and also Janet Blenkinship, Margaret Burbeck, Beth Chatto, Gordon Collier, Susan Dickinson, Helen Dillon, Leon Doyen, Susan Farquhar, John Godsen, Chris Grey-Wilson, Don Jacobs, Günther Jürgl, Ursula Key-Davis, Hans Kramer, Roy Lancaster, Alan Leslie, Tony Lord, Richard Nutt, Piet Oudolf, Frank Perring, Erich Pohle, Koen van Poucke, Roger Poulett, Martyn Rix, Mick Sandell, Gisela Schiemann, Joe Sharman, Mike Sinnott, Geoff Stebbings, Jane Sterndale-Bennett, Graham Thomas, Piers Trehane, Mamie Walker, Anne Watson and James Wood.

The authors and publishers would also like to thank the following for their invaluable help in providing the photographs reproduced in this book: Roger Phillips: pages 1, 45, 53, 64, 77, 81, 93, 97, 101, 104, 120, 129, 132, 141, 144; John Fielding: pages 21, 57, 72; Chris Grey-Wilson: page 48; Phil Lusby: pages 49, 108; Mikinori Ogisu: page 60; Valerie Finnis: pages 4, 29, 109; Graham Gough: page 33.

All other photographs are by Graham Rice.

PERSONAL ACKNOWLEDGEMENTS

I would like to give special thanks to Graham Gough and Barbara Keuning for their practical support and enthusiastic encouragement, and to my co-author for doing all the work. Thank you, Graham.   *Elizabeth Strangman*

First of all I would like to thank Elizabeth for suggesting this collaboration; it's been a privilege to work with her. I would also like to thank Sue Jackson for covering the draft with pertinent queries and for her support throughout the turbulent gestation of the book. Thanks also to Graham Gough who scrawled awkward but useful questions in the margins of the draft, 'Why?' being the most frequent and the most useful.   *Graham Rice*

Finally we would both like to thank our agent, Gloria Ferris, for all her work on our behalf.

INDEX

Page numbers in *italic* refer to illustrations

159

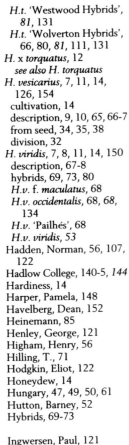